"I have been instructed and often moved by these scholarly and pastorally perceptive expositions. Barry Webb opens up the texts carefully and accessibly, and does so with the sensitivity of an experienced pastor. Such pastoral scholarship is powerful and edifying."

Christopher Ash, Former Director of the PT Cornhill Training Course,
The Proclamation Trust; author, *The Priority of Preaching*

"Expository preaching involves much more than defining Hebrew and Greek words, or cool and collected explanations of obscure issues raised by biblical texts. It involves grasping both the theological message of the Scriptures and letting that message grasp us who preach week in and week out. Barry Webb is not only the finest interpreter of the book of Judges; he is also the book's finest expositor. His presentation of the principle enduring theological points of each literary unit in Judges and Ruth is clear, practical, and passionate. This book is a great gift first to preachers, but ultimately to God's people who will hear from them the living and life-giving Word of the Lord from these books."

Daniel I. Block, Gunther H. Knoedler Professor of Old Testament,
Wheaton College

"These are insightful, stimulating, often challenging expositions from the pen of a great exegete and preacher."

James Hely Hutchinson, Director, Institut Biblique Belge, Brussels

"In his homiletical commentary, Professor Webb's sermons lead us through the chaotic waters of Judges until we arrive at the end of Ruth where the storm finally settles with the birth of a baby in Bethlehem. In this exegetically accurate, highly engaging, and master-fully accessible commentary, a seasoned scholar with a pastor's heart captains us to the only surety of our souls—the great Redeemer, Jesus Christ."

Douglas Sean O'Donnell, Senior Lecturer in Biblical Studies and
Practical Theology, Queensland Theological College; author, *The Beginning and End of Wisdom*

"Barry Webb has a special skill for a comprehensive interpretation of Scripture: solid exegetical scholarship is combined with deep theological insights and relevant pastoral wisdom applied to our present day situation. The narrative style of the commentary makes it easy to read. Webb's prudent work clarifies in an astonishing manner the theological meaning of Judges and Ruth as a part of the entire Biblical canon testifying to God's work of creation and redemption, to his sovereign grace and faithfulness. This is Biblical theology at its best, and very helpful for preachers and all believers."

Miikka Ruokanen, Professor of Systematic Theology, University of Helsinki;
Guest Professor, Nanjing Union Theological Seminary and Fudan University,
Shanghai

"What happens when a society turns its back on God? *Judges and Ruth* opens up the era of Israel's judges in a way that resonates in so many ways with the social, religious, and moral crises of our own age. This is a book worth recommending to anyone interested in leadership. Many commentaries are good for reference, but difficult to read. Barry Webb has given us one that you will find difficult to put down. Making Christian sense of Ehud, Deborah, Gideon, Samson, and the rest of the judges and bringing them alive so that they "still speak" is a task beautifully executed by one who looks back over a lifetime of study of the Bible, experience of life, and observation of the world. It is a seamless blend of scholarship, devotion, life-wisdom, and understanding of modern society."

David Seccombe, Former Principal, George Whitefield College, Capetown

"In this careful reading of the text within the immediate context of Judges and Ruth, the wider Old Testament message, and ultimately the whole story of the Bible, Barry Webb gives us what we need most from a commentary—a gospel driven encouragement to love and serve our Lord more deeply."

Peter Sholl, Director, MOCLAM, Monterrey, Mexico

"Barry Webb's teaching and preaching have been a gift to the churches. Barry preaches the Word with a gentle clarity that shows he deeply understands both the text and the people to whom he is preaching. This expository commentary on Judges and Ruth bears all the hallmarks of Barry's scholarship and much-loved preaching. Those preparing to preach on these two wonderful books will benefit greatly from Barry's expositions, as will all who read them. This is the kind of preaching that nourishes faith as we advance in the knowledge of God and of the Savior he has provided."

Mark D. Thompson, Principal, Moore Theological College

JUDGES AND RUTH

PREACHING THE WORD
Edited by R. Kent Hughes

(((PREACHING *the* WORD)))

JUDGES
and RUTH

GOD *in* CHAOS

BARRY G. WEBB

R. Kent Hughes
Series Editor

 **CROSSWAY**

WHEATON, ILLINOIS

Judges and Ruth

Copyright © 2015 by Barry G. Webb

Published by Crossway
      1300 Crescent Street
      Wheaton, Illinois 60187

Cover design: Jon McGrath, Simplicated Studio

Cover image: Adam Greene, illustrator

First printing 2015

Printed in the United States of America

Hardcover ISBN: 978-1-4335-0676-5
ePub ISBN: 978-1-4335-2330-4

PDF ISBN: 978-1-4335-0677-2
Mobipocket ISBN: 978-1-4335-0678-9

Library of Congress Cataloging-in-Publication Data

Webb, Barry G.
Judges and Ruth : God in chaos / Barry G. Webb.
  pages cm.—(Preaching the word)
    Includes bibliographical references and index.
    ISBN 978-1-4335-0676-5 (hc)
    1. Bible. Judges—Commentaries. 2. Bible. Ruth—Commentaries. I. Title.
BS1305.53.W435   2015
222'd.307—dc23   2014026742

Crossway is a publishing ministry of Good News Publishers.

TS		25	24	23	22	21	20	19	18	17	16	15
15	14	13	12	11	10	9	8	7	6	5	4	3	2	1

To Abi, Jakey, Nate, Maggie, and Tom—
five precious gifts from God

And after that he gave them judges until Samuel the prophet. Then they asked for a king, and God gave them Saul the son of Kish, a man of the tribe of Benjamin, for forty years. And when he had removed him, he raised up David to be their king, of whom he testified and said, "I have found in David the son of Jesse a man after my heart, who will do all my will." Of this man's offspring God has brought to Israel a Savior, Jesus, as he promised.

ACTS 13:20b–23

Contents

RUTH

A Word to Those Who Preach the Word

There are times when I am preaching that I have especially sensed the pleasure of God. I usually become aware of it through the unnatural silence. The ever-present coughing ceases, and the pews stop creaking, bringing an almost physical quiet to the sanctuary—through which my words sail like arrows. I experience a heightened eloquence, so that the cadence and volume of my voice intensify the truth I am preaching.

There is nothing quite like it—the Holy Spirit filling one's sails, the sense of his pleasure, and the awareness that something is happening among one's hearers. This experience is, of course, not unique, for thousands of preachers have similar experiences, even greater ones.

What has happened when this takes place? How do we account for this sense of his smile? The answer for me has come from the ancient rhetorical categories of *logos*, *ethos*, and *pathos*.

The first reason for his smile is the *logos*—in terms of preaching, God's Word. This means that as we stand before God's people to proclaim his Word, we have done our homework. We have exegeted the passage, mined the significance of its words in their context, and applied sound hermeneutical principles in interpreting the text so that we understand what its words meant to its hearers. And it means that we have labored long until we can express in a sentence what the theme of the text is—so that our outline springs from the text. Then our preparation will be such that as we preach, we will not be preaching our own thoughts about God's Word, but God's actual Word, his *logos*. This is fundamental to pleasing him in preaching.

The second element in knowing God's smile in preaching is *ethos*—what you are as a person. There is a danger endemic to preaching, which is having your hands and heart cauterized by holy things. Phillips Brooks illustrated it by the analogy of a train conductor who comes to believe that he has been to the places he announces because of his long and loud heralding of them. And that is why Brooks insisted that preaching must be "the bringing of truth through personality." Though we can never perfectly embody the truth we preach, we must be subject to it, long for it, and make it as much a part of our ethos as possible. As the Puritan William Ames said, "Next to the Scriptures, nothing makes a sermon more to pierce, than when it comes out of the inward affection of the heart without any affectation." When a preacher's *ethos* backs up his *logos*, there will be the pleasure of God.

Last, there is *pathos*—personal passion and conviction. David Hume, the Scottish philosopher and skeptic, was once challenged as he was seen going to hear George Whitefield preach: "I thought you do not believe in the gospel." Hume replied, "I don't, but he does." Just so! When a preacher believes what he preaches, there will be passion. And this belief and requisite passion will know the smile of God.

The pleasure of God is a matter of *logos* (the Word), *ethos* (what you are), and *pathos* (your passion). As you preach the Word may you experience his smile—the Holy Spirit in your sails!

R. Kent Hughes
Wheaton, Illinois

Preface

Writing this book has been a real treat, not just because Judges and Ruth are so rewarding to study (so are all the other books of the Old and New Testaments), but because they belong so naturally together. It's not just that they are both set "in the days when the judges ruled" (Ruth 1:1), but that they complement each other so beautifully. I have always been aware of this in a general way, but haven't appreciated the full significance of it until now, and it has been a discovery that has delighted and uplifted me.

Judges is a very confronting book, especially for contemporary Christian readers. It is full of violence and has some horrifying stories of women, in particular, being abused. Worst of all, it is about the people of God behaving abominably again and again and again and suffering the consequences. There is chaos in Judges, caused by the almost unbelievable perversity of human beings, but there's also the powerful presence of God who intervenes again and again to pull them back from the brink of oblivion. But the chaos keeps returning, and by the end things seem to be going from bad to worse. There's a muted hope for a king who will be able to bring some order out of the chaos (21:25). But that's all—a kind of wistful longing that one day it might all be over, and Israel will be able to look back to the days of the judges as a nightmare from which they have finally awakened. And then we come to Ruth, with its message of redemption. It too, begins with pain—especially for Naomi and her family—but then it quickly turns into a story of love and inclusion, restoration and blessing. It's like moving from darkness to light and from chaos to calm. Judges ends with the faint hope of a king, Ruth with the birth of a baby in Bethlehem who turns out to be the ancestor of King David. And that, of course, opens out toward the New Testament and the glorious gospel of God's redeeming grace in Christ. Judges by itself is depressing, but Judges and Ruth together are full of hope. I have called this series of sermons "God in Chaos" as a way of distilling in one memorable phrase the struggle that is at the heart of these two books and the light that eventually breaks through because of God.

It's also been a treat for me to write this book because it's a contribution to the Preaching the Word series, and I'm a preacher. I'm other things as well, but I never feel as fully myself as when I'm preaching. This book has enabled me to be myself, and there's a special joy in that, especially when you believe, as I do, that what I am I am by the grace of God. I was converted as a teenager under the strong preaching of the then young evangelist Billy Graham. It wasn't his rousing oratory that saved me, of course, but the gospel he preached, the message of God's grace to us in Jesus Christ. And with that went the quiet but powerful work of the Spirit, who convicted me of its truth and moved me to respond. I had never found it hard to believe in God or to conform to my Christian parents' expectations of me. I was already a cultural Christian. But that day I knew I had become something more—a disciple of Jesus Christ, heart and soul committed to him and his service. I had experienced the transforming power of the gospel and wanted nothing more in the years that followed than to tell that same gospel to others. I had also become a preacher. I had a lot to learn, of course, but I began preaching right away, and the Plymouth Brethren among whom I had been raised gave me ample scope to express my new passion. Every Sunday night, with a few companions, I began to preach in the open air, in the streets around our church. Soon opportunities opened up for me to preach indoors as well at the weekly "gospel meetings" in the church building. My preaching ministry developed from there and has continued to this day.

My philosophy of preaching was shaped to a large extent by the way I began. Preaching should be passionate and engaging. In the open air, if you're not arresting no one will stop and listen, and even inside a captive audience will only *appear* to be listening. Their minds will quickly drift elsewhere. This is particularly so today, when audio and visual communication has become so varied and stimulating, and people's attention spans are shrinking. The preacher should not try to compete with this directly, of course. He will simply not be able to do so and will be boring by default. Instead he should offer his hearers something they *can't* get elsewhere. But the bottom line is that he must be engaging. Monotonous, dispassionate, lecture-style preaching is simply a waste of time.

Second, the preacher must have confidence in the Word of God. It is God's Word, not our rhetoric, that is "living and active, sharper than any two-edged sword, piercing to the division of soul and of spirit, of joints and of marrow, and discerning the thoughts and intentions of the heart" (Hebrews 4:12), and it is by "the living and abiding word of God," not our oratory, that people are born again (1 Peter 1:23). We may sway people by our rhetoric if we are gifted enough, but if that is all we do, others who are more gifted will sway them more. And if we have not built strong Biblical foundations into people's lives by the faithful preaching of God's Word, they will eventually go wherever the most charismatic speakers take them. There are two main implications of this. The preacher who has confidence in the Word of God will not shrink from preaching the whole of Scripture, not just the bits he feels most comfortable with or that he feels will be most acceptable to his audience. He will believe that "*All* Scripture is breathed out by God and profitable for teaching, for reproof, for correction, and for training in righteousness, that the man of God may be complete, equipped for every good work" (2 Timothy 3:16–17). He will be committed to preaching all of it because he knows his people need all of it. He will also not try to jolly it up with jokes or so overload it with illustrations that people are diverted from it instead of taken deeply into it. This is not to say that there is no place in preaching for a judicious use of humor or apt illustrations, especially if they are drawn from the preacher's own experience of the things he is talking about. Readers will find plenty of examples in what follows. But these must never give the impression that the preacher thinks the Bible is boring and needs to be made interesting by copious embellishment. The preacher who has confidence in the Word of God will not be driven by a need to *make* the Bible interesting, but by a conviction that it *is* interesting, and that the best way to convince people of this is to open its riches to them and let the text itself do the work.

Finally, the Christian preacher will be convinced of the unity of Scripture and that its central theme is God's great work of salvation that reaches its fulfillment in Christ. I have always believed this, but my understanding of it was deepened enormously by the fine theological education I received at Moore College, Sydney. This consolidated my understanding of what Christian preaching should be and has guided my practice ever since. In particular it taught me how to preach the gospel from every part of Scripture, including the Old Testament with all its breadth and depth and variety, without artificially forcing it to say things it doesn't. Not every Old Testament passage speaks directly of Christ, and it is bad exegesis to try to make it do so. However, every passage is part of a story that leads to him, and along the way each has much to teach us about the character and ways of the God we have come to know in Christ as our heavenly Father. Each also has much to teach us about ourselves and about the struggle to live a life of faithful obedience to God in a world that daily tests our resolve to do so. So the Bible has many secondary themes as well as its primary one. It has an inexhaustible richness that will never disappoint the patient reader and preacher. But I am persuaded that however many other things we may speak about along the way, our preaching should always be taking people on a journey that leads to Christ, just as the whole Bible leads to him. In other words, the Bible as a whole is the gospel writ large, and therefore all Christian preaching can and should be evangelistic. Which brings me back, really, to my conversion as a youngster under the preaching of Billy Graham. That is what ignited my passion for preaching and made me want, whatever else I became, to be an evangelist. And I believe that is what I have always been at heart and still am today. What my theological education and experience has shown me is that there is absolutely no conflict between that and being an evangelical scholar and expository preacher.

I am most grateful for the opportunity that Kent Hughes gave me to write this volume. Judges and Ruth are both books for our times, an age of individualism when every man or woman does what is right in his or her own eyes, when love has been divorced from commitment, and when people need more than ever to discover, or rediscover, the redeeming love of God in Christ. May this book help inspire the kind of preaching that will lead them to him.

Barry G. Webb
Moore College
Sydney, Australia
September 3, 2014

JUDGES

1

After Joshua: The Legacy of a Great Leader

JUDGES 1:1–21

THERE ARE MOMENTS in the lives of people and nations that change everything. The birth of a first child is like that—his or her parents' lives are changed forever. So is the death of one's last surviving parent, the passing of a generation. We call such things boundary events because they are moments of irreversible transition. In the life of a nation it may be the passing of a great leader or the achievement of independence. Sometimes transitions to a new situation are traumatic and fill us with foreboding. The dropping of the first atomic bomb on Hiroshima on August 6, 1945, the year I was born, was an event like this. No longer could nations look to merely conventional weapons to protect them. A change had taken place that was irreversible, and those who understood this and had the means to do so began to arm themselves with new weapons. We had entered the nuclear age. The Second World War was ending, but another had already begun, and there was no going back. Those born after August 6, 1945, were born into a world that was radically changed from the one their parents had known.

The book of Judges opens with a boundary event of this kind. Joshua has died. An era of progress and confidence has ended, and the future is uncertain. Joshua was not just anyone. He had been a man of tremendous importance for Israel. By his personal example of courage, faith in God, and military leadership, he had brought Israel into its promised inheritance in Canaan. He was not perfect, but he was unquestionably great—the greatest man of his generation—and Israel would feel the loss of him keenly. As its name suggests, the book of Joshua is dominated by Joshua from beginning to end. It begins with the death of Moses, Joshua's mentor, an even more towering figure than Joshua himself. That, too, was a mammoth boundary event. But by the time Moses died Joshua was already in place to take Israel forward. Moses had personally commissioned him. Deuteronomy 34:9 tells us that "Joshua the son of Nun was full of the spirit of wisdom, for Moses had laid his hands on him." So after Moses there was Joshua. But after Joshua there was no one in particular. There was a leadership vacuum, and Israel was in crisis.

Joshua's Influence

The crisis was mitigated to some extent by Joshua's legacy—the imprint he left on Israel. Great people exert a powerful influence on others, an influence that often outlives them. But even great people have flaws, and their legacy can sometimes be more harmful than good. That was the case with Solomon, for example, whose failures in the latter part of this reign left Israel compromised and divided (1 Kings 11, 12). Joshua's legacy, on the other hand, was positive: "the people served the LORD all the days of Joshua, and all the days of the elders who outlived Joshua" (2:7). Joshua had been the greatest man of his generation, and those who knew him aspired to be like him. Even after his death they followed his example of godly living. Several things in 1:1–21 show the impact his life had made.

Unity (v. 1)

We have all witnessed the sad spectacle of divided families. Thoughtless words have been said or selfish actions taken. People have been hurt and found it hard to forgive. Strong people have gotten their way at the expense of weaker ones. Quarrels over money, especially disputed wills, have split families into warring factions that have led to stalemate rather than settlement. Bitterness has set in, and blighted relationships, and the damage done to the family can last for generations. The same thing sometimes happens in nations. Leaders maintain their hold on power by playing factions against one another, resulting in an appearance of unity without any real concord. When they finally die or fall from power, open warfare ensues as competing factions struggle for supremacy in the vacuum left behind. For all they may have achieved militarily, economically, and so on, their legacy is disaster—a nation divided against itself. Not so with Joshua. After his death what we find is not this or that faction vying for supremacy, but the Israelites acting as one: "*the people of Israel* inquired of the LORD" (v. 1). Joshua was the kind of leader who drew people together rather than setting them against one another, and that is a mark of true greatness.[1]

People Who Seek God (v. 1)

A leader has to lead, and to do that he must stand out in some way from others. He must exercise authority and have that authority respected. But Joshua had never claimed to have absolute power or focused attention on himself as though he was Israel's supreme leader or as if they would be lost without him. He had always directed his followers to the Lord as the one to whom all alike were accountable, including himself. This was something that had been impressed on him by his predecessor Moses (Deuteronomy 31:1–8, 23) and powerfully reinforced by his own encounter with God, the true "commander of the army of the Lord," in Joshua 5:13–15. So although Joshua left a huge gap when he died, the Israelites knew they were not leaderless. They "inquired of the Lord," seeking direction from him as their supreme commander. They knew they were *his* people, *his* army. Joshua had never eclipsed God in their vision, and it is a central part of his legacy that they continued to look to God as their leader after Joshua himself was no longer with them.

It's not clear how the inquiry was made. Perhaps it was through a priest, using oracular stones (the Urim and Thummim) as in 20:27, 28.[2] According to Numbers 27:18–21 this is how Joshua had been given instructions about Israel's movements in the wilderness. But the nature of the response here (a whole complex sentence rather than a simple yes or no) suggests that in this case something more was involved than the use of the Urim and Thummim—most likely the delivery of a spoken oracle by the priest himself or (as elsewhere in Judges) a prophet or the mysterious "messenger of the Lord."[3] We're simply not told. What is significant is not how the inquiry was made, but the attitude it reveals. The Israelites inquired of the Lord because they recognized him as their supreme leader, as Joshua had done, and believed he had not abandoned them now that Joshua was gone. This, too, shows the powerful impact Joshua had made on their lives. We will return later to the significant response to Israel's inquiry in verse 2.

People Who Know They Need One Another and Work Together (vv. 3–21)

This is another aspect of the national unity that was part of Joshua's legacy. Joshua had never been an autocrat. He believed in teamwork. He was a man who knew how to delegate responsibility and work cooperatively with others and had modeled this in his leadership. Again and again in the book of Joshua we see him exercising leadership along with Eleazar the priest, the elders, and heads of families and tribes.[4] The phrase "he and the elders of Israel" is particularly revealing about the way Joshua had shared his leadership with these key men. He had mourned with them when Israel suffered a heavy defeat at Ai (Joshua 7:6) and literally walked with them "before the people" as they went up to Ai a second time (Joshua 8:10). It was a great and courageous example of team leadership that put humility, trust, and cooperation before self-seeking, personal status, and competitiveness. These were the men who would eventually have to shoulder the responsibility of leading in their own right, and the book of Judges indicates just how profoundly their understanding of what that entailed was shaped by Joshua's example: "And the people served the LORD all the days of Joshua, and all the days of *the elders who outlived Joshua*" (2:7). Furthermore, as we are about to see, Joshua's example of noncompetitive, cooperative leadership impacted not only the elders of Israel but the whole nation.

In the time of the judges the major people groups that made up Israel were the twelve tribes, named after their ancestors, the twelve sons of Jacob. This gave the people of each tribe an identity more specific than simply "Israelites." This was a good thing in itself, because people need to feel they belong to something smaller and more strongly kinship-based than a nation. In the modern world this is expressed (among other ways) in the need many feel to do genealogical research and produce a family tree that shows their connectedness to others sharing the same forebears. But there are dangers when the desire for a distinct identity goes too far. Kinship connectedness can descend into a kind of tribalism that threatens the unity of the larger community to which the tribes belong. It can set tribe against tribe in a way that leads to rivalry and the kind of fierce competitiveness that destabilizes nations and can ultimately destroy them. This very nearly happened in the period of the judges, as the closing chapters of the book show. In the period immediately following Joshua's death, however, and no doubt due to his influence, relationships between the tribes were marked by cooperation rather than rivalry.

Joshua had led Israel in a series of military campaigns that broke the back of Canaanite resistance and then divided up the land by lot, giving each tribe a specific part of Canaan as its inheritance in the land the Lord had given them (Joshua 1:10—12:24; 13:1–51). But in his farewell speech he had made it clear that much remained to be done. Canaanites still lived in the allocated territories, and each tribe faced the challenge of taking possession of what had been assigned to it and establishing its presence there. This would not be easy, and some territories would be harder to occupy than others, especially those with large Canaanite populations and fortified cities. Nor were all the tribes equally capable of such an undertaking. Some were larger than others, with more manpower and resources. If Israel as a whole was to accomplish the task Joshua had left them, they would have to work together, which is exactly what we see them doing in the first half of Judges 1.

In response to Israel's inquiry in verse 1, Judah is named as the tribe that should go first (v. 2). But the men of Judah do not launch out on their own. On the contrary, the very first thing they do is to ask the men of Simeon, their "brother" Israelites, to go with them and help them fight the Canaanites in their territory, and they offer to help the Simeonites do the same in theirs, an offer the Simeonites readily agree to (v. 3). This is referred to again in verse 17, and these two verses frame everything in between. In other words, the cooperation between these two tribes was basic to the whole series of campaigns fought by Judah and its fellow Israelites in the southern part of Canaan (vv. 9–17). The smaller tribes and clans, such as the Kenites and Benjaminites (vv. 16, 21), had the most to gain from this kind of partnership, but so did Judah, and ultimately all Israel, because it set a pattern that made the nation stronger whenever and wherever it was repeated. The way ahead was going to be difficult and would put the unity of Israel under severe strain. But the fact that they started this way was a good sign and another indication of the powerful influence that Joshua had had on the nation.

The Blessing of God

Joshua's legacy was good, but it was not the fundamental cause of the success enjoyed by the men of Judah and those associated with them. That lay in God, not in them, just as Joshua's own achievements were not in the end attributable to Joshua himself but to the God he served. That was certainly how Joshua had seen things at the end of his long life: "And now I am about to go the way of all the earth, and you know in your hearts and souls, all of you, that not one word has failed of all the good things that the LORD your God promised concerning you. All have come to pass for you; not one of them has failed" (Joshua 23:14). God had been faithful; he had made promises to his people and had kept them. The same is true for the good things that happen after Joshua's death here in Judges 1. God promised victory to Judah (v. 2), and he was true to his word: he "gave" the Canaanites into the hand of Judah and Simeon (v. 4), and the Lord was "with Judah" (v. 19). God doesn't send people into battle without being with them. He blesses those he sends with his presence and help.[5] The real reason the men of Judah were successful was not their good strategy or military might, or even their unity and cooperative leadership, but the evident blessing of God upon them in fulfillment of his promise.

Two mini-narratives embedded in the passage show us this blessing of God at closer range. Like a good camera man, the author doesn't just sweep across the scene of Judah's battles to show the general direction and shape of things. He also zooms in at a couple of points to give us a closer look at two representative examples of what was happening. The first scene we are shown at close range is military (vv. 4–7); the second is domestic (vv. 11–15).

Victory (vv. 4–7)

The first joint operation of the men of Judah and the men of Simeon was at Bezek, near Jerusalem. It was an ambitious campaign that penetrated enemy territory in the high country at the center of Canaan and resulted in a massive victory (v. 4). But the battle itself is reported in only one verse and is clearly not what the writer most wants us to dwell on. His main interest lies elsewhere. He quickly narrows the focus to one man, Adoni-bezek (the "lord" or "ruler" of Bezek), and shows us the kind of man he was and the fate he suffered (vv. 5–7). It is a gruesome passage, but what it's about is not revenge. Israel had not suffered at the hands of this man. Others had, though, and now God brings terrible, just retribution on him for what he has done (v. 7). Among other things, this mini-narrative shows us that much more is going on than God's giving the land to Israel. He is also judging the Canaanites, especially their rulers, for their evil lifestyle. The men of Judah and Simeon are his agents in this case, but it is fundamentally God's doing. It is God who gives this tyrant into their hands, and what they do to him is God's judgment on him (v. 4). This is the negative, flip side of God's blessing on his people; they share in his judging of the world. It is a high honor that all his people are destined one day to share (1 Corinthians 6:2).

But as Christians who now stand on the other side of the cross, what are we to make of the *form* that God's justice took in this particular case (v. 6), especially in view of Jesus' command to love our enemies and do them good, not harm (Luke 6:27)? We have already noted that it is not revenge. But what more can be said? Positively, it is a case of the principle of justice enshrined in the Law of Moses: "If anyone injures his neighbor, as he has done it shall be done to him, fracture for fracture, eye for eye, tooth for tooth; whatever injury he has given a person shall be given to him" (Leviticus 24:19, 20).

The responsibility to dispense justice of this kind lay with duly appointed judges (Exodus 21:22), not private individuals, and limited punishment to what was fair: the offender got no more and no less than he deserved. Given the extreme brevity of the account, it's not clear whether or not there was any judicial process involved in Adoni-bezek's case; probably not. That is the nature of warfare; it delivers summary justice in situations where the normal processes of justice have broken down. But that does not make the punishment meted out to Adoni-bezek unjust. In view of the sheer volume of suffering he had inflicted (by his own admission he had mutilated seventy) he was actually treated rather leniently!

Finally, we should note that though Jesus forbade personal revenge, he upheld the principle of just retribution and the right and responsibility of judges to administer it (Matthew 7:2; 5:25, 26). We may be glad that in the gospel age in which we live the administration of justice is the role of the state rather than of the church (Romans 13:1–4) and that, on the whole, wrongdoers are dealt with less severely than Adoni-bezek was. But this passage stands as a reminder that cruel tyrants are not all-powerful. Unless they repent, God will call them to account, and his people will share in his victory over them.

Marriage (vv. 11–15)

The blessing of God is more immediately apparent in this second scene. It features not a cruel tyrant who gets his just deserts but a young man who is richly rewarded for his bravery. Othniel distinguishes himself in battle at Kiriath-sepher and wins the hand of Achsah, Caleb's daughter, as his wife. And what a prize she is! Caleb had been a close associate of Joshua. They were among the twelve men chosen to spy out Canaan in preparation for the conquest, and the only two of their generation who were promised that they would enter it because of the faith they had shown in God's promises (Numbers 13:6; 14:6, 30). Caleb in particular had been commended by God as one who had "a different spirit" and fully followed the Lord (Numbers 14:24). So Achsah had a rich heritage, which she brought with her when she became Othniel's bride.

But she also brought herself, and her sterling qualities show through in verses 14, 15. She urges her new husband to ask her father for a field as her dowry, and when the field turns out to be in the Negeb, the dry area in the south of Canaan, she herself presses him to also give her springs to irrigate it. Achsah is no shrinking violet. She's hardheaded and practical. She knows what is needed and is not backward about making a reasonable request. And her father, far from being affronted by her boldness as a lesser man might be, gives her what she has asked for and more: "And Caleb gave her the upper springs and the lower springs" (v. 15). So we end with a picture of the desert blooming. Not just victory in battle, but marriage, land, and fertility—the rich blessing of God. Othniel is truly a blessed man. And to cap it all, Caleb himself, who has blessed Othniel and Achsah with their inheritance, at last, in his extreme old age, receives Hebron as his own promised inheritance, a fitting reward for a lifetime of wholehearted service to God (v. 20).[6]

Not everything is perfect, of course. There are some disquieting indications in verses 19b, 21 that some things did not go according to plan, and we will have more to say about this in due course. Darker days will come. But the overwhelming impression of verses 1–21 is of God's faithfulness to his promise: "And the LORD was with Judah, and he took possession of the hill country" (v. 19a; cf. v. 2). Israel's experience in the period immediately following Joshua's death was one of manifest, abundant blessing.

The Shape of Things to Come

But before we move on, let us reflect again on the question that was asked back in verse 1 and the answer it received: Who will lead us? Judah. This is one of those very pregnant verses of Scripture. It's heavy with significance, and a great deal is going to emerge from it. Of course, the announcement that Judah should take the lead shouldn't have surprised anyone. Way back in the time of the patriarchs Jacob had said this about his fourth son:

> Judah, your brothers shall praise you;
>> your hand shall be on the neck of your enemies;
>> your father's sons shall bow down before you.
> Judah is a lion's cub;
>> from the prey, my son, you have gone up.
> He stooped down; he crouched as a lion
>> and as a lioness; who dares rouse him?
> The scepter shall not depart from Judah,
>> nor the ruler's staff from between his feet,
> until tribute comes to him;
>> and to him shall be the obedience of the peoples. (Genesis 49:8–10)

Judah had always been destined for leadership, but until this time none of that nation's leaders had been Judahites. Moses was not from the tribe of Judah, nor was Joshua. But in the longer term the leadership Israel would need to bring it into the full enjoyment of its inheritance would come from Judah—not just from the tribe of that name, but from one who would arise from it, and the statement made at the beginning of Judges is in effect an announcement that the time has come for this to begin to happen. Not only did the tribe of Judah lead the other tribes after Joshua's death, but Othniel, the first judge, was from Judah (3:7–11).[7] And scarcely are the Judahites named as leaders in chapter 1 than they advance against Jerusalem and subdue it (1:7, 8), the city that was later to become the city of David (2 Samuel 5:6–10). So something begins here in Judges that has its outworking in David, and eventually in Jesus, the great Son of David, Israel's Messiah, and the One hailed in the book of Revelation as "the Lion of the tribe of Judah" (Revelation 5:5).

Time to Reflect

This passage has been about the legacy of a great man. Joshua made a great impact on his generation and left behind him people who worked together, called on God, moved at his command, and experienced his blessing. They coped well with the transition to life without Joshua, in part at least because he had prepared them well for the challenges they would face. Those of us who have been fortunate enough to have godly parents and grandparents have had a similarly great preparation for life. I am reminded of Paul's memorable words to his young protégé, Timothy: "I am reminded of your sincere faith, a faith that dwelt first in your grandmother Lois and your mother Eunice and now, I am sure, dwells in you as well" (2 Timothy 1:5). To be on the receiving end of such a legacy is a great privilege, and it is an equally great privilege to be able to give it to our children and grandchildren. But whether or not we have been blessed in this way, as Christians we all share in a far greater legacy. For the whole church of which we are a part is the legacy of Jesus Christ. It is the fruit of his work and still impacts the world in which we live in incalculable ways. At its worst the church is a scandal, but at its best it bears the imprint of Christ's own character and brings delight to his heart (Ephesians 5:22–32; Revelation 19:6–8; cf. Isaiah 62:5; Jeremiah 32:41; Zephaniah 3:17). And where it honors him as its Lord and is obedient to him, his abundant blessing is evident and brings glory to God.[8]

More importantly, the passage has been about God's providing leadership for his people. It is always a shock when someone who has made a massive impact on the church and on us personally is taken from us. Many of my generation were powerfully impacted by the evangelistic vision and preaching of Billy Graham, now over ninety years of age. We wish our children could have experienced what we did in the 1950s and 1960s when his ministry was at its height and thousands of people came to Christ at his meetings. For us, his death will mean the end of an era in which we saw God move in amazing ways and saw victories that we had scarcely thought possible. On a smaller scale similar loss is felt with the death or departure of a pastor whose faithful ministry has impacted whole families and helped raise up another generation of committed gospel-minded young men and women. All of us know people whose influence on us has been so profound that we feel they are simply irreplaceable. But the reality is that *no human being* is indispensable. Time moves on, and God remains faithful to his people, and in every generation he raises up godly leaders to care for them. But none of them is perfect, and idolizing them can be a snare. It can lead us into a kind of hero-worship that makes it hard for us to see beyond the leaders God gives us to God himself. The fact is that if all those we admire and feel dependent on were taken from us tomorrow we would not be bereft and leaderless.

After Joshua had died God provided the tribe of Judah to lead his people, confirming that Judah was destined to play a central role in God's future purposes for his people. The kind of leadership they would need in the years ahead to enter into all that God had promised them would come from the tribe of Judah. And that larger purpose of God has now been realized in Jesus. He is our supreme leader. He is the perfecter of our faith. He has promised never to leave or forsake us. It is to him we must look, and in his name we must go forward to possess all that God has for us. If we do that, we will not only be greatly blessed ourselves but, like Joshua, will leave a rich legacy to those who come after us.

2

Judgment Day: What Went Wrong?

JUDGES 1:22—2:5

WE LIVE IN A WORLD WHERE things go wrong, and many of the things that do so are beyond our control. Accidents happen. People that are well and strong and in the prime of life are suddenly struck down by cancer. Earthquakes and tsunamis happen without warning and kill thousands. We do our best in work or ministry, but somehow our dreams are never realized. A church plant fails. Things seem to conspire against us, and our plans end in disappointment. People long for marriage, but it never happens for them. A baby is conceived but miscarries. Crops are sown, but the rain never comes. Things go wrong, and we ask why but receive no answers. Things are just not right, and we are powerless to change them.

It is not always so, however. Sometimes there are reasons—reasons that deep down we know but find hard to acknowledge. We bring trouble on ourselves by what we do or fail to do; but instead of accepting responsibility for our misfortune we attribute it to others or to bad luck or the general state of the world or (worst of all) to God. But in the end this is self-destructive. It traps us in a delusion of our own making, damages us morally and spiritually, and cuts us off from the only real source of healing. There is no hope for us until we face up to what really went wrong and our own part in it.

I have always been fascinated with aircraft and for some time now have been an avid watcher of the documentary series *Air Crash Investigations* on the National Geographic channel UK. It's unsettling to say the least, especially when you're about to embark on another overseas trip! Most episodes follow the same basic pattern. A plane is preparing to take off. We are shown the pilots discussing the flight and doing all the appropriate pre-flight checks. They are highly professional and completely in command. There may be some concerns about the weather or other matters. But everything is under control. It's a normal beginning to a normal flight. Then we're shown the passengers boarding the aircraft, making their way down the aisles, finding their seats and storing their luggage. The occasional one is new to flying and looks a little apprehensive, but most look totally relaxed. Sometimes we're told a little about them. This family is going on a vacation. Someone else is visiting a relative she hasn't seen for some time. Another is a businessman on an interstate trip he's done a hundred times. Everyone is settling in. The regular announcements are being made. Everything is routine. No one has any reason to think this flight will be different from any other.

Then a ways into the flight, unusual things begin to happen. They are scarcely noticeable at first—an unexpected warmth in the cabin, a puzzling noise somewhere, lights on the instrument panel that make no sense and begin to confuse the pilots, then difficulty in controlling the aircraft, and finally (too late) a sickening lurch to one side or a plunge, followed by screams, chaos, and darkness. The rest of the program describes the search for survivors and answers. Meticulously, piece by piece, the events that led up to the disaster are retraced, and every scrap of recoverable wreckage is examined in a search for the probable cause. Sometimes no explanation is found, but more often than not there comes a moment of truth when the reason at last comes to light, and measures are taken to ensure, as far as possible, that what happened in this case never happens again. The arrival at the point of explanation is empowering because it enables effective action to be taken.

In the passage we examined in the previous chapter the book of Judges got off to a great start. Joshua's influence lived on. The tribes of Israel inquired of God and worked together. They moved at God's command and were victorious. They experienced God's blessing at both the national and personal level. God was with them. But toward the end of the passage there were some disquieting indications that not everything has gone according to plan. Judah could not dislodge the Canaanites from the coastal plain (1:19), and the Benjaminites did not expel the Jebusites from Jerusalem (1:21). The result was a kind of stalemate: "so the Jebusites have lived with the people of Benjamin in Jerusalem to this day" (1:21). It may not be a disaster on the level of a plane crash. It is more like the first puzzling warnings of one. These revelations pose questions for which no satisfactory answer is yet at hand. If the Lord was with the men of Judah, why were the iron chariots of the

Canaanites such a problem (1:19)? And why, after Jerusalem was conquered, did the Benjaminites allow the Jebusites to remain there (1:21)? Deeper probing of these questions is needed if the real nature of what went wrong is to be understood and appropriate lessons learned from it. This deeper probing happens in the rest of chapter 1, and the full revelation of the underlying causes comes in 2:1–5.

In his "Poem in October" the Welsh poet Dylan Thomas spoke of his thirtieth birthday as a turning point in his life. He likened it to an October day when the chill of approaching winter made itself felt in the air, and he became aware that his life, too, was changing. The carefree days of his childhood were over, and the troubles of his more mature years had begun to darken his horizons. Something similar happens when we get to verse 22 of Judges 1. The focus shifts from Judah and the other southern tribes to "the house of Joseph" (Manasseh and Ephraim)[1] and their allies in the north. All seems well at first. The Joseph tribes go up to Bethel, a strategic town nine miles (fourteen and a half kilometers) north of Jerusalem. The Lord is with them as he had been with the men of Judah, and they too are successful (v. 22). But what follows makes us wonder just how real their achievement is (v. 26). There is a distinct chill in the air, and as we read on we can no longer ignore the negatives—there are just too many of them. They begin to take over the account and dominate it. As in Dylan Thomas's poem, the good times are over, and the bad times have come.

A Claytons Victory (1:22–26)

There is no denying that the victory at Bethel was a significant one. Bethel was a strategic town north of Jerusalem, and taking it opened up the whole northern hill country as far as the Jezreel Valley to potential occupation by Israel. Furthermore, the way it was taken showed a great deal of military skill. Spies were sent to check out its defenses. A man who was leaving the city was approached and promised that his life would be spared if he cooperated with them. With his help they gained access and took the town's defenders by surprise. They struck down the town's inhabitants but, true to their word, spared the collaborator and his family. There are clear echoes here of Joshua's victory at Jericho and the sparing of Rahab the prostitute (Joshua 6). But there is a twist—a totally unexpected development that brings this story to a completely different kind of ending. Bethel's pre-Israelite name was Luz (v. 23), and when the man is spared, he goes to the land of the Hittites (Syria)[2] and builds a new Luz as a memorial to the old one (v. 26)! Was it an act of penance or defiance or simple nostalgia? We don't know. What is clear, though, is that this man, unlike Rahab, does not become an Israelite. He remains a citizen of Luz and therefore still a Canaanite at heart. He retires to a safe distance, but does not go away into oblivion. He builds something that is within the sphere of awareness, and contact, of future generations of Israelites: ". . . Luz. That is its name to this day" (v. 26). In other words, it's not just a man and his family that survive, but Canaanite culture in a very tangible form—a city. Luz has not so much been conquered as moved. The end result is that two cities, one Israelite and the other Canaanite, exist side by side, so to speak. The victory at Bethel turns out to be what Australians would call a Claytons victory—no real victory at all.[3] But there's a riddle here. Why did things turn out this way if "the LORD was with them" (the northern tribes) when they went up against Bethel (v. 22)? What went wrong? The answer is not clear at this point. Only subsequent events will bring it to light.

A Deteriorating Situation (1:27–36)

This passage summarizes the fortunes of the individual northern tribes, from Manasseh (v. 27) to Dan (v. 34), and it's not a pretty story. But there are some successes—"When Israel grew strong, they put the Canaanites to forced labor" (v. 28) and similar statements in verses 30, 35. The Israelites did eventually get the upper hand in some places. But the passage as a whole begins on a negative note (v. 27a), and as it runs its course it becomes clear that in general Israel's position is deteriorating alarmingly. First, the Canaanites hold out in certain areas and end up living among the Israelites (vv. 27, 29, 30, 32); then the Israelites live among the Canaanites (v. 33); and finally the Amorites (another name for Canaanites) stop the Israelites from coming down into the coastal plain and push them back into the hills (v. 34). What began with a victory at Bethel ends with a humiliating defeat and a general situation that can at best be described as a standoff, with Israel living in a land they have not been able to take complete control of. And again we ask, what went wrong? If God was with them (v. 22), what can account for their failure?

This time an explanation of sorts is given. Five of the six paragraphs in this section begin with the same bald statement: the Israelites "did not drive out" the Canaanites—Manasseh didn't (v. 27), nor did Ephraim (v. 29), nor did Zebulun (v. 30), Asher (v. 31), or Naphtali (v. 33). The expression "did not" implies choice and therefore culpability. But couldn't their choice be seen as a simple concession to reality? After all, even Judah, the tribe designated leader by God back in verse 2, had not been able to drive out the Canaanites from the coastal plain "because they had chariots of iron" (1:19).

The Canaanites had superior equipment, military hardware that gave them an unbeatable advantage on low, flat territory. Couldn't the decision of the northern tribes not to drive out the Canaanites from some areas have simply been a piece of military realism—better to settle for what is achievable than risk heavy losses trying to do the impossible? And the experience of the Danites in verse 34 (being pushed back into the hills) seems to confirm that the decision of the other tribes was right. Still, though, the question lingers: if God was with them (v. 22), why should iron chariots have been decisive? Why were concessions necessary? The *real* cause of Israel's failure is still not apparent. Further probing of exactly what went wrong is needed. As in the case of air crash investigations, the search for an answer is still ongoing. The chief investigator has not yet submitted his final report. But he is about to do so. Enter "the angel of the LORD" (2:1)!

Judgment Day (2:1–5)

This first appearance of "the angel of the LORD" (2:1) marks a very special moment in the book of Judges. He "went up" from Gilgal to Bochim (v. 1), just as Judah "went up" to Bezek in 1:4 and the house of Joseph "went up" to Bethel in 1:22. In fact this is the last of a series of goings up that have spanned the whole of chapter 1 as the various tribes have moved up from Israel's encampment near the Jordan to take possession of their respective territories throughout the land.[4] This final "going up" (v. 1) by the angel of the Lord brings us to the moment when all that has gone before is to be reviewed and assessed. It's judgment day.

But who exactly is this "angel of the LORD" (v. 1)? This is the first time we meet him in Judges, but it will not be the last. He will appear again, briefly, in 5:23, then again in 6:11ff. and 13:3ff., but his identity remains mysterious. The best clues come in chapters 6 and 13, and we'll reserve further comment until then. Suffice it to say that here in chapter 2 he speaks as though he is God himself: "*I* brought you up from Egypt . . . *I* will never break *my* covenant with you . . ." (v. 1) and so on. And the response of the Israelites as soon as he stops speaking is to offer sacrifices "to the LORD" (v. 5). In other words, he is a messenger like no other in the Old Testament. The fact that he goes up from "Gilgal" (v. 1), near Jericho, suggests he may be the very one who appeared to Joshua in the same place as "the commander of the LORD's army" in Joshua 5:13–15. To encounter him is to encounter God. The one who appeared to Joshua at the beginning of Israel's campaign to occupy Canaan now appears again to review how things have gone and to give his verdict on whether or not his orders have been followed. It's a tense moment for Israel.

The verdict is not positive, and this is not a happy day for those being called to account. Bochim (v. 1), which means "weeping," is another name for Bethel. It is not its real name, but what the Israelites came to call it because of what happened there (v. 5). They will come to Bethel and weep again near the end of the book (20:26). The place where God had promised to give Jacob the land (Genesis 28:10–19) and where the Joseph tribes had had a significant victory (1:22–26) became a place of sorrow and bitter memories because of things that began to go wrong there and got worse as time went by.

The key word in the angel's speech is "covenant": "I said, 'I will never break my covenant with you, and you shall make no covenant with the inhabitants of this land'" (vv. 1, 2). A covenant is a promise confirmed in a ceremony of some kind, a wedding, for example, in which people solemnly promise to be faithful to each other. God had made such a covenant with Israel when he promised to give the land of Canaan to Abraham's descendants, and he had acted on that promise when he brought them out of slavery in Egypt and led them through the wilderness to the promised land (v. 1). Israel's responsibility, as beneficiaries of this covenant, was to be faithful to the Lord by keeping his commandments. One such commandment was that they should not make a covenant with the people of Canaan, but rather break down their altars (v. 2; cf. Deuteronomy 7:1–5). They could not be in two covenants at once—one with the Lord and the other with the people of Canaan and (by implication) their gods. To do so would be unfaithful to the Lord. And the accusation brought by the angel is that this is exactly what Israel has done. The Lord had promised never to break his covenant with them, and they had promised the same, but they had not kept their promise. In becoming covenant-makers with the Canaanites they had become covenant-breakers with the Lord who had brought them out of Egypt. This is God's own analysis of what went wrong and led to the failure described in 1:22–36.

It began at Bethel, or Luz as the Canaanites called it. "The LORD was with" the Israelites (1:22), but instead of simply going ahead and trusting him to give them victory, they made an agreement with a Canaanite, and from there it was downhill all the way for Israel. The verdict of the angel of the Lord is that it was not the superior might of the Canaanites that defeated Israel or their determination to remain in the land, but Israel's unfaithfulness to the Lord—their making a covenant with the people of the land. Those who are unfaithful to the Lord cannot expect to have his continued presence with them. By that unfaithfulness they forfeited the full possession of what God had promised them. What began with making covenant with a Canaanite at Bethel ended with bitter weeping there before the Lord they had betrayed.

But let us think again of that expression they "deal[t] kindly" with the informer (1:24). It sounds so innocuous, doesn't it? Even good and right. But the underlying Hebrew expression is, "we will do *chesed* with you," and the word *chesed* is a word that has to do with making a covenant. To "do *chesed*" with someone is enter into a bond with them, to pledge loyalty to them (Genesis 21:23; Deuteronomy 7:9; etc.), and to do this in a way that compromises your loyalty to God is wrong, however innocent and right it may seem. That is the substance of the angel's rebuke to the Israelites at Bethel. "What is this you have done?" (v. 2) echoes the question God put to Adam in the garden of Eden. And Adam's feeble excuses, like the pathetic fig leaves he and Eve had put on, only made the truth more apparent. They had disobeyed the God who made them. They had been unfaithful to the One to whom they owed everything. They had sinned, and they knew it.

And just as their sin had terrible consequences, so would Israel's. The Lord would no longer drive out the Canaanites before his people. They had already had a taste of this in chapter 1; now they were to experience it in full measure. They would not just share the land God had given them with Canaanites, but the gods of those they had failed to dispossess would dispossess *them* of the integrity they could have had as faithful worshipers of Yahweh: "they [the Canaanites] shall become thorns in your sides, *and their gods shall be a snare to you*" (v. 3). Their covenant with a Canaanite became an accommodation with the whole Canaanite way of life, including their religion, and the wrong once committed became a besetting sin that they fell into again and again throughout the entire period of the judges. The book will tell the sorry story of what a harvest of bitter consequences they reaped from their unfaithfulness to God. So "Bethel" ("house of God") became "Bochim" ("place of weeping"). The weeping Israelites offered sacrifices to God there (v. 5), but it was too late. Sacrifice is no substitute for obedience, as Saul was later to learn (1 Samuel 15:22).

A Warning

The situation we see Israel in at the end of this passage did not come about suddenly. It was the result of a slow process that began with one act of compromise. Doing something that is inconsistent with being faithful to God can always be made to sound reasonable, but it is always wrong. And in our own day the temptations to do so are legion, and often very subtle. Under the pressure to act "kindly" (1:24), to be tolerant, we can begin to compromise our commitment to the uniqueness of Christ and the truth of the gospel, especially in the pluralistic context in which most of us now live, in which truth is relativized and tolerance is promoted as the supreme virtue. But, of course, it is all a lie. Tolerance is a relative, not absolute virtue. Whether or not it is good depends on what is tolerated. To tolerate evil, however attractively it is packaged, is to bed with the devil and make a covenant with death. It is to be unfaithful to the Lord who saved us and rightly demands our obedience, and when we do it we lose strength, vitality, and victory. We lack moral strength, find ourselves weak in the face of the enemy, and end up weeping and ashamed. And if we manage to preserve some appearance of virtue in this life, a day will come when we will stand before the God we have betrayed and be exposed for the shams we have become.

This is also a warning for the churches to which we belong. The church at Ephesus did not abandon its first love all at once. Nor did the Laodiceans become lukewarm overnight. It was by slow degrees. The shift from faithfulness to compromise was barely perceptible at first. For a long time they were able to ignore the warning signs and pretend that all was well, and they fed their self-deception by the positive comments of their undiscerning admirers. But the word of the risen Christ, sent by his faithful apostle, ended all that. The truth was out, and it was hard to hear: they were loveless, wretched, pitiable, poor, blind, and naked (Revelation 3:17). It was judgment day, and they were as exposed as Israel was before the angel of the Lord. The Apostle Paul put the same basic issue as follows: "Do not be unequally yoked with unbelievers. For what partnership has righteousness with lawlessness? Or what fellowship has light with darkness?" (2 Corinthians 6:14). The world offers us infinite opportunities for compromise. Israel's world was Canaan, with its false gods and beguiling culture. Ours is the fast-paced, hedonistic, pluralistic, consumer culture in which everything is possible and nothing forbidden except intolerance. The opportunities to compromise are well-nigh overwhelming; the pressure to do so is immense.

Nor can we pretend that the issues are straightforward or that what loyalty to Christ requires is always transparently clear. Christian young people sometimes have to choose between being true to God's call on their lives or conforming to their parents' expectations of them. What does it mean to "honor your father and your mother" (Exodus 20:12) in such circumstances? Pastors have to deal daily with relationship issues that are complex and painful, and it's hard to know which course of action is truer to what Scripture teaches. What some see as compromise, others see as the kind of wisdom needed to avoid putting unnecessary obstacles in the way of the gospel. Faced with the difficult issues posed by homosexuality, whole Christian denominations become polarized between those who see themselves as being faithful to Scripture and those who understand themselves as being sensitive to the leading of the Spirit.[5] And so on. These issues will not go away, and there are no easy answers to many of them. We must all answer to our own consciences before God and allow others to do the same. What we must never do, though, is close our ears to the Word of God or harden our hearts when God speaks to us. Because in the end it is not to the world with its strident voices and insistent demands for our acquiescence that we must answer, but to Christ the Lord and the Word of God that he honored as Scripture. For one day we, like Israel, will have to stand before the divine Judge and hear his verdict on how faithful we have been to him (2 Corinthians 5:9, 10; 1 John 2:2). It will be too late then to change what we have done, and no excuse will bear his scrutiny if we have failed him. Better to be faithful now than to weep then.

3

Losing Our Children: "Another Generation . . . Who Did Not Know the Lord"

JUDGES 2:6-15

GENERATIONAL CHANGE is a reality that none of us can avoid. As the Preacher of the book of Ecclesiastes has put it so memorably, "A generation goes, and a generation comes" (Ecclesiastes 1:4a). Only the earth "remains for ever," and even that will pass away one day and be replaced by a new and different one (Ecclesiastes 1:4b; Revelation 22:1). Change is inevitable and must be embraced, including the changes that take place from generation to generation. Gen X follows baby boomers, to be followed in turn by Gen Y and Gen Z, and each generation is shaped by the circumstances and experiences of its own time. Generations overlap, and those of one generation have to live with and try to understand those of another. But eventually the last of each generation passes away. Only the memory and legacy of that generation remains, and with time even that begins to be marginalized and diminished. The new generation must make its own way in life, engaging with its own world and shaped by its own values.

All this can cause great anxiety, because the values of our own generation, inculcated in our upbringing, seem so obviously right to us. We fear for our children, who live in such a different world and are influenced by things that pull them in a different direction from the one we feel they should take. This is a special anxiety for Christian parents, who believe that the most basic values of their lives are not simply passing fashions but eternal truths. The anxiety can become extreme when parents feel that any departure from these truths by their children must be because of some failure in their raising of them. The faithfulness or otherwise of their children is read as success or failure on their own part, and parents can carry heavy burdens of guilt all their lives if some of their children do not turn out to be believers. Losing their children can mean losing self-respect and sometimes the respect of others, including other Christians. All this is extremely painful. It's a kind of death, just as real in some ways as actual bereavement, but often it doesn't attract the same kind of sympathy. Losing our children is no light thing. Losing a whole generation is incalculably worse.

Losing Joshua (vv. 6–9)

> When Joshua dismissed the people, the people of Israel went each to his inheritance to take possession of the land. (2:6)

The passing of Joshua's generation began with the passing of Joshua himself. The book of Judges opens by drawing attention to his death as a boundary marker between two eras. It is surprising, therefore, to say the least, to meet Joshua again here in chapter 2 still very much alive! With that we are suddenly back at the beginning of the judges period again, or more correctly before the beginning, because the assembly from which Joshua dismisses the people here in 2:6, "each to his inheritance to take possession of the land," is not the assembly of 1:1, 2 at which Israel had inquired of the Lord after Joshua's death. Nor is it the one that has just been described in 2:1–5. It is the much earlier assembly of Joshua 24 at which Joshua himself had presided. Joshua knew, at that time, that his own death was near and that with it Israel would approach a critical moment. Much had been achieved in his lifetime. Major battles had been fought and won. God had given victory after victory—so much so that at the end of those battles Joshua had been able to say that "not one word has failed of all the good things that the LORD your God promised concerning you. All have come to pass for you; not one of them has failed" (Joshua 23:14). God had broken the back of Canaanite resistance. Israel had prevailed. The land was subdued before them and had been allocated to the various tribes as their inheritance, a different part for each tribe (Joshua 13—21). God had been faithful to Israel, and under Joshua's leadership they had been faithful to him. Much remained to be done (Joshua 13:1), but the decisive battles were over. All the tribes had to do now was take possession of what was already theirs.

But Joshua's long life was coming to an end, and it was handover time, time for Joshua to commission the next generation as Moses had commissioned him. He told them to revere the Lord and serve him alone, and they promised to do so (Joshua 24:14–22). But it would be harder to do this when he was no longer there to inspire them by his example and strong leadership. And Joshua knew it. That's why he had renewed the covenant in a solemn assembly at Shechem and bound Israel by a solemn oath never to forsake the Lord (Joshua 24:14–25). He knew that the time after his death would be a testing time for Israel. Without his firm, guiding hand they would become vulnerable to the huge temptations to unfaithfulness that life in the land of Canaan would present. It's like a father anxious about how his children will fare when they leave home and have to make their way in a world that is alluring but often hostile to Christian faith. Or like an aging pastor pondering his retirement and concerned for those he has invested his life in and must now leave to the care of others. Subsequent events will show that Joshua's concerns were not unfounded. The loss of Joshua would be a great loss to Israel.

For a time, though, all appeared to be well. Those Joshua dismissed from the great assembly at Shechem went with purpose, "each to his inheritance to take possession of the land" (v. 6). They knew where they were going and were confident they would be able to accomplish what Joshua had entrusted to them. The territories that had been assigned to them were their "inheritance," something God had determined they should have and that Joshua had bequeathed to them by the victories he had won. They went fired by Joshua's exhortations and by his own sterling example. Joshua himself entered his own inheritance as described in verse 9, and they expected to do the same. And why not? Joshua was dead, but Joshua's God certainly wasn't. There was no reason at all why the loss of Joshua should mean the loss of God or the loss of what he intended for them. So they carried on, motivated and shaped by the example Joshua had left them. "And the people served the LORD all the days of Joshua, and all the days of the elders who outlived Joshua, who had seen all the great work the LORD had done for Israel" (v. 7). Joshua's words and example were powerful. But the Israelites had something far greater to give them confidence as they faced the future: the memory of the "great work" (v. 7) *God* had already done and that they had personally experienced under Joshua.

Memory is a powerful thing. In an important sense we are defined by our history. We are what our history has made us, and without a clear memory of it we can forget who we are. Without anchorage in the past we can become adrift in the present, without any clear sense of what our destiny is. Those who had experienced the great things the Lord had done for Israel under Joshua had the kind of foundation that gave stability and purpose to their lives, and it showed in how they lived: they "served the LORD" (v. 7) all their days. But memory is also a fragile thing. If it is not reinforced by constant teaching and recall, it can grow weak—too weak to keep us anchored to what is foundational to our existence. And when that happens we begin to drift. That is what happened to those who came after Joshua and his contemporaries had passed away.

Losing the Next Generation (v. 10)

The first thing we are told about the next generation is that they "did not know the LORD or the work that he had done for Israel" (v. 10). It's not entirely clear how we are meant to take this. At the very least it seems that the two things mentioned here must be closely related. There is a necessary connection between knowing the Lord and knowing the "work" he has done. To "not know" this great work was to "not know" the One who did it, and according to verse 7 the "great work" being referred to is the victory over the kings of Canaan that God had given to Joshua and those who fought under his leadership. This began with the remarkable conquest of Jericho (Joshua 6) and continued with the fall of Ai (Joshua 8) and the subsequent successful campaigns in the south and north of Canaan (Joshua 10, 11). The results are documented in the list of kings defeated by Joshua in Joshua 12.

In Joshua 21:43–45 all of this is attributed to God and his faithfulness to the promises he had made to Israel. None of it, in the final analysis, was Joshua's work. All of it, from beginning to end, was a "great work" that *the Lord* had done for Israel in fulfillment of his covenant promises (Judges 2:7). To experience that "great work" was to experience firsthand the mighty power and trustworthy character of God, just as an earlier generation had experienced them in the exodus from Egypt in the time of Moses. Such experiences do not happen every day, but when they do they are powerful enough to shape a whole generation and even a whole people for generations to come—if they are remembered. And there is the challenge for each generation—to make sure, as best they can, that what is foundational to their faith is not forgotten by those who come after them.

In Israel this responsibility fell first of all on parents.

> And these words that I command you today shall be on your heart. You shall teach them diligently to your children, and shall talk of them when you sit in your house, and when you walk by the way, and when you lie down, and when you rise. You shall bind them as a sign on your hand, and

they shall be as frontlets between your eyes. You shall write them on the doorposts of your house and on your gates. (Deuteronomy 6:6–9)

The annual celebration of the Passover was meant to keep memories alive and give parents the opportunity to answer vital questions.

And when your children say to you, "What do you mean by this service?" you shall say, "It is the sacrifice of the LORD's Passover, for he passed over the houses of the people of Israel in Egypt, when he struck the Egyptians but spared our houses." (Exodus 12:26, 27)

The importance of this was even rehearsed in public worship, so that each generation of worshipers would remember the solemn responsibility God had entrusted to them.

He established a testimony in Jacob
  and appointed a law in Israel,
which he commanded our fathers
  to teach to their children,
that the next generation might know them,
  the children yet unborn,
and arise and tell them to their children,
  so that they should set their hope in God
and not forget the works of God,
  but keep his commandments. (Psalm 78:5–7)

But instructing and warning the next generation was not the responsibility of parents alone. They were to be supported in this by the nation's leaders, especially the Levites:

Then Moses wrote this law and gave it to the priests, the sons of Levi, who carried the ark of the covenant of the LORD, and to all the elders of Israel. And Moses commanded them, "At the end of every seven years, at the set time in the year of release, at the Feast of Booths, when all Israel comes to appear before the LORD your God at the place that he will choose, you shall read this law before all Israel in their hearing. Assemble the people, men, women, and little ones, and the sojourner within your towns, that they may hear and learn to fear the LORD your God, and be careful to do all the words of this law, and that their children, who have not known it, may hear and learn to fear the LORD your God, as long as you live in the land that you are going over the Jordan to possess." (Deuteronomy 31:9–13)

On such occasions all Israelites, parents and children alike, were to be reminded of the Law of God and their solemn duty to obey it. And that Law was not bare commandments, but also the story of God's saving acts, especially of his deliverance of Israel's ancestors from slavery in Egypt: "I am the LORD your God, who brought you out of the land of Egypt, out of the house of slavery. You shall have no other gods before me" (Exodus 20:1–3). There were laws to be kept. But there were also things that must never be forgotten, and it was the duty of each generation to remind the next generation of them.

Given all this, should the blame for the loss of the judges' generation be laid squarely at the feet of Joshua and his contemporaries? Had they been so taken up with the task of conquering Canaan that they had neglected the most vital task of all, teaching their own children the Law of God and instilling in them the memory of the great things he had done for Israel? Some have thought so.[1] But a careful reading of the passage does not support this. First, as we have already noted, God's "work" on view in verse 10 is not the exodus from Egypt, which was central to the rehearsing of the Law, but the God-given conquest of Canaan under Joshua referred to in verse 7. The next generation did not "know" the Lord because they had not seen *this* "work." Second, since not knowing and not seeing are linked in this way, we cannot take the not knowing as ignorance caused by a lack of instruction. The point is not that they had no awareness of the things in question, but simply that they had not experienced them firsthand. Finally, and most importantly, in what immediately follows it is the next generation themselves, not their parents, who are blamed for what happened: they "did what was evil . . . they abandoned the LORD" (vv. 11, 12). In other words, their not knowing was willful rather than innocent. It was rebellion, a deliberate refusal to acknowledge the obligations entailed in their covenant relationship with God.

The next generation were no less ignorant of their calling as a nation than Samson was of his calling as a Nazirite (16:17). Their "evil" (v. 11) did not arise from a failure on the part of their parents, but from their own choice. Not having experienced firsthand what their parents had experienced was a contributing factor, but it was no excuse. If that were the case all generations later than Moses could be excused for *their* wrongdoing because they had not experienced the exodus from Egypt. These things were known and placed each succeeding generation under the same obligation to be faithful to Yahweh. But the post-Joshua generation repudiated this obligation, and the author of Judges lays the blame squarely on them themselves rather than on their parents. They were the rebellious children of faithful parents.

There are other notable examples of this in Scripture. The godly Hezekiah is followed by the godless Manasseh. The reforming Josiah is followed by Jehoahaz, who "did what was evil in the sight of the LORD" (2 Kings

13:11). And even where parents clearly do sin, the character of their children varies. Adam and Eve had Abel, whose offering pleased God, and Cain, who murdered his brother. Even Jesus, who had no children, had a Judas among his disciples. Instructing children in the ways of the Lord is a very serious responsibility. However, careful readers of the Bible will be wary of drawing too direct a connection between the faithfulness or unfaithfulness of parents in doing this and the eventual character of their adult children. We will return to this below.

Apostasy (vv. 11–13)

The language used of the next generation's behavior here is very strong: they "did what was evil . . . they abandoned the LORD" (vv. 11, 13). It may not have happened all at once; such things seldom do. There is probably foreshortening in the text; what took some time is spoken of in summary fashion. Some of the compromises involved are described in chapter 1 and summarized in the angel's speech in 2:1–5. The present passage speaks only of the end result. However it came about, and however long it took to happen, what the next generation did was to turn away from the Lord, and in the end it was quite conscious and deliberate. Apostasy is a choice: it is to choose evil over good, and to forsake the Lord for something or someone else. Apostasy is the renunciation of something you once professed to believe. And apostates are self-made; they are not the victims of others' choices. They are what they have chosen to be.

We have all seen it happen. Perhaps a pastor or high-profile Christian leader abandons his calling for an immoral relationship and ends up justifying his choice by attacking the faith he once preached. Or a son who was an apparently ardent disciple of Jesus in his teens now disdains Christianity as something he has outgrown in his adulthood. There are always contributing circumstances, and in some cases these may include what others have done or failed to do. But in the end those who have turned away must accept responsibility for their own actions. Seeing themselves as victims will not save them. Nor will it help for others to excuse them by shifting the primary responsibility from the wrongdoers to themselves. The truth must be told if recovery is to happen: they have done what is evil; they have abandoned the Lord.

The Anatomy of Evil

The term "evil" damns apostasy with a single word. Apostasy is evil; no other term is strong enough to capture its gravity. And this judgment is justified for several reasons, as verses 11–13 indicate. To do what is evil "in the sight of *the LORD*" (v. 11) is to sin absolutely, because the Lord is the absolute moral authority. What is evil in the eyes of human beings is a matter of personal judgment: what one person considers evil another person may not. But what is evil in the sight of the Lord is unambiguously evil—it is that simple. The Lord is the one described in Genesis 2 as the Lord God, the Creator of human beings, and therefore one who has the absolute right to distinguish right from wrong and determine the bounds within which life is to be lived. He who ordered the physical universe by his word, separating heaven from earth, light from darkness, and land from sea (Genesis 1), also separated right from wrong by that same word (Genesis 2). To do what is evil in his sight is to repeat what Adam and Eve did in Genesis 3. It is to commit the primal sin, the one sin that is the source of all others, to declare one's solidarity with fallen humanity in its defiance of its Creator. It is to choose moral autonomy. But in reality this is not to choose another good—an alternative and equally valid morality—but to do evil. Everything one does from then on is tainted by the underlying evil of rebellion against God and even becomes a justification for it (we do not need God because we are "good" people). To do evil in the sight of the Lord is to commit the ultimate sin, and nothing can compensate for it.

For the Israelites, though, such behavior had a particularly heinous quality. For them it was not simply to sin against their Creator, but to abandon "the LORD, the God of their fathers, who had brought them out of the land of Egypt" (v. 12). In other words, it was the basest ingratitude. The truth is that there was nothing in how the Lord had treated them as a people that justified such behavior. He had chosen them in Abraham as an act of pure grace. He had persevered with the patriarchs through their frequent failures and occasional perverseness with astonishing patience. And when their descendants found themselves enslaved in Egypt and cried out to him for help, he "heard their groaning" and "remembered his covenant with Abraham, with Isaac, and with Jacob" (Exodus 2:23, 24). He sent Moses to lead them and brought them out with signs and wonders to live as his free people. In other words, he was not just their Creator, but their gracious and powerful Redeemer, the one who above all others had the right to their grateful obedience. And this is the one they "abandoned" (v. 12). What other word is there for that but "evil" (v. 11)?

Astonishingly, though, evil can nearly always be justified in some way, at least by those who commit it. What is evil in the eyes of the Lord seems right in their own eyes (17:6; 21:25). People abandon the Lord because some other course of action seems better, more attractive in some way, or required by the circumstances. People rarely just turn away from God; they turn from him to something else. For the Israelites it was "the Baals," "other gods, from among the gods of the peoples who were around them" (vv. 11, 12). The fact that they were in this situation at all, of course, was a result of *previous* disobedience. Instead of dispossessing the Canaanites and destroying their places of worship as they had been told to do, they had chosen accommodation with them. And the angel of the Lord had told them in no uncertain terms what the result would be: "they shall become thorns in your sides, and *their gods shall be a snare to you*" (2:3). And now we see that beginning to happen. The Israelites abandon the Lord and begin to "[go] after" these other gods, "bow down" to them, and "serve" them (vv. 11, 12).

But why did they do so? What made these gods so seductive to the Israelites? I remember some years ago visiting a museum that had an exhibition of artifacts from pre-Israelite Canaan—statuettes of male and female gods, sacrificial vessels, images of sacrificial animals, miniature altars, and so on. It was a remarkable collection, and as an Old Testament scholar I was fascinated by these things. But I never once felt inclined to fall down and worship them. To Israel's neighbors, however, these things were powerful symbols of the forces that shaped their whole lives for good or ill, the spiritual powers behind what we would regard as natural phenomena—the changing seasons, the autumn and spring rains, the things that determined the fertility of the soil, and animals they depended on for their food and welfare. And the worship of these nature gods seemed to work for the Canaanites. They had lived in the land a long time and knew its ways. They knew how to raise the kinds of crops that fed their families and made them prosperous, and they attributed their success to the worship of their gods. In contrast, the newly-arrived Israelites had no experience of such things. Their ancestors had been slaves in Egypt, where they depended on Pharaoh to feed them. In the wilderness they had been fed manna by God. But now that they were in Canaan the manna had stopped falling from Heaven (Joshua 5:12). They had to farm the soil and feed themselves as their neighbors did, but they didn't know how to. What could make more sense, in these circumstances, than to learn from the native inhabitants of the land? And what harm could there be in "enriching" their worship by incorporating some elements of the local culture? But Yahweh saw it differently. They could not have him and Baal too. They had to choose and had chosen wrongly. They had chosen the way of unfaithfulness to their covenant Lord and became spiritual adulterers. What they did was "evil in the sight of the Lord," and he would no more tolerate it than a husband would tolerate his wife taking other lovers (v. 11). Israel would learn, to its cost, that the Lord took his relationship with them seriously.

Anger (vv. 14, 15)

This is a very confronting paragraph. Everything in it flows from the "anger" of verse 14a—the giving over, selling, and powerlessness of verse 14, the "harm" of verse 15a, and the "terrible distress" of verse 15b. From beginning to end it shows us the terrible consequences of Israel's apostasy, and the anger that makes it all happen is God's: "the anger of *the Lord* was kindled against Israel" (v. 14a). This is not an easy aspect of the Bible's teaching for us. But we dare not shrink from it. To do so would be to make the same mistake that Israel made in the period of the judges. To fail to take the anger of God seriously is to court disaster.

This passage has several things to teach us about this important subject. First, the anger of God is real. Verse 14a reads literally, "Yahweh's nose became hot against Israel!" To us this is a quaint, even humorous word picture. But it is anything but a laughing matter. It conveys in a typically concrete and vivid way the fact that Yahweh is a *passionate* God. He has powerful emotions. Things move him, and he reacts! Historically this has been a problem for many Christian thinkers. How can God be all-powerful, totally sovereign, if he is moved by things outside himself? Doesn't the ascription of emotion to God detract in some way from his Godness? Mustn't we understand the language to be metaphorical and its real referent to be something other than emotions? There are at least two problems with this line of thought, however. First, whatever aspect of God's nature the language refers to, the verb "was kindled" implies change. God *reacted* to Israel's apostasy. He was *moved* by it in some way. So the underlying "problem" of God being moved by something outside himself remains, whether or not the language is metaphorical. Second, too much is lost if we back away from the belief that God has emotions. Along with his anger, we would also have to deny his love, his grief, and his compassion. We would be left with a God utterly unlike the one we actually meet in the Bible, and especially in Jesus Christ who has most perfectly revealed him to us. The truth is not that God does not have emotions, but that he has *perfect* emotions—emotions that are not faulty as ours are and do not lead him into errors of judgments as ours sometimes do.

The second thing we need to note here is that God's anger is not without cause. It is aroused by Israel's apostasy. We will never be able to see God's anger as right until we understand the true nature of apostasy. Forsaking the Lord is not a mistake or misdemeanor that can be easily excused. It is not an error of judgment; it is a deliberate breach of trust, every bit as deep and hurtful as marital unfaithfulness. In other words, it is deeply personal and wounding. Perhaps only those who have experienced this kind of betrayal by one they love can fully appreciate how justified God's anger is and how strange it would be if it were absent.

Thirdly, the way God's anger is expressed is not capricious but measured and in complete accord with what he had said he would do. See, for example, the following warnings Joshua had given Israel as God's spokesman:

> And now I am about to go the way of all the earth, and you know in your hearts and souls, all of you, that not one word has failed of all the good things that the LORD your God promised concerning you. All have come to pass for you; not one of them has failed. But just as all the good things that the LORD your God promised concerning you have been fulfilled for you, so the LORD will bring upon you all the evil things, until he has destroyed you from off this good land that the LORD your God has given you, if you transgress the covenant of the LORD your God, which he commanded you, and go and serve other gods and bow down to them. Then the anger of the LORD will be kindled against you, and you shall perish quickly from off the good land that he has given to you. (Joshua 23:14–16)

> If you forsake the LORD and serve foreign gods, then he will turn and do you harm and consume you, after having done you good. (Joshua 24:20)

God had shown himself to be true to his word by fulfilling the promises he had made to his people, and he would also be true to his word in fulfilling the warnings he had given them. There is nothing capricious about that. The God of the Bible gets angry, but he does not throw tantrums!

Fourth, God's anger has terrible consequences for those who are the objects of it. For Israel it meant being given over, "plundered," "sold," "harm[ed]," and ending up in "terrible distress" (Judges 2:14). It is an awful thing to have God angry with you, and the New Testament warns us of this in no less graphic terms than the Old. In his "wrath" against ungodly people, God "gave them up" to impurity, dishonorable passions, and a debased mind (Romans 1:18–28). Such people are "children of wrath" and without hope according to Ephesians 2:1–12. And the final consequence of being in that state is "the punishment of eternal destruction" (2 Thessalonians 1:9). No wonder Jesus told us to "fear him who can destroy both soul and body in hell" (Matthew 10:28). Hell is the *ultimate* "terrible distress" (Judges 2:15), the final consequence of having God against you. And if that is a warning for the world, it is also a warning for those who profess to be followers of Christ.

Jesus spoke his most terrible warnings about Hell to his twelve disciples, one of whom, Judas, proved to be a "son of destruction" (John 17:12). And the frightful warning of Hebrews 10:26–31 was written to Christians who were tempted to do what Judas did:

> For if we go on sinning deliberately after receiving the knowledge of the truth, there no longer remains a sacrifice for sins, but a fearful expectation of judgment, and a fury of fire that will consume the adversaries. Anyone who has set aside the law of Moses dies without mercy on the evidence of two or three witnesses. How much worse punishment, do you think, will be deserved by the one who has trampled underfoot the Son of God, and has profaned the blood of the covenant by which he was sanctified, and has outraged the Spirit of grace? For we know him who said, "Vengeance is mine; I will repay." And again, "The Lord will judge his people." It is a fearful thing to fall into the hands of the living God.

The Israelites who "abandoned the LORD" (Judges 2:12) in the period of the judges were playing with fire. The "terrible distress" (v. 15) they experienced was not Hell, but it was certainly a foretaste of it. Apostasy is no small matter. It arouses God's righteous anger, and the consequences are severe.

Hope

What hope is there for rebels and those who care deeply about them? What consolation is there for one generation that sees the next generation turn away from God? What hope is there for a church or nation that abandons the Lord? And what solace is there for godly parents who see a dearly loved child walk away? No consolation is offered in this passage, which speaks only of apostasy and God's anger. But there is hope—slim perhaps, but real nonetheless—in the place of this passage in the book. It is not the end! There is more to Israel's story than is told in these verses, and more to God's character than his anger. So those who must bear the pain of seeing others abandon the Lord are not alone. They stand with others who suffer as they do. And they stand with God, who has been abandoned as they have. And they hope in him.

4

The Program

JUDGES 2:16—3:6

ATTENDING A THEATER to watch a performance is usually enjoyable, which is why we go. But it can also be frustrating and confusing, especially if the performance is in a foreign language (as often with opera) or in archaic rather than contemporary English (as with Shakespeare) or in a genre with which you are not familiar (as in some kinds of music or dance) or if the story line is complex. In these circumstances it can be very helpful to have an introduction of some kind. A good introduction can enhance your comprehension and enjoyment of what you are about to see. To meet this need, theater companies and producers normally provide a program that is available on arrival. It is often overpriced and has more advertising than we would like, but most theatergoers accept it as indispensable to their enjoyment of the performance and a nice souvenir to keep and take home. So sales are generally strong and provide additional income for those involved in the production. Programs work well.

Of course, the book of Judges is no theater piece; it was never intended for the stage. It has a much more serious purpose than to entertain or make money. But it certainly is a drama of considerable complexity, with some exciting, tension-filled, and even humorous moments, and a host of colorful characters. Most of them make only a temporary appearance, some for as little as one or two verses. The scene is constantly changing, and the various acts are more or less complete in themselves, with little clear connection between them. The variety and constant change can be bewildering. What is it all about? Fortunately, in 2:16—3:6 the author has given us a program that answers this question for us. It gives us the broad outline of the story, without spoiling it by giving us any of the detail. At heart, what we are about to experience is a tussle between two principal characters, the Lord Yahweh and his people Israel, who have pledged loyalty to one another, but whose relationship is in trouble. As act follows act, scene follows scene, and each episode of the story gives way to the next, the crisis in their relationship deepens, until Yahweh is faced with a decision he had hoped to avoid. The relationship seems unsustainable. But the program has not told us everything; we are in for some surprises.

Grace

The outline the program gives us begins with an action of God: "Then the LORD raised up judges, who saved them out of the hand of those who plundered them" (v. 16). This tells us that the story to be unfolded in the body of the book, beginning with the account of the first judge in 3:7–11, is fundamentally a drama of grace. Israel has sinned, God is angry, Israel suffers. But God's basic disposition toward them is one of grace: he raises up "judges" (v. 16) to save them—not one judge, but many; not on one occasion, but again and again. Notice how astonishing this grace is.

First, it is grace in the face of the most shameful betrayal. After delivering Israel from slavery in Egypt, God had made a covenant with them at Sinai (Exodus 20—24). It was not a covenant that was imposed, but was graciously given and freely accepted. It was in effect a marriage that Israel had entered into with Yahweh that day, solemnly swearing to be faithful.

> Moses came and told the people all the words of the LORD and all the rules. And all the people answered with one voice and said, "All the words that the LORD has spoken we will do." . . . And Moses took half of the blood and put it in basins, and half of the blood he threw against the altar. Then he took the Book of the Covenant and read it in the hearing of the people. And they said, "All that the LORD has spoken we will do, and we will be obedient." And Moses took the blood and threw it on the people and said, "Behold the blood of the covenant that the LORD has made with you in accordance with all these words." (Exodus 24:3, 6–8)

Furthermore, when Yahweh had fulfilled his promises to them by giving them Canaan through Joshua, Moses' successor, they had voluntarily renewed the covenant and again vowed to be faithful.

> Then Joshua said to the people, "You are witnesses against yourselves that you have chosen the LORD, to serve him." And they said, "We are witnesses." He said, "Then put away the foreign gods that are among you, and incline your heart to the LORD, the God of Israel." And the people said to Joshua, "The LORD our God we will serve, and his voice we will obey." (Joshua 24:22–24)

But then, when the last of Joshua's generation is dead, they do exactly what they had vowed never to do. Those who have received Canaan as a gift forget their duty to those who gave it to them and become focused on the present and the new opportunities life in Canaan presents to them. Prosperity beckons, and the new ways seem better. They abandon Yahweh as yesterday's god.[1] And what does Yahweh do when it doesn't work out? He raises up judges to save them. That's grace.

Second, it's grace that springs from compassion. The statement about Yahweh raising up judges comes immediately after the "terrible distress" of verse 15, *with nothing in between.* There is no confession of sin on Israel's part, no repentance, no putting away of their alternative gods, not even a cry for help! These things do happen from time to time in the stories of the judges that follow, but what the program is telling us is that they are never the cause of Yahweh's gracious rescue missions, because Israel's repentance, if it happens at all, is always shallow and temporary. It never signals a true change of heart and never leads back to true and lasting loyalty. And Yahweh is never fooled by it. The only thing that stirs his heart and moves him to intervene is their distress. He sees it, he cares about it, he remembers they are his, and he raises up judges to save them. That's grace—grace that reaches out in compassion. "The LORD was moved to pity by their groaning" (v. 18).

Third, it's grace that persists. Here we note again the plural of verse 16 and the "whenever" of verse 18: "the LORD raised up *judges*," and "*Whenever* the LORD raised up judges . . . he saved them." There were many judges raised up and many acts of salvation over a period of more than two hundred years,[2] and, of course, that was only the latest chapter in God's grace to Israel. From the beginning the story of his dealings with them had been one of grace. It had survived the waywardness of the patriarchs, the worship of the golden calf, and the ungrateful grumbling of the wilderness generation. It was a patient grace, and a long one. It continued up to and through the whole period of the judges. He raised up judges to save them again and again. It was grace that went the distance. Grace that outlasted disappointment and betrayal and saved again and again and again. Persistent grace.

Finally, though, it was grace that was abused, which brings us to another recurring theme of the program and another, perverse, kind of persistence.

Willfulness

Parents do not need a dictionary to tell them what willfulness is. A willful child is intent on having his or her own way, "headstrong,"[3] "obstinately and often perversely" rebellious.[4] A willful child will not be corrected, however foolish, dangerous, or downright bad his behavior is. God's children, too, were willful, and never more so than in the time of the judges. But willful is perhaps too mild a term for them, for perverseness was not an occasional feature of their obstinacy, but the essence of it. They were willfully persistent in doing *evil*, and nothing even Yahweh could do could halt their headlong pursuit of it for long. Every description of Israel's behavior in verses 16–19 speaks of willfulness: they "did not listen," they "turned aside" (v. 17) "turned back," went "after other gods," "serv[ed] them," "bow[ed] down to them," and finally "did not drop any of . . . their stubborn ways" (v. 19).

The pattern that emerges in these verses has commonly been described as circular and represented in illustration 4.1.

But this is not accurate. We have already noted that there is no reference in the overview here in chapter 2 to Israel "crying out to the LORD." They are not rescued because they appeal to the LORD, but solely because God cannot bear their distress. More significantly, the pattern is one of deterioration rather than mere repetition. This is particularly clear in verse 19: "Whenever the judge died, they turned back and were *more* corrupt than their fathers." In other words, with each turn of the wheel the situation got worse; each generation behaved more badly than the preceding one. What we have is not a repeating cycle, but a downward spiral, a vortex in which Israel is drawn ever more deeply into the grip of the evil it has chosen. And this was in spite of the discipline God repeatedly brought to bear and the attempts of the judges themselves to bring them to a better mind: "they did not listen to their judges" (v. 17).[5] In the judges period Israel was characterized by sheer, mind-boggling, willful persistence in self-destructive rebellion.

It used to be common in evangelical circles to speak of departure from godly living as "backsliding" or falling prey to some "besetting sin." The language is quaint these days and rarely heard, but it refers to problems that are still very much with us. The latter expression was derived from the reference to "sin which doth so easily beset us" in the King James wording of Hebrews 12:1. A "besetting sin" was a particular sin that a person seemed powerless to resist. Try as they would, the temptation to commit it overcame them again and again, so that eventually (unless they were delivered) they remained in the grip of it and it became a permanent blot on their Christian character and testimony. People who found themselves in this state were urged to make open confession of their sin, cry out to God for deliverance, and seek help and counsel from others in the Christian fellowship. "Backsliding" referred to a (usually gradual) departure from practicing a Christian faith that a person had once claimed to have. It was normally attributed to a lack of discipline, circumstances that had overtaken the person and caused him or her to lose confidence or commitment, or the attraction of other things, such as a career or a compromising relationship they were reluctant to give up. Backsliding could be a euphemism for apostasy, but was more often thought of as a tendency in that direction, not yet confirmed by outright abandonment of the faith. Backsliders generally still professed to be Christians, though their behavior called their profession into question. The recommended remedy was a public recommitment to Christ, often at an evangelistic meeting.

"Backsliding" and "besetting sin" were and still are serious problems. But neither term is fully adequate to describe Israel's behavior in Judges, because both are fundamentally sins of weakness rather than willfulness. The Israelites of the judges period returned again and again to the same sin, but they were not backsliders—they were persistent, willful sinners. And according to both Testaments, willful sin is an abuse of God's grace that is without remedy. It cannot be atoned for by sacrifice. It is inexcusable and exposes those who commit it directly to God's wrath (Numbers 15:30; Hebrews 10:26–31). It should not surprise us, therefore, that this passage about willful sin is followed immediately by an announcement of judgment.

Judgment (2:20–23)

These verses bring us to the end of the preview of the judges period as a whole that the author has given us in verses 11–19 and to the decision Yahweh made in the light of Israel's persistent sin in spite of all the grace he had shown them. The time has come for God's final verdict on their behavior to be given and appropriate action to be taken.

Verse 20 brings us back to the solemn fact of God's anger. Israel has aroused it again and again and suffered terrible consequences. But each time God has eventually relented and rescued them. Now Israel is to learn a hard lesson: it's possible to provoke God once too often and to incur something far more serious than temporary chastisement. The formal language in verses 20, 21 indicates that we must imagine a court in session, but with a difference. In this court Yahweh is both the prosecuting attorney and the judge. First he reads out the charge: ". . . this people have transgressed my covenant that I commanded their fathers and have not obeyed my voice" (v. 20). Everything about this stresses the seriousness of the offense and the situation to which it has led. Israel is not addressed directly, as they were back in 2:1–3, but is spoken *about* in the third person: "this people." Their willfulness has caused their relationship with Yahweh to break down. Now they face him as their judge rather than their deliverer.

Furthermore, their offense has not been merely against "the law" in an abstract, impersonal sense. It has been against Yahweh personally. They have broken "[his] covenant," which he "commanded" their fathers (v. 20). Moreover, the word "fathers" is a reminder of generational responsibility. They are not just any people, but the children of those to whom God made gracious promises, promises that had been fulfilled under Joshua (Joshua 21:43–45). This entailed an obligation to honor God and their fathers by grateful obedience; but they have dishonored both. So what will the judge do?

The facts before him are: a covenant has been broken (v. 20), and a test has been failed (vv. 21, 22). Let's consider the test first.

The Failed Test (vv. 21, 22)

The test concerned "the nations that Joshua left when he died" (v. 21). The incompleteness of Joshua's conquest of Canaan is frankly acknowledged both here and in the book of Joshua. Joshua himself had referred to this repeatedly in his address to Israel in Joshua 23:

> Behold, I have allotted to you as an inheritance for your tribes *those nations that remain.* (v. 4)

> *These nations remaining* among you. (v. 7)

> The remnant of *these nations remaining among you.* (v. 12)

But verses 22 and 23 of our present passage tell us that this was not due to some failure or oversight on Joshua's part. He left those nations for a purpose (v. 22), and his action in doing so was not his alone, but at the same time God's: "*the Lord* left those nations, not driving them out quickly, and *he* did not give them into the hand of Joshua" (v. 23). The purpose was "to test Israel by them, whether they [would][6] walk in the way of the Lord as their fathers did, or not" (v. 22). We are now at a point, after the summary of Israel's willful sin throughout the whole judges period in verses 11–19, when that test has been failed. Israel has clearly *not* "walk[ed] in the way of the Lord as their fathers did." They have failed the test of faithfulness that God and Joshua had set for them and must now face the consequences.

The Broken Covenant (v. 20)

Israel's failure was not just a legal thing but a relational one, which brings us to the most painful aspect of the dilemma that God as their judge faces here. "Covenant" is the framework for all the proceedings in this courtroom scene. But it is not a covenant that some other person or agency has framed. The judge refers to it as "*my* covenant that *I* commanded" (v. 20). So the offense is personal; it is against God himself.

This is always what sin is in essence: an offense against God. It is also an offense against ourselves as moral beings, and often also an offense against others. But it is fundamentally an offense against God, because he is the Creator of us all and the One who rightly holds us accountable to him for our actions. There is a covenant relationship between God and human beings inherent in creation itself and in our being made in the image of God.[7] The offense is greater, though, for those (like Israel in the Old Testament and Christians in the New Testament) who have been brought into a special relationship with God by his gracious redeeming work for them and in them. This is a covenant relationship more akin to a marriage or to a relationship brought about by birth, like that between children and their parents. So there is more to God's relationship with his guilty people than the relationship between a judge and an offender. The relationship is much more multifaceted, deep, and painful than that. And something worse than failing a test has happened. A covenant of the most personal kind has been broken. Justice must be done, but also something more than justice, and in fact the very nature of the covenant that God had made with Israel recognized this.

God's covenant with Israel had two basic aspects: a promise aspect and a law aspect. The promise aspect was the more fundamental and entailed, among other things, God's commitment to give the whole land of Canaan to Abraham's descendants. This commitment was unconditional.

> The LORD said to Abram . . . "Lift up your eyes and look from the place where you are, northward and southward and eastward and westward, for all the land that you see I will give to you and to your offspring forever. . . . Arise, walk through the length and the breadth of the land, for I will give it to you." (Genesis 13:14–17)

> [God] said to him, "I am the LORD who brought you out from Ur of the Chaldeans to give you this land to possess." But he said, "O Lord GOD, how am I to know that I shall possess it?" . . . Then the LORD said to Abram, "Know for certain that your offspring will be sojourners in a land that is not theirs and will be servants there, and they will be afflicted for four hundred years. . . . And they shall come back here in the fourth generation, . . . To your offspring I give this land, from the river of Egypt to the great river, the river Euphrates, the land of the Kenites, the Kenizzites, the Kadmonites, the Hittites, the Perizzites, the Rephaim, the Amorites, the Canaanites, the Girgashites and the Jebusites." (Genesis 15:7–21)

> And God said to him, "Behold, my covenant is with you, and you shall be the father of a multitude of nations. . . . And I will establish my covenant between me and you and your offspring after you throughout their generations for an everlasting covenant, to be God to you and to your offspring after you. And I will give to you and to your offspring after you the land of your sojournings, all the land of Canaan, for an everlasting possession, and I will be their God." (Genesis 17:3–8)

> Jacob left Beersheba and went toward Haran. And he came to a certain place and stayed there that night, because the sun had set. Taking one of the stones of the place, he put it under his head and lay down in that place to sleep. And he dreamed, and behold, there was a ladder set up on the earth, and the top of it reached to heaven. . . . And behold, the LORD stood above it and said, "I am the LORD, the God of Abraham your father and the God of Isaac. The land on which you lie I will give to you and to your offspring. . . . I am with you and will keep you wherever you go, and will bring you back to this land. For I will not leave you until I have done what I have promised you." (Genesis 28:10–15; cf. Genesis 35:11, 12)

This is the promise referred to by the angel of the LORD (speaking as God) in Judges 2:1: "I brought you up from Egypt and brought you into the land that I swore to give to your fathers. I said, 'I will never break my covenant with you.'" The commitment to give Israel the whole land of Canaan was fundamental to his covenant with them, and he had promised never to break it.

However, the covenant also had a law element. This is particularly clear in the form in which it was given at Mount Sinai—commandments with blessings and curses attached. These did not replace or overturn the promise God made to Abraham but presupposed it.[8] The people God brought out from Egypt and gave his law to were Abraham's descendants, and he rescued them from slavery precisely because he "remembered his covenant with Abraham, with Isaac, and with Jacob" (Exodus 2:24). The Law gave clear instruction about how Israel was to live as the redeemed people of God and spelled out what the consequences of their obedience or disobedience to God would be. In particular Moses had warned the Israelites of his day what would happen if they angered the LORD by turning away from him and worshiping other gods: "evil will befall you, because you will do what is evil in the sight of the LORD" (Deuteronomy 31:29). And Joshua had repeated this warning to the next generation: "if you transgress the covenant of the LORD your God, which he commanded you, and go and serve other gods and bow down to them . . . the anger of the LORD will be kindled against you, and you shall perish quickly from off the good land that he has given to you" (Joshua 23:16). None of this would mean the absolute end of the covenant relationship: they would still be God's people, and the promise on which his relationship with them was based would never be revoked. It did mean, though, that any particular generation could miss out on the enjoyment of what God had promised. One generation would die in the wilderness, another would fail to get full possession of the land, and another would lose it altogether. The complete fulfillment of the promise would come only through the Messiah, Jesus Christ. But at any time the covenant relationship could be experienced as blessing or curse, the enjoyment of what was promised or forfeiture of it by disobedience. That is inherent in the covenant as law, the covenant that, God says, "I *commanded* their fathers" (v. 20).

The Judge's Decision (vv. 21–23)

There are many judges in this book, but only one supreme Judge. He is later acknowledged as such by Jephthah in 11:27 in a situation where negotiation has failed: "The LORD, the Judge, [will] decide this day." We have reached a similar point here in 2:21. Testing has failed, discipline has failed, the covenant has been broken, and God the righteous Judge must decide what to do.

It has been said that God doesn't have problems. Nonsense! You can't have children without having problems, and God has lots of children! Furthermore they are recalcitrant children who refuse correction.[9] The whole world is a problem; the human race as a whole has rebelled against God. But the rebelliousness of God's own people is the problem within the problem; it is the family problem, and the most painful one of all for God. God's biggest problem is his covenant people, the descendants of Abraham, because they stand at the center of his purposes for the world (Genesis 12:1–3). In New Testament terms, God's biggest problem is the church, the spiritual children of Abraham. They are his children, and he cannot simply disown them or break his promises to them without violating his own integrity. But *something* must be done!

God's problem in dealing with sinners, whether his own people or not, is how to be both gracious and just. It is not a problem beyond God's competence, but the solution will not come quickly or without pain. The complete solution is found only in the cross of Christ, where perfect love and perfect justice meet (Romans 3:21–26; cf. Psalm 85:1). Here in Judges 2 a ruling is made that is much less far-reaching but perfectly in accord with God's character and suited to the immediate situation. The people of Israel have abused the grace God has shown them in promising to give the whole land to Abraham's descendants and putting the attainment of that within their reach through Joshua. They have forfeited their right to the enjoyment of the covenant promise and will have instead what was foreshadowed in the covenant law. This generation will not enjoy full possession of the land. The nations that were initially left to test their faithfulness will now be left as a punishment for their unfaithfulness. Yahweh will "no longer drive out before them any of the nations that Joshua left when he died" (v. 21). The fulfillment of the promise will be deferred; this faithless generation will not experience it. This is a carefully measured judgment. God does not give full vent to his anger by revoking the promise and disowning his people. In that sense it is a gracious judgment. But neither does he ignore their willfulness; he punishes them as he said he would. In that sense it is a just judgment. It is only an interim solution, but a just and gracious one. This same blend of grace and justice will characterize all God's dealings with his rebellious people in the judges period and beyond. It's why the history of salvation does not stop here, but continues through all the ups and downs of Israel's history until it reaches its climax in Christ.

Assimilation (3:1–6)

This last part of the passage largely repeats what has gone before. In that sense it's an epilogue, a tailpiece that rounds off the action without adding much to it. It lists the nations the Lord left by not giving them into Joshua's hand (v. 3) and reminds us why he did so: to test Israel (vv. 1, 4). And it reminds us that Israel failed the test by worshiping Canaan's gods (v. 6). We've heard all this before. If we received a theater program that described the final scene of the play in such terms we'd know we could leave before it without missing much. But it also adds a couple of things that we would be the poorer for not staying to hear. First, it gives us another reason why God left those nations. It was so the new generation would not simply receive what others had fought for but would learn something valuable by having to struggle for it themselves (vv. 1, 2). Second, and more important, it tells us of a fatal step that was crucial in Israel's slide into apostasy: they intermarried with the Canaanites (vv. 5, 6). In some ways this tailpiece is a rather wistful reflection on what could have been. Israel could have passed the test and continued to have God's blessing, but they didn't. They could have grown through the struggle to fully claim what was theirs and be the better for it, but they didn't. They could have transformed Canaan from a place of idolatry into a place of God-honoring monotheism, but they didn't. In short, they capitulated to Canaanite culture. In New Testament terms, they became "conformed to this world" (Romans 12:2). The program of conquest became a program of assimilation, and the critical factor, in the end, was intermarriage.

It was a problem that was to plague Israel throughout the time of the judges and on into the rest of the Old Testament period. The first judge, Othniel, married Achsah, the daughter of Caleb, but the last judge, Samson, married a Philistine. Solomon brought ruin on Israel by marrying "many foreign women" (1 Kings 11:1), and even the exile did not cure Israel of the problem. The leaders of the restored community did the same, and only drastic action by Ezra saved it from the ruin that would have inevitably followed (Ezra 9). But let's be clear: the issue was never primarily, or even essentially, a racial one. Rahab the harlot, who broke solidarity with her Canaanite past, became a worshiper of Yahweh and a member of his community with no harm to Israel. Boaz married Ruth the Moabitess, who took refuge under Yahweh's wings and went on to be an ancestor of King David and of Jesus. The issue was not race but covenant unfaithfulness: Israelites pledging themselves in marriage to women who worshiped the gods of Canaan and eventually doing so themselves (v. 6). It has ever been so. The surest way to end up "lov[ing] the world" (1 John 2:15, 16) yourself is to bind yourself to someone who already does. Hence the apostle's solemn warning, "Do not be unequally yoked with unbelievers. For what partnership has righteousness with lawlessness? Or what fellowship has light with darkness? What accord has Christ with Belial? Or what portion does a believer share with an unbeliever?" (2 Corinthians 6:14, 15).

The Bible's teaching on this issue is consistent and clear, but the application of it in the modern world is far from straightforward. On the one hand "lov[ing] the world" (1 John 2:15) requires engagement with it in evangelism and acts of compassion. God himself "loved the world" in this sense; it's what motivated him to send Jesus into the world to be our Savior (John 3:16). And Jesus sent his disciples into the world as salt and light (John 17:18; Matthew 5:13–14). So the way to avoid the kind of entanglements Paul has in mind cannot be to remove yourself from the world and live a completely separated existence, as some Christians (both Catholic and Protestant) have done over the years, and still do. But engagement with the world in a good sense inevitably involves us in relationships with people that put us at risk of the very thing Paul is warning us about: forming alliances (especially with the opposite sex) that are incompatible with faithfulness to Christ and may in the end make us no longer identifiable as his followers at all. In short, it can lead to assimilation into the world rather than transformative engagement with it. Intermarriage is just one aspect of a more general problem, but since it's the one that our passage highlights it's right we reflect on that in particular here.

Satan knows that sexual attraction is a particular point of vulnerability, especially for young people longing for love and parenthood. Within the particular Christian community to which they belong the opportunities to find a suitable Christian partner can be limited, and with the passing of time the need to find one can become urgent, especially for women. Furthermore, not all who marry unbelievers end up becoming unbelievers themselves; in a minority of cases it is the unbeliever who is changed and eventually becomes one in Christ with his believing partner.

So what should be done for Christians who are contemplating taking such a step or have already done so? First, they need to know that we understand their situation and need. The reality is that in many Christian communities there is a serious imbalance between the number of mature and godly young women and the number of similar young men. Second, we need to do all we can, through hospitality and other means, to provide opportunities for young Christian men and women to meet. A little discreet matchmaking is not out of place, provided it does not put people under pressure. Third, while acknowledging their desires as normal, we should encourage them not to make finding a marriage partner their first priority, but to "seek first the kingdom of God and his righteousness" (Matthew 6:33). Loving service to God and others is the way to true fulfillment, whether or not that includes marriage. Fourth, we should remind them that Scripture is clear that intermarriage with unbelievers is not God's will for us and that to take that path is an act of willful disobedience. It is not apostasy, but it may lead to it, as it did in Israel's case. At the very least it will make complete oneness with their partner impossible and will create other difficulties: "the way of transgressors is hard" (Proverbs 13:15 KJV). The book of Judges provides sobering examples of this, especially in the case of Samson and in the disasters that follow in chapters 17—21 when "everyone [does] what is right in his own eyes" (17:6; 21:25). The occasional happy outcome (as in a partner being converted) should be seen as an extraordinary act of grace, and not as something the person has any right to expect. Finally, we should not abandon those who go their own way in this area, but continue to be committed to them in love and do all we can to help them, as God does for Israel in the book of Judges. In this, as in so many other ways, Judges is a text for our times.

We have read the program. Now we are ready for the performance itself. We have already learned some valuable lessons, and these will be reinforced and expanded in what follows.

5

Othniel: A Model Savior

JUDGES 3:7–11

LEADERSHIP IS OBVIOUSLY a huge issue in Judges. It begins with the question, who will lead? and it ends, or nearly so, with the same question (1:1; 20:18). It is not a book without leaders; there's a whole series of them in chapters 3—16, but they increasingly fail to come up to expectations, and the last verse hints that a new kind of leader (a king) will be needed to rescue Israel from collapse. God's people need good leaders, but they have always been in short supply.

Every now and then, though, someone exceptional arises. Moses was such a leader. So was Joshua. But after Joshua? We have to read well into Judges 1 before any individual appears who seems to have the qualities required, but he is very old and represents a generation that is rapidly passing away. Caleb featured prominently in the book of Joshua. He and Joshua had been inseparable. They had shared in the spying out of Canaan and claiming it for Israel. And though Caleb had never led Israel as Joshua did, he had shown the same faith and fighting spirit. But in Judges 1 Caleb is less prominent. It is "Judah," Caleb's tribe, rather than Caleb himself that captures Hebron and drives the Anakim out of it (1:10).[1] And when they reach Debir, Caleb seeks a younger man to capture it on his behalf. So Caleb recedes into the background, and Othniel takes his place as battle leader. It is a sign of generational change and provides us with our first glimpse of the man who is to be Israel's first judge.

Generational change is inevitable, but it's often hard to predict what it will lead to. The Moses generation, which missed out on entering the promised land because it failed to believe the promise of God, was followed by a generation that did believe the promise and entered the land under Joshua. But though that generation continued to serve the Lord all the days of Joshua and those who outlived him, they were followed by one that did not (2:7–10). Given the dangers of generational change, appropriate management of it is important, and can be critical. Late in his life Moses paved the way for positive change by choosing and commissioning Joshua as his successor (Deuteronomy 31:1–8). Joshua solemnly charged all Israel to remain faithful to Yahweh after his death, but left no clear successor. So momentum was lost, and as Joshua's contemporaries aged and passed from the scene the question of leadership became critical. It is at this crucial moment that Othniel comes into view because Caleb was wise enough, in his old age, to know his limitations and to give the opportunity for new leadership to emerge. It was a master stroke, because when Caleb and his contemporaries were all gone and Israel needed saving, Othniel was the man to do it. With Othniel's rise to national leadership in 3:9, the transition from the age of Joshua to the age of the judges is complete. This is an issue that leaders of God's people still need to heed today. Too many vibrant Christian ministries and organizations, including churches, falter or even die because generational change has not been managed well.

The Need for a Savior

Apostasy (v. 7)

With the statement that "the people of Israel did what was evil in the sight of the LORD" in verse 7, we are back at the point where the overview of the judges period began in 2:11. It is the moment of deliberate rebellion against God and the beginning of a downward spiral that will get worse and worse throughout chapters 3—16. There is no need to repeat here what we have already said at some length in previous chapters, except to underline again the seriousness of the situation. To do evil by turning away from the Lord to other gods is always a disaster of the first order. It means that the very identity and continued existence of the people of God is at stake. Israel was nothing before God saved them, and they will become nothing again without him. Those who were once slaves to Pharaoh will becomes slaves again if they continue on this path, slaves not just to the false gods they have chosen, but also to the whole lifestyle that goes with them. They will simply become Canaanites and cease to be the people of God at all. Apostates are in deep trouble. They need saving.[2]

Double Trouble (v. 8)

People who turn away from God often don't think they are in trouble. Becoming worldly is not something they perceive as dangerous. They've gone that way because they find the world and its ways attractive. They feel liberated, like the prodigal son heading out from the father's house to a far country full of exciting new opportunities for pleasure and fulfillment. But trouble is sure to come sooner or later, and it is no accident that it does because the gods of this world are in reality no gods at all, with no power to save or satisfy. Such people are also in trouble for a deeper reason, however. Those who turn their backs on God anger him and will sooner or later face his judgment. If they will not come to their senses and come home of their own accord, he will go after them and teach them the error of their ways by punishing them as they deserve.

We must be careful, though, to distinguish between God's dealings with his children and his acts of judgment in general. Retribution—pure punishment, unmitigated by grace—is for those who are, and remain, *outside* his covenant: "having no hope and without God in the world" (Ephesians 2:12). The final, permanent expression of God's retributive justice is Hell (Revelation 14:9–11). But within God's covenant with his people (which he has promised never to break, 2:1) a different kind of judgment takes place. The most appropriate term for it is discipline, because it is corrective rather than retributive, and always tempered by grace. It can be severe, but its aim is always to reclaim rather than destroy (Hebrews 12:5–11). Only those who utterly refuse to be disciplined become subject to retribution, because (as their conduct shows) they are reprobate and are not true children of God at all. At times in Judges, Israel comes very close to reaching this point, and some individuals such as Abimelech in chapter 9 actually do so. As we will see, his personal story is wholly one of retribution. But whatever the fate of individuals like Abimelech may be, God's covenant with Israel stands, and his grace again and again draws the nation back from the brink of destruction. In the present passage Othniel is the special agent of that grace.

The agent of God's discipline is a terrible tyrant. We are not told very much about him. We are given his name, "Cushan-rishathaim," and are told his nationality, "king of Mesopotamia," or in Hebrew, "king of Aram-naharaim" ("king of Aram of the two rivers") (v. 8). We're also told the length of his domination of Israel, "eight years" (v. 8). But this is meager data from which to construct a picture of him. He's a very enigmatic figure. He presents the kind of problem about whom pedantic scholars like to write learned articles. Some suggest he was an early Babylonian ruler from Mesopotamia (which means "two rivers"), in what is now southern Iraq.[3] Others, for various reasons, suggest he was a Nubian from southern Egypt or an Edomite from the region south of the Dead Sea (which requires a slight emendation of the Hebrew text). Still others think he was an Asiatic, or a Midianite, or even a chieftain of southern Judah (a kind of rogue, homegrown warlord). My own best guess is that he was Syrian, given that Aram was the ancient name of Syria, and that "two rivers," the Abana and Pharpar, are referred to as "the rivers of Damascus" in 2 Kings 5:12. But no one knows for sure, and in fact the quest to establish his identity precisely is a rather pointless exercise, because it has been deliberately withheld from us. The text itself tells us all we need to know. He is God's instrument to discipline Israel (v. 8), and he is terrible. The mystery surrounding him actually adds to the sense of dread we feel at his presence, and his name deepens this foreboding. Like the statement about his origins it teases us by hiding as much as it reveals.

The second part of his name, *rishathaim*, means "doubly wicked" and rhymes with the second part of his place of origin. He is "Cushan-*rishathaim* king of Aram-*naharaim*," and for maximum impact the name is mentioned four times in only three verses (twice in v. 8 and twice again in v. 10). That's enough to unnerve us even before we know what it means! In Hebrew he is literally "Cushan the doubly wicked." It can hardly be his real name; no parent would call their baby that! So we don't actually know who he was. Cushan-rishathaim was probably a name coined for him by those who suffered at his hands. In this name we see him through the eyes of his victims—a wicked, wicked tyrant. No details are given; those are left to our imagination. But the very generalness of the description enhances rather than detracts from Cushan's stature. He is a *type* we recognize, because history is punctuated by men like him, from Israel's day to our own, and on to the end of time. Antiochus Epiphanes, Nero, Hitler, Stalin, Pol Pot, Idi Amin, the Antichrist, Satan—there have been many embodiments of evil. Cushan-rishathaim has lived many times.

At its deepest level, the mystery surrounding Cushan-rishathaim is the mystery of evil itself. Like him, evil has many names and incarnations, and its origin, like his, is largely hidden from us. The serpent simply appears in Eden without explanation. He is made by God, like the other beasts of the field (Genesis 3:1). But why then is he so different? Likewise Satan, who appears among the "the sons of God" in Job 1:6, 7. He comes from "going to and fro on the earth" (Job 1:7). Yes, but before that? From Heaven (Jude 6)? But if so, we are back to the same problem: evil in paradise. From where does it arise? From God? But what then of his moral perfection? From the fact that he has given his creatures the ability to choose? But whence, then, even the *thought* of rebellion? The answer to these questions is not revealed. What we do know, from the Othniel story and from Scripture as a whole, is that when evil appears it is never ultimate. It never rules the world as God does. God's complete mastery of it is seen particularly in the way he causes even evil people to serve his good purposes for his people. Here he hands them over to Cushan-rishathaim to be disciplined (v. 8). They are not snatched from God's hand (no tyrant has the power to do that), but (literally) "sold" by him in a deliberate transaction that he initiates and controls. It is a carefully measured act of discipline, in which the punishment fits the crime. Those who "serve" foreign gods are made to "serve" a foreign ruler (vv. 7, 8), and those who do "evil" are handed over to one who is "wicked." And the One who determines the punishment also determines its duration. He initiates it by handing his people over to Cushan and ends it after "eight years" by raising up Othniel to save them from him (vv. 8, 9). Even in their darkest moments Israel is never simply in the hands of Cushan-rishathaim; they are also, still, in the hands of God, who is sovereign over evil and committed to their good.

The Cry for a Savior

The eight years of suffering at the hands of Cushan-rishathaim ended, or *began* to end, when "the people of Israel cried out to the LORD" (v. 9). They would not *actually* end, of course, until God did something. But a cry to the Lord is a good thing, and a hopeful sign that the discipline God has administered to his rebellious people is starting to bear fruit. At the same time, however, this "cry" comes as a bit of a surprise, because no appeal to the Lord was mentioned in the overview of the judges period as a whole in 2:11–19. So we should not attach too much importance to it. It is not an essential element in what happens here or anywhere else in Judges. In the Samson story, for example, God provides a savior for Israel even when they *don't* cry out to him. Nor does crying out to the Lord necessarily indicate sorrow for sin and a serious intention to change (see 10:12, 13). As far as we know, it is purely a cry of pain and desperation here. It is a hopeful sign, though, that the Israelites realize that the gods they have turned to are useless in their hour of need.[4] In their extremity it is Yahweh to whom they cry out, and not "the Baals and the Asheroth" of verse 7. And God, in his mercy, is quick to respond, as he was to the similar cry of their ancestors back in Egypt (Exodus 2:23, 24). There is hope for people who cry out to God (Jeremiah 33:3; Psalm 50:15; Jonah 2:1, 2; Romans 10:13).

The Savior God Provided (vv. 9b, 10)

We know more about Othniel than we do about Cushan-rishathaim. We are reminded that he is Caleb's nephew,[5] and we know from chapter 1 that he's daring, has initiative and flair, and is a proven fighter. We also know that he is married to Caleb's daughter, which is not insignificant here because we've just been told in verse 6 that intermarriage with Canaanites was a critical factor in Israel's apostasy. Not so Othniel! He is completely untainted by that sin, for what more "Israelite" wife could one have than the daughter of the illustrious Caleb? Furthermore, Othniel, like Caleb himself, is from the tribe of Judah (1 Chronicles 4:13), the tribe that was singled out for leadership in the opening two verses of the book and performed so creditably in the first half of chapter 1. Othniel is a man of character, with all the right background and connections, someone eminently suitable to lead Israel. Othniel, of the tribe of Judah, occupies a position in the lineup of Israel's judges similar to David's role in the lineup of their kings. Othniel stands at their head and is in many respects an ideal figure. Nor are we disappointed when he takes to the field of battle as Israel's champion: he "went out to war" and "prevailed" (v. 10). What he did at Debir in 1:13 he now does on a much grander scale. Othniel has come of age, so to speak. He has answered the challenge, risen to higher responsibilities, and emerged as a fully fledged national hero.

For all this, however, the account of Othniel's career here is remarkably brief and surprisingly lacking in color. There is no detailed description of either scene or character or action. Where did the battle take place? What size was the enemy army? What Israelite tribes took part? What tactics were used? How did God intervene to turn the tide against the enemy? And so on. We simply don't know, because nothing is said about any of the things that would made this a vivid narrative. In fact, the Othniel "story," if we can call it that, is astonishingly bland, which is probably why it never turns up in children's Bible story books or Sunday school lessons. It's just not interesting enough to hold anyone's attention. Most of the expressions used here have already been used in chapter 2 and will continue to appear with monotonous regularity throughout the book: the Israelites did evil, they served other gods, the Lord was roused to anger, he gave them over to an oppressor, and so on, until the formulaic ending is reached: "So the land had rest" (v. 11). It's all so general, even boring, like a small picture with almost no detail, in a big, plain frame. Even the intriguing Cushan-rishathaim is described in only the most general terms, as we have seen. The preacher, if he dares preach from this passage at all, will have to work hard to make it engaging.

What then are we to make of this strange disparity between Othniel's impressive credentials and the minimalist way his story is told here? Two things. First, it shows us that it is not the author's intention to glorify Othniel. He "saved" Israel to be sure (v. 9), but it is not Othniel's initiative or courage or prowess in battle that is featured, but God's activity through him. The Lord "raised [him] up" (v. 9). "The Spirit of the LORD was upon him" (v. 10), and when he went out to war, the LORD "*gave* Cushan-rishathaim . . . into his hand" (v. 10). In other words, the *real* Savior of Israel was the Lord, not Othniel, and Othniel's impressive credentials and personal charisma would have counted for nothing without the Lord. Second, the sparseness of the account enables us to see the basic features of judgeship as a gracious provision of God more clearly. At this perilous time in Israel's life, judges were basically deliverers in a military sense rather than routine administrators of justice. They did the latter too, as we see for example in Deborah (4:4, 5). But the essential way they administered God's justice was by bringing his judgment to bear on Israel's enemies, by breaking their power and driving them out, thereby lifting their heavy yoke from his people's shoulders and giving them "rest" (v. 11).

The "how" of judgeship will be shown in detail in subsequent episodes; in this first one the focus is on the "what." It shows that in Judges judgeship is not essentially about administration or retribution (although it involves both) but about salvation. The book of Judges is a book of saviors, and behind each of them, raising them up, empowering them, and giving them victory, is Yahweh, without whom they would be nothing. "Salvation belongs to the LORD!" (Jonah 2:9). That's the key message of this passage, and everything is stripped back to basics to let that message stand out in all its stark simplicity. It's basic to all that follows.

The Fruit of Salvation

At the end of our passage, the salvation achieved through Othniel issues in "rest" (v. 11). We'll get accustomed to this kind of ending in the chapters that follow. It also occurs at the end of the Ehud, Barak, and Gideon stories (3:30; 5:31; 8:28). The danger is that because it's frequent and because, by its very nature, it's a quiet ending that comes after the main action is over, we may miss its importance. So let's spend a while on this first occurrence of it here at the end of the Othniel episode to make sure we don't miss any of its riches. Several observations are appropriate.

First, the rest spoken of here is a gift rather than an achievement. It came about because God "gave" Cushan-rishathaim into Othniel's hand (v. 10). We have spoken about this already and won't labor the point here. But it's important! It's fundamental to the whole Biblical understanding of salvation. Second, this "rest" (v. 11) is the enjoyment of something God promised.

All your men of valor shall cross over ahead of your brothers . . . until the LORD gives *rest* to your brothers, as to you, and they also occupy the land that the LORD your God gives them beyond the Jordan. (Deuteronomy 3:18–20)

You have not as yet come to the *rest* and to the inheritance that the LORD your God is giving you. (Deuteronomy 12:9)

When you go over the Jordan and live in the land that the LORD your God is giving you to inherit, and when he gives you *rest* from all your enemies around, so that you live in safety . . . (Deuteronomy 12:10)

When the LORD your God has given you *rest* from all your enemies around you, in the land that the LORD your God is giving you for an inheritance to possess . . . (Deuteronomy 25:19)

This promised rest was forfeited by the wilderness generation because of their unbelief (Psalm 95:8–11). It was enjoyed for a time by the Joshua generation (Joshua 11:23; 23:1), but was lost again by the next generation, as we've seen in the opening two chapters of Judges. The principle stands, however: rest is the promise of God. The enjoyment of it is given by God to the faithful and obedient, as we see in the book of Joshua, but also, as we see in the present passage, to the oppressed and desperate, to those who simply "cry out" to God for it. Third, this rest is given through a man God chooses to use, in this case Othniel. Presumably, since he has all power God could have given it directly, without any human involvement at all. This is how he gave the rest of the seventh day to human beings in Genesis 1, 2. In the context of salvation, however, God's chosen means is to use a man he raises up and on whom he places his Spirit (vv. 9, 10). Fourth, this rest is generous. The "forty years" of rest in verse 11 is five times as long as the "eight years" of discipline in verse 8. In a very concrete way this underlines the point made earlier: the book of Judges is fundamentally a book of salvation rather than judgment. God judges, but Biblically speaking we cannot say that "God *is* judgment" in the way we can say that "God *is* love" (1 John 4:8, 16). In a fallen world judgment is a necessary work of God, but salvation, which flows from his love (John 3:16), is his natural or preferred work, the work that most expresses who he is.[6]

Fifth, this rest is concrete and comprehensive. It is not just an inner peace in the midst of trouble. That kind of rest is wonderful and precious. Here, however, it is "the land" that had rest, standing here for Israel's total environment. War brings destruction of crops, the cessation of normal agricultural production, and with that, famine. We see this particularly in the Gideon narrative.[7] Rest from war enables the agricultural cycle to begin again, village life to be resumed, and communities to flourish, with all the physical, social, and emotional benefits that follow from this, as we see in the book of Ruth. So "rest" here does not just mean the absence of something (war), but the presence of *shalom*, total well-being, or at the least the conditions that make it possible. Finally, however, the "rest" of this verse is limited; it lasted only *until* "Othniel the son of Kenaz died" (v. 11). It need not have ended then; the real cause that it ended is given in 3:12—the subsequent lapse of Israel back into apostasy. In its own subtle way, though, the limited nature of the rest of verse 11 hints at a deeper truth. Rest can never be permanent in a world where death reigns. Othniel, for all his excellent qualities and all that God accomplished through him, was a fallen man in a fallen world and therefore could not bring permanent rest to God's people. For that a greater Savior and a greater salvation was needed.

Beyond Othniel

The brief account of Othniel's career in 3:7–11 is about a man who was outstanding in his generation. Read against its background in 1:11—15, it's the story of a person who had potential for leadership and was given the opportunity to show it by an older man who knew the time had come for him to step back and make way for new talent to emerge. Othniel's appearance as a national leader in 3:9 vindicates Caleb's wisdom: God chose the man Caleb had mentored.

Yet the story of Othniel is very much a beginning rather than an end. Othniel is not just the first judge; he is a model judge. He shows us what judgeship at its best is and what God can accomplish through it—relief from oppression, salvation, and rest. Othniel sets a high standard. He is the Mr. Right who leads the way. All who follow will be variations on the pattern he has set and will disappoint to one degree or another, leaving us wondering in the end whether judgeship itself must finally be written off as a failure, an experiment with a style of leadership that simply could not work long-term. However, that's where the way the book ends is so significant: "In those days there was no king in Israel. Everyone did what was right in his own eyes" (21:25).This acknowledges the limitations of judgeship: it was unable to stem the tide of lawlessness, and thus the salvation it could provide was only temporary. But at the same time it provides hope by pointing the way ahead. Judgeship was only one phase in the history of salvation. After the judges would come the kings, and after them would come the Messiah, Jesus Christ,

God's perfect King and the bringer of complete, permanent salvation. Which brings us back, with richer insight, to the question and answer that opened the book: Who will lead? Judah! Othniel, judge from the tribe of Judah, was the first leader in whom that divine decree was embodied, and Jesus, King from the same tribe, was the last. So sinful though we are, we are not leaderless or abandoned to the enemy. God has provided a Savior who has defeated Satan and provided a deliverance for us that is greater by far than anything the judges could achieve (Hebrews 2:3; 5:9).

What this means for us experientially is that the elusive "rest" of Old Testament promise has been secured and expanded into an eternal rest that we enter now by faith and will experience eternally in Heaven (Hebrews 4:1–10). The Israelites of the wilderness generation failed to enter the promised rest through unbelief. The Joshua generation experienced it temporarily. Their successors in the judges period experienced it intermittently. But the fullness of it always eluded them. Like the ever-receding horizon or a mirage in the desert, it was always beyond them—always hoped for, but never fully reached. What they needed to enter it fully was a leader who would never die, who could break the vicious cycle of self-destruction by dealing with their sin once and for all. The good news for us is that at last that Leader has come, the One in whom the promise of rest is at last realized. Beyond Othniel lies the whole ongoing epic of God's perseverance with his people in judgment and grace, until its climax is finally reached in the coming of Jesus Christ, who is not just Mr. Right, but the perfecter of our faith, the Savior and Judge of us all (Acts 17:30, 31; Titus 3:4; Hebrews 12:2). And beyond that, in eternity, lies the full enjoyment of all he has won for us—a rest that will never end (Hebrews 4:9).

6

Ehud: Holy Laughter

JUDGES 3:12-30

TO PUT IT MILDLY, Ehud comes as a bit of a shock after Othniel. Othniel was an ideal figure—well-connected, heroic, upright, the kind of man we can understand God choosing to lead Israel. Now, straight after him, we have a devious assassin, also chosen by God to save Israel (vv. 15, 21). That's disturbing. It's not the only disturbing thing in Judges, of course. The whole book is disturbing. It's a very violent book, about Israel doing "what was evil in the sight of the LORD" again and again and suffering the consequences. It's about a dark period in Israel's history that makes pretty uncomfortable reading. Of course, it's no bad thing in itself to be disturbed. The fact that people do evil *should* disturb us, especially when they are God's people. So far, though, it's been the rank and file who do evil. The leaders, Caleb and Othniel, have been exemplary. Now we have a *leader* who is devious and whom God apparently approves of. That's even more disturbing. God's own integrity seems to be at stake here. This is not unique to the Ehud story. From here on in Judges, most of the people God uses to rescue Israel use methods that are morally questionable. Consider Jael, for example, or Jephthah or Samson. But the Ehud episode is not simply one of a kind. There is something *uniquely* disturbing about it that we will become increasingly aware of as the story unfolds. We will find ourselves laughing, but feeling uncomfortable in doing so. What is especially disturbing about this story is its humor.

Let's start, though, where the story itself does, with something that is definitely no laughing matter—Israel's lapse back into apostasy, defeat, and misery.

What's Not Funny at All

Sin (v. 12a)

"And the people of Israel again did what was evil in the sight of the LORD" (v. 12). We've heard this before, and we'll hear it many more times in Judges. The danger, of course, is that we'll become used to it, and it will cease to shock us. But the very prevalence of it is telling us three important things. First, sin is boring. It happens again and again, and there's nothing particularly creative or original about it. Israel returns to the same thing again and again. Second, the fact that it always follows something for which Israel should be grateful, in this case the forty-year "rest" of verse 11, shows us that sin is perverse. At heart it is ingratitude to God, to whom we owe everything. Paul makes this point powerfully in the way he describes the rebelliousness of human beings in Romans 1:21: "Although they knew God, they did not honor him as God *or give thanks to him*." Third, it shows us that sin is an addiction.[1] There are times in Judges when Israel seems to break free from it, most notably in the exuberant song of praise in chapter 5 and in the apparent repentance in 10:15, 16, but sooner or later it comes back and claims them again. It's as addictive as any of the toxic substances that enslave people today, and just as destructive. It's the master drug, and it's no laughing matter.

Its Consequences (vv. 12b–14)

The consequences in this case are Israel's enslavement to Eglon, king of Moab, for eighteen years. First we are told of this in terms of God's response to their sin: "the LORD strengthened Eglon the king of Moab against Israel" (v. 12). Then we are told about it in terms of Eglon's own actions: "He [Eglon] gathered to himself the Ammonites and the Amalekites, and went and defeated Israel" (v. 13). In other words, the consequences of sin are neither simply natural nor simply supernatural. Sin weakens people and nations and makes them vulnerable, sooner or later, to collapse or conquest. But this is part of how God set up the world, and in some cases, like this one, such calamities are specific acts of judgment. In most cases we simply do not know how God is involved or why he causes or allows such things to happen.[2] But every time they do happen should be taken as a challenge to humble ourselves before God and seek his forgiveness for every way we have offended him and contributed to the world's ills (Lamentations 3:26–29, 40; 1 Corinthians 11:28–30; James 5:13–16). The world has paid a high price for its rebellion against God, and so has the church for its failure to be faithful to his word. And each of us, in one way or another, is part of the problem. At one level Eglon's conquest of Israel was like the similar conquests of tyrants the world over and is capable of being explained in terms of simple opportunity, ambition, and military capability. But in this case the veil is drawn back, and we are allowed to see that it was also a specific act of God (v. 12). The people of Israel had to learn that their special relationship with God did not give them license to sin with impunity. Indeed, it put them under greater obligation than others to respect God's just requirements, and if they failed to do so it made them liable to more severe punishment. Amos was later to remind the Israelites of this truth in a particularly confronting way:

> You only have I known
>> of all the families of the earth;
> therefore I will punish you
>> for all your iniquities. (Amos 3:2)

It was a hard lesson for Israel to learn, and eventually they had to be taught it through the bitter experience of exile. Sin has consequences, especially for God's own people, and in the present passage Eglon is God's means of teaching them that. Sin and its consequences are both deadly serious matters.

What's Amazing (v. 15a)

What God Does Again

"Then the people of Israel cried out to the Lord, and the Lord raised up for them a deliverer" (v. 15a). We've heard this before too (2:16, 18), and while the way God does it will vary, we'll see him doing this same thing several more times before the book is finished. He will commission Barak and Gideon, empower Jephthah, and stir up Samson—always with the same end in view—to deliver his people. And he will do it even when they *don't* cry out to him (13:25; cf. 2:15, 16). This is not at all boring in the way the repetition of sin is. But the frequency of it carries the same danger—namely, that we become used to it and fail to recognize its importance. Isn't it *astonishing* that God keeps saving his people even though they keep sinning against him? And shouldn't every new instance of it cause the most profound gratitude to well up within us? Without this we would all be lost, because the fact is that this side of Heaven we *will* go on sinning, even though it is not our intention to do so, and if God should ever abandon us to the full consequences of our sin all hope would be gone. There are two amazing things in Judges: Israel's persistence in sin and God's persistence in saving them, and the second is the most astonishing by far.

The Man God Uses

"Ehud, the son of Gera, the Benjaminite, a left-handed man" (v. 15b). It's easy to understand why God chose Othniel. But why Ehud the Benjaminite? Othniel's tribe, Judah, was destined for leadership from the time of the patriarchs (Genesis 49:8–10). They were designated the leading tribe at the beginning of the book (1:1, 2) and performed very creditably in the first chapter (1:1–21). In contrast, Benjamin's record has been abysmal. Benjamin gets only one mention in Judges 1, not for overcoming the enemy, but for *not* driving out the Jebusites from Jerusalem (1:21). In other words, Benjamin, has nothing to commend it, making "Ehud, the son of Gera, the Benjaminite" (v. 15) a most unlikely deliverer. The mention of his origin evokes the kind of surprise Nathanael later felt at the news that the promised Messiah was Jesus of Nazareth: "Can anything good come out of Nazareth?" (John 1:45, 46). The equivalent question here would be, "Can anything good come from Benjamin?" Ehud is not only from the wrong tribe, however; he is also wrong physically—he's "a left-handed man," (v. 15) or literally, a man who was "bound up" or "restricted" in his right hand. It's not clear whether this was simply an idiomatic expression for left-handedness or whether Ehud had a literal deformity. In either case it made him peculiarly unsuited to be Israel's deliverer, because a strong right hand or arm was regarded as a warrior's greatest asset. It was the sword-bearing arm, symbolic of military might (Psalm 44:3; 89:13; 98:1; Isaiah 62:8). So Ehud was weak at the very point where a warrior should be strong. God's choice of Ehud is surprising to say the least.

What's Concealed (vv. 15c, 16)

The long, central part of the story actually begins quite seriously. It's not clear at this stage whether anyone, including Ehud himself, knows that God has chosen him to deliver Israel or even whether God is involved at all in what happens at this point. The only conscious actors are human beings— "the people of Israel" and "Ehud" respectively (v. 15). Ehud is chosen not to deliver Israel but to carry tribute, and he is chosen not, apparently, by God but by his fellows. From a Biblical point of view, however, things are never as simple as that. Events can never be divided neatly into things that human beings do and things that God does, as though we control parts of the world and

God others. The Joseph story, for example, shows this very clearly (Genesis 45:5; 50:19, 20), and the crucifixion of Jesus even more so. The latter was both a dreadful deed done by men and a most gracious and sovereign act of God (Acts 2:23). So in the present passage what human beings do contributes to God's "rais[ing] up" of Ehud (v. 15), though they were probably unaware of it. What the Israelites *were* aware of was their servitude to Eglon, and the necessity of sending tribute to him. But why choose Ehud to take it? Possibly because, as a left-handed man, he would not be mistaken for a warrior and therefore as a provocation. His incapacity mirrored that of his people, making him a perfect person to be sent as their representative. They have cried out to the Lord to save them, but they see no evidence of any response on his part. So they do what must be done. Choosing Ehud to carry tribute indicates that they have no expectation of deliverance in the foreseeable future.

Ehud sees things quite differently, however. He realizes that he is being given a rare opportunity to cross the border and penetrate deeply into enemy territory, perhaps into the very presence of the tyrant himself, and that his handicap may actually be an asset. So he prepares to make the most of his chance to strike a blow for freedom. He makes for himself a two-edged sword, "a cubit" (eighteen inches) long, and fastens it "on his right thigh under his clothes" (v. 16). The absence of any mention of his fellow Israelites at this point confirms that the idea is entirely his own. They have no idea what he is planning. The sword is custom-made, double-edged for maximum effect, and short enough to be concealed on Ehud's right thigh for easy access with his left hand. He will only have one chance to strike, so surprise and having exactly the right weapon are both critical. Ehud is a smooth and daring operator. Most of all, he is a trickster, a master of the art of concealment. This is what most sets him apart from the other judges and the seed from which the distinctive humor of the story develops.

What's Laughable (vv. 17–29)

Eglon's Bulk (v. 17)

At first Ehud simply does what he was sent to do: "And he presented the tribute to Eglon king of Moab" (v. 17a). But now the way Eglon is depicted in the story begins to change. In a way that's quite unusual in Biblical stories, we are shown Eglon's bulk: "Now Eglon was a very fat man" (v. 17b). In an age like our own where slimness is valued as a sign of fitness, beauty, and self-discipline, and obesity is a major problem, this immediately registers as a negative comment. But it's not easy to know how we are meant to take it here. It certainly doesn't immediately mark Eglon as a laughable figure. In Israel's world fatness was not generally regarded as something negative. More often than not it was seen as a sign of prosperity and good fortune (Isaiah 17:4; 55:2; Jeremiah 31:14; cf. Job 36:16; Psalm 36:8; 63:5; 65:5, 11;109:24; Romans 11:17 [ESV margin, "richness"]). The specific term for "fat" in verse 17 (the Hebrew word *bari'*) is used in Daniel 1:15 to describe how the young Jewish heroes flourished physically in spite of their refusal to eat the king's rich food! The description of Eglon as "*very* fat," though, does make us wonder. Was he fat to excess? The best clue to how we are meant to view him lies in the meaning of Eglon's name ("calf" or "young bull") and the kind of tribute that Ehud has brought to him. The agricultural nature of Israel's economy at the time and the specific term used for the tribute (*minchah*, a grain offering) (Leviticus 2:8; 6:14 (Hebrew 15); 7:12; 23:16; Numbers 5:25; 6:16; 15:9) imply that Ehud has brought agricultural produce—food! In other words, Eglon has been fattening himself on the produce he has extorted from Israel and has unwittingly turned himself into a fattened calf ripe for slaughter![3] Israelites reading the story would have a wry smile on their faces at this point, relishing what is about to take place.

His Gullibility (vv. 18–20)

As he hoped, Ehud is allowed to present the tribute to Eglon in person (v. 17a), but instead of using his dagger at once he leaves. So the tension builds. What is Ehud up to? This starts to become clear in what he does next. On the road back there are some "idols" (v. 19; literally "carved objects"). Since they are "near Gilgal," close to the border between Israel and Moab (Judges 2:1; Joshua 4:19), they may have acted as boundary markers as well as objects of worship.[4] In any case Ehud chooses this place to dismiss the porters who had helped him deliver the tribute and return alone for a *second* meeting with Eglon. He is gambling on being given a further audience with the king, and if it works this strategy has a number of advantages. His first visit has left Eglon falsely assured that he has nothing to fear from Ehud. Second, since his porters were not aware of his plot, their presence could cause unnecessary complications. By dismissing them and returning alone he has removed that danger. Finally, since he must now act quickly and escape quickly, working alone is preferable.

When he gets back, Eglon receives him again without any qualms. Perhaps he has had Ehud followed and is curious to know why he has turned back, especially from the place of idols. If so, Ehud is quick to build on this curiosity. And now the full cleverness of this plot is revealed. His words are double-edged, like his dagger: "I have a secret message for you, O king" (v. 19a).

The expression translated "message" here is the Hebrew word *dabar*, which can mean "a word" (and therefore a message) or "a thing" (and therefore something else). Eglon is intrigued, especially by the additional word "secret." Has Ehud consulted the gods whose idols he has visited? Does he bring an oracle? Has he decided to change sides and bring Eglon a juicy piece of intelligence? In either case a "secret" is not for sharing, so he does exactly what Ehud hoped he would do: he commands, "Silence," which his attendants take as a dismissal and quietly slip out (v. 19b). Now Ehud has his enemy exactly where he wants him, alone and completely oblivious of the danger he is in. Before the blow is struck, though, we are given a few more details to heighten our satisfaction at Eglon's plight. Eglon is "sitting alone in his cool roof chamber" (v. 20). He is completely at ease, in a room that he has probably had purposely built on the roof of his palace where he can relax and catch refreshing breezes to cool himself on hot summer days. He even has a private privy attached for his comfort and convenience (v. 24)! Eglon is the complete tyrant—smug, self-satisfied, enjoying to the full his ill-gotten gains, and sublimely confident that no one can touch him. He is about to find out, too late, how wrong he is.

Ehud moves closer and repeats what he said before, but with an important addition: "I have a message *from God* for you" (v. 20). In an age when everyone is religious this raises the stakes significantly higher for Eglon. Kings regularly consulted the gods for guidance in matters of state (2 Samuel 5:22–25; 7:1–3; 1 Kings 22:13–15; 19:1–7; etc.); so if Ehud has an oracle for him, Eglon cannot afford to ignore him. And if he knows that Ehud has turned back from a place of religious significance (v. 19) he has added reason to take the Israelite's claim seriously. However this may be, what the king does next shows us how completely he has been taken in by Ehud's clever words. He stands up to receive Ehud's "message from God" (v. 20) and in so doing positions his huge belly perfectly as a target for Ehud's strike. Eglon is a gullible fool, and he's about to become a dead one.

His Downfall (vv. 21, 22)

What happens now happens quickly but is described in slow motion, almost like a series of stills rather than one blurred action. Here is what everything has been building toward, and the writer clearly wants us to be able to savor all the gruesome details. Ehud's left hand reaches under his cloak, draws the murder weapon from his right thigh, and thrusts it into Eglon's belly, which is so huge that it swallows the sword so completely that Ehud leaves it there. All that comes out is "dung" (v. 22). Eglon is finished, but not the story, because the writer, and Ehud, have more fun to make of him yet.

His Servants (vv. 23–25)

Ehud quickly makes his escape, but not before locking the doors of Eglon's room behind him. How he managed to do this is not explained. Was there a key already in the lock? Was he assisted by an informer? Whether he planned it beforehand or just did it on the spur of the moment, it is a master stroke—the crowning detail of the writer's presentation of Ehud as a master of deception. He concealed his plan from his fellow Israelites; he hid his sword on his body; by his clever words he hid the real nature of his "message/thing from God" (v. 20), and now he hides the dead king in his private room. At the very least it gives Ehud added time to escape, but it also presents Eglon's servants, when they return, with a very embarrassing predicament. Why are the doors to the king's quarters locked? Perhaps their portly master is asleep? Or is he busy and doesn't want to be disturbed? Or perhaps he is on the toilet? They know he has one in there (v. 24), and the thought that he is using it is perhaps prompted by the smell beginning to issue from the room. So they wait, trying to look relaxed, but becoming increasingly anxious. Why so long? Is he constipated? Has he had a fall? Is he unconscious? They too have a key to the king's chamber, but are reluctant to use it for fear of breaking court etiquette and incurring the king's wrath. It's exactly the kind of confusion and indecision on which Ehud has counted. But finally they can wait no longer. When he *still* doesn't open the doors, they at last unlock them themselves and rush in, and what they see confirms their worst fears: "there lay their lord *dead* on the floor" (v. 25). It is not a pretty sight (or smell). And for Eglon's servants it is an unmitigated disaster. They shared his life; now they share his humiliation. Like him they have been made to look like utter fools, and without him they too are nothing.

His Soldiers (vv. 26–29)

Meanwhile, Ehud has made good his escape.[5] He passes by the "idols" again, back into territory still held by Israel, and heads for "Seirah" (v. 26). This place is otherwise unknown but must have been somewhere in "the hill country of Ephraim," north of Jerusalem, because that is where Ehud blows his trumpet (v. 27). By going there Ehud has positioned himself outside the relatively small allotment of his own tribe, Benjamin, at the highest and most central point in the whole region, to make it clear that his trumpet blast is a rallying call to all Israel. It is also a very deliberate public presentation of himself to Israel as their deliverer, the one God has given them in answer to their cry of verse 15. He may have known himself to be this from the start, but it was tactically important for him to appear as nothing but a tribute-bearer until he had struck the decisive blow. Now, though, it was time to go public, and his trumpet blast was his way of doing so. Word must have spread quickly because soon he is ready to go back again, this time with fighters instead of porters, and finish what he has begun: "the people of Israel went down with him from the hill country, and he was their leader" (v. 27).

The way the action now unfolds, from the central hills toward the Jordan Valley, shows that the Moabites are already fleeing from Israelite territory. Ehud sees this as confirmation that the Lord has given them into Israel's hand and spurs on his followers by telling them so (v. 28). There is no mention of Eglon's allies, the Ammonites and Amalekites, of verse 13. In the moment of crisis they are nowhere to be seen. It is one more indication of the hopeless position in which the Moabites now find themselves. Their complete destruction follows as a matter of course. The Israelites cut them off at "the fords of the Jordan"—the only crossing point that gave them any hope of escape—and slaughter them there until not one is left (vv. 28, 29). Ten thousand Moabites are killed. It's either terrible or glorious, depending on how you view it.

In contrast to the account of Eglon's downfall in verses 17–25, everything seems to be told now in a compact, matter-of-fact fashion except for one detail that is impossible to detect in most English translations. The vanquished Moabites were "strong" (*shamen*) and "able-bodied" (*'ish chayil*) according to verse 29. But both words can be read in more than one sense. Like the word *bari'*, used of Eglon back in verse 17 ("Eglon was a very *fat* man"), *shamen*, too, can mean "fat."[6] It has the same kind of meaning possibilities as *stout* in English—either "brave" or "large" (overweight). And *'ish chayil* ("substantial") is capable of the same kind of double entendre—substantial in importance, strength, or just size. Like Eglon, his followers have prospered at Israel's expense, and in a way that now works against them. They are too fat to run fast! In other words, while they might once have seemed strong and able-bodied, now, in defeat, they look merely obese and cumbersome. They have been demoralized and stripped of their dignity like the fat Eglon himself back in verses 17–22 and like his bumbling servants in verses 24, 25. Eglon's fall has prefigured and ensured the downfall of all of them. Ehud has made all of them look laughable. He has brought down the oppressor, rid the land of his lackeys, and secured eighty years of rest for Israel (v. 30).

The Exposure of a Tyrant

There was nothing funny about Eglon during the eighteen years of his tyranny over Israel (v. 14). He was a commander of men. He was able to form a coalition of nations with competing interests and somehow unify and command them (v. 13). He was a military leader who knew how to strategize and achieve victories. He knew how to make conquered people serve him and pay tribute. He knew how to get power and wield it to his advantage. He knew how to consolidate his hold on power and enrich himself at the expense of those he ruled. He was a strong, ruthless leader, and Israel had been powerless to resist him. And as long as Eglon was strong, so were his servants and his warriors. They were his agents and enforcers, and there was nothing funny about any of them. They *became* laughable only when they were confronted with Ehud, the deliverer God had "raised up" (v. 15). Then they began to look entirely different. They were exposed for the fools they were, and their power was brought to an end so suddenly and completely it was laughable. And as Eglon's followers shared his downfall, Ehud's followers shared his victory. They were like those, much later, who saw God break the power of mighty Babylon and set his people free.

> When the LORD restored the fortunes of Zion,
> we were like those who dream.
> *Then our mouth was filled with laughter,*
> and our tongue with shouts of joy. (Psalm 126:1, 2)

This was not cheap gloating over someone they had beaten. It was the laughter of sheer delight at something God had done. The story of Ehud rings with the same kind of laughter.

Laughing with God

Laughter is not the normal emotional language of God's people in the Bible. More often they groan and weep, as Israel often does in Judges.[7] This is the normal experience of sinful people living in a fallen world (Romans 8:18–23). But every now and then laughter breaks through, as it does here in the Ehud story. It breaks through because suddenly we are shown things as God sees them instead of how we have become accustomed to seeing them. From our point of view tyrants like Eglon are terrifying. They do evil, and good people seem powerless to resist them. They fill us with despair. But to God they are laughable.

> Why do the nations rage
>   and the peoples plot in vain?
> The kings of the earth set themselves,
>   and the rulers take counsel together,
>   against the LORD and against his Anointed, saying,
> "Let us burst their bonds apart
>   and cast away their cords from us."
>
> *He who sits in the heavens laughs;*
>   the Lord holds them in derision. (Psalm 2:1–4)

It is not that God is indifferent to the evil such people do or the suffering they inflict. Otherwise he would not judge them as this psalm goes on to say he will. Rather, it is because he knows that their claims to be able to defy him with impunity are absurd, because they are no match for "his Anointed" (Psalm 2:2). God's Anointed (his messiah) was his chosen king, especially David and the kings of Judah that followed him (1 Samuel 16:1–3, 11–13; 2 Samuel 7:8–13). In the Old Testament Psalm 2 was fulfilled in the victories God gave to David, bringing hostile nations under his rule (2 Samuel 8:1–14). But the New Testament points to a far greater fulfillment in Jesus Christ, the great Son of David and God's Messiah par excellence. The New Testament writers quote Psalm 2 four times with reference to the victory Jesus won over sin and Satan and the evil powers of this world by his death and resurrection (Acts 4:25, 26; 13:33; Hebrews 1:5; 5:5). Who could have imagined that when Jesus stood before Pilate, who represented the awesome might of the Roman Empire, he was about to establish a kingdom that would conquer Rome and outlast it for more than two thousand years? How laughable, from this perspective, were Rome's pretensions to absolute power!

Ehud's deliverance of Israel for eighty years is miniscule in comparison to this, and his story is so different from the account of Christ's victory that it may seem preposterous to compare the two. Ehud's character and methods are utterly unlike those of Jesus. Ehud was devious—Jesus was guileless (1 Peter 2:22), Ehud was a man of violence—Jesus a man of peace, and so on. But there are also significant points of similarity. Both were deliverers raised up by God. Both were unlikely deliverers, with unpromising origins and an appearance of weakness rather than strength. Both faced the enemy alone and overcame him. Both were later revealed as victorious and summoned others to share in their victory. Both overcame the world (represented by Moab and Rome respectively) and achieved rest for God's people. Both, in a sense, made a spectacle of the evil powers. We have seen this as a major theme of the Ehud story. Paul makes the same point in relation to the victory of Christ: "[God] disarmed the rulers and authorities and *put them to open shame*, by triumphing over them in him" (Colossians 2:15).

The main difference is the role that humor plays in the way Ehud's victory is described, and especially the nature of that humor. It is coarse, and may embarrass us, but should not do so. It is what one recent commentator has called "a literary cartoon,"[8] intended to make a powerful point. Like Hans Christian Andersen's famous fairy tale, it encourages us to look with childlike simplicity and see the truth that everyone around us either can't or won't see: "The emperor has no clothes!"[9] In other words, the posturings of the apparently invincible are ridiculous. But in this case the humor has theological grounding. The tyrants of this world do have real power. They may be used by God to discipline his people, as Eglon was, but they do not have absolute power, and their days are numbered. Their assumption that they are invincible and will never be called to account for their actions is absurd, for it is God, not they, who rules the world and determines the fate of his people. And the One who gave them their power can and will end it when he chooses to do so. In fact he has already exposed their hollow claims for what they are in the death and resurrection of his Messiah (Acts 17:30, 31). "He who sits in the heavens *laughs*; the Lord holds them in *derision*" (Psalm 2:4). By its humor the Ehud story invites us to see the tyrants of this world as God sees them and to join in the laughter of Heaven. This is not whistling in the dark. It is holy laughter, and perhaps the only thing that can keep us sane in our darkest days. Let's receive it thankfully and rejoice that, however overwhelming evil may sometimes seem, we have something to laugh about.

7

Shamgar: The Man from Nowhere

JUDGES 3:31

SHAMGAR IS A MAN OF MYSTERY, and he is part of the larger mystery of salvation in the book of Judges. Shamgar appears suddenly, as though out of nowhere, does what he does in one verse, and disappears just as suddenly, leaving scarcely a trace behind (5:6). But as the writer of Judges tells us, "he *also* saved Israel" (3:31). In other words, this strange man and what he did is part of something bigger than himself—the saving and therefore survival of Israel in the judges period—something that is no less mysterious, in its own way, than Shamgar himself. Perhaps no one has expressed the mystery of God's ways more memorably than the English poet William Cowper: "God moves in a mysterious way his wonders to perform." What Cowper primarily had in mind was the mystery of creation and God's providential workings through apparently natural events. An even greater mystery, though, is God's saving work in history, something that confounds human wisdom and is fully revealed only in Christ (1 Corinthians 1:20–24; Romans 16:25). In Judges perhaps nothing illustrates the impenetrable nature of this mystery more than the brief note about Shamgar here in 3:31. It raises more questions than it answers. However, if we carefully follow the few clues it gives us we will find they lead us to the greatest mystery of all, not with all our questions about it answered, but with our appreciation of it enhanced by the journey we have taken.

The Mystery of Shamgar's Time and Circumstances

Judges 3:31 locates Shamgar between Ehud's victory over the Moabites in 3:12–30 and Ehud's death in 4:1. This means that his act of saving Israel by killing six hundred Philistines belongs in the eighty years of peace of verse 30. But how can this be? Here is the first element of the mystery surrounding Shamgar. To get some insight into it we need to know something about the Philistines and the backward reference to "the days of Shamgar" in 5:6.

Ehud's victory over the Moabites happened in the lower Jordan Valley, on the far eastern extremity of Israelite territory. With Shamgar we not only move forward in time, but also westward across the central highlands to where the mountains come down to meet the coastal plain bordering the Mediterranean Sea, close to the area we know today as the Gaza Strip. It is here that we meet the Philistines for the first time in the book of Judges and the beginning of a conflict between them and Israel that was to continue with various levels of intensity for about two hundred years, from the time of Shamgar to the time of King David.

The Philistines arrived in Canaan not long after the Israelites. The Israelites had entered overland, from the east. The Philistines arrived by sea, from the west. They came from Crete and other places in and around the Aegean Sea[1] and arrived in Canaan after an unsuccessful attempt to enter Egypt. They settled in the coastal area of southern Canaan, eventually forming a federation of five major city states: Ashdod, Ashkelon, Ekron, Gath, and Gaza. They brought with them the new skill of iron smelting, which gave them a technological advantage over both the Israelites and the native Canaanites. This was especially so on the coastal plains where their iron chariots (or perhaps iron-enhanced chariots) could be used to devastating effect against foot soldiers. In time they would emerge as Israel's main competitors for control of Canaan. The mention of iron chariots in 1:19 is an early indication of their presence. Sisera, with his nine hundred iron chariots (4:3), was probably from another wave of sea people closely related to them, and we will hear much more of the Philistines in the Samson story in chapters 13—16.

But Shamgar's clash with them is the first time we meet them directly in Judges. Most likely Shamgar came upon them as they were making exploratory probes up into the hills bordering the coastal plain as part of a reconnaissance mission prior to launching an all-out assault on Israel. By successfully repelling them he saved Israel, for the time being, from being further troubled by them and stopped the eighty years of rest referred to in verse 30 from being interrupted. If this is so, then the expression "After him" that opens verse 31 means "after Ehud's victory against the Moabites," but before his death in 4:1. Later, after Ehud's death but while Shamgar was still living, things got much worse, especially in northern Israel as described in

5:6, 7. This is the setting for the Deborah-Barak episode that we will come to in the next study.

The Mystery of Shamgar's Origins

Probing into Shamgar's background only deepens the mystery surrounding him. We are given none of the other kinds of background information normally supplied for Israel's judges—his tribe, place of birth or hometown, place or places where he fought, how long he lived or ruled, when and where he was buried, or what followed his death. He seems to come from nowhere and simply disappear rather than die. The sole piece of data we have to work with is his name, but that, too, is a riddle. "Shamgar" occurs frequently as a name in non-Israelite texts,[2] but only here in the Bible. It does not have the normal form of a Hebrew name,[3] suggesting that he may not even have been an Israelite. This startling possibility is made even more likely by the phrase "the son of Anath" (v. 31) that is attached to his personal name. It is unusual in several ways. With Hebrew names it is normal to have a patronymic here (a phrase indicating the person's father). But since "Anath" is feminine, it seems to link him with his mother. However, in Canaanite texts from the period before Israel's arrival in the land, Anath (or Anat) is the name of a god rather than a human being. She was worshiped by the Canaanites as a goddess of war, and her activities are described in particularly gruesome and bloodthirsty terms. Bronze arrowheads from early Iron Age Palestine, inscribed with names of the type, "X son of Anath," seem to indicate the existence of a warrior class associated with Anath as their patron deity.[4] Shamgar's improvised weapon, though, makes it more likely that he was a farmer than a professional fighter and that Anath was his real, human mother rather than a goddess. But why, then, was she called this? All things considered, it seems that Shamgar's family must have been either Canaanite or an Israelite family that had become involved in some way in worshiping the Canaanite gods. Even this is surmise, however. The reality is that probing into Shamgar's background leads to nothing about which we can be certain. It just becomes more and more murky.

The Mystery of Shamgar's Victory

Shamgar's weapon was not the sword or spear of a professional soldier, nor a purpose-made weapon like Ehud's dagger. It was an "oxgoad" (v. 31), a long, pointed stick used to prod reluctant animals, especially as they pulled a plow. How he managed to kill six hundred Philistines with it we are not told, and it's probably best not to speculate. Nor do we know whether he did it in one encounter or several spread over some time, perhaps years. Neither do we know whether he did it alone or not, although the natural sense of the verse suggests the former. All we can safely say, I think, is that the Philistines' flashy iron chariots would have been useless in the Judean foothills with their narrow ravines and that Shamgar's intimate knowledge of the area would have given him an advantage that might have compensated to some extent for the extreme odds that were stacked against him. Beyond that we only have a couple of clues from elsewhere in the book. They are significant, however. The overview in Judges 2 indicates that the various rescues Israel experienced in the judges period were fundamentally Yahweh's doing. Furthermore, there is an intriguing review in 10:11 of the particular deliverances Israel had experienced to that point. Included there is the question, "Did I not save you from . . . . *the Philistines?*" (v. 11), and the only deliverance from the Philistines in the preceding chapters is the one involving Shamgar. So we're on safe ground in assuming that Shamgar's amazing victory was not achieved simply by his own skill, but with the help of God. It is one of those moments in the book when God stepped in and made the impossible possible. As the lowly ox goad became a powerful instrument in Shamgar's hand, so did Shamgar in God's hand. Here at last the fog surrounding Shamgar parts, and one shaft of light breaks through—not the brilliance of Shamgar, but the astonishing freedom and power of a God who could use such an obscure and tainted person to save his people.

The Mystery of God

Thank God that not everything about God is mysterious. There is a fascination with mystery in some religions, including some branches of Christianity, that so distances God from us that all we are left with is a sense of awe and religious experiences that become a substitute for really *knowing* God. God is immeasurably greater than us, yes. *But he is knowable.* He has revealed himself to us in his mighty acts of creation and redemption, in the inspired words of Scripture that explain his character and ways and purposes to us, and supremely in Jesus Christ, the Word made flesh. The folly of trying to connect with God by experiences not based on God's revelation of himself is powerfully expressed by Paul in his marvelous letter to the Romans.

> But the righteousness based on faith says, "Do not say in your heart, 'Who will ascend into heaven?'" (that is, to bring Christ down) "or 'Who will descend into the abyss?'" (that is, to bring Christ up from the dead). But

what does it say? "The word is near you, in your mouth and in your heart" (that is, the word of faith that we proclaim); because, if you confess with your mouth that Jesus is Lord and believe in your heart that God raised him from the dead, you will be saved. (Romans 10:6–9)

In this sense God is not distant from us. The gap between him and us has been bridged from his side. He has come to us, spoken to us, and made relationship with him possible. The "mystery of godliness" (God's plan of salvation, centered on Jesus Christ) has been revealed.

Great indeed, we confess, is the mystery of godliness:

> He was manifested in the flesh,
>   vindicated by the Spirit,
>   seen by angels,
> proclaimed among the nations,
>   believed on in the world,
>   taken up in glory. (1 Timothy 3:16)

The mystery Paul speaks of here is something wonderful beyond anything we could imagine, but it is something that has been *revealed* and is to be confessed, proclaimed, and believed.

However, passages like the brief note about Shamgar in 3:31 are there to remind us that God has not so given himself into our hands that our knowledge of him is exhaustive, that we have no more to learn, or that he does not still have the freedom to act in ways that may surprise us. Far from it. The same apostle who spoke so forthrightly about the clarity of God's self-revelation in Romans 10 speaks in the very next chapter of the unknowability of God's ways.

Oh, the depth of the riches and wisdom and knowledge of God! How unsearchable are his judgments and how inscrutable his ways! "For who has known the mind of the Lord, or who has been his counselor?" (Romans 11:33, 34)

The traditional way of describing this paradox is in terms of the contrast between God's revelation of himself in the history of salvation (special revelation) and his behind-the-scenes ordering of all things (providence). True to its character, however, the account of Shamgar's victory in Judges 3 doesn't fit neatly into either of these categories. In terms of its content (an act of "saving" Israel) it belongs on the trajectory of salvation history. But in terms of the way it is described it belongs more to the category of providence. There is no mention at all of God in 3:31 itself. Shamgar's victory over the Philistines *appears* to be entirely his own doing. But 2:16 and 10:11 show us indirectly the hidden hand of God behind it. The mystery of Shamgar is traceable finally to God, but only indirectly, leaving most of our questions unanswered.

Shamgar and Us

We can take three main lessons from this mini-story of an enigmatic savior.

First, as for Shamgar, the basic facts of the Christian gospel are clear, but it is not a message that dispels all mystery. Our reaction to forms of spirituality that obscure the gospel should not be so extreme that we lose our sense of wonder at the astonishing strangeness of God veiled in infant flesh or of a crucified Messiah. The person God used to save us is not from nowhere, but he is certainly One whose origins (if we can even use such a term of him) are ultimately mysterious.[5] That should keep us humble before the mystery of God.

Second, the brief note about Shamgar should make us grateful that no one is too obscure or tainted for God to use. Shamgar, with his murky background and his ox goad, is one element of a pattern of God using unlikely people that runs right through Judges, from left-handed Ehud to hesitant Barak to fearful Gideon to the outcast Jephthah to the wild man Samson. If God could use these people he can use anyone, even you and me.

Finally, in Shamgar we catch a glimpse of unbroken rest. He prevented the eighty-year rest that Ehud had won for Israel from being disturbed by a Philistine incursion, and like all the deliverances won by Israel's judges that is a signpost on the way to something greater—a rest in which there will be no need for emergency action to keep the enemy at bay. Jesus has already put us beyond Satan's power to condemn us (Romans 8:1, 33, 34; cf. Zechariah 3:1, 2) and will one day put us beyond his power to touch us or even to threaten to do so. Swords will be beaten into plowshares and spears into pruning hooks, and farmers will be able to relax at last (Micah 4:3, 4). Ox goads will just be ox goads.

8

Barak: Captain Lightning

JUDGES 4:1–24

HUMAN BEINGS have a timeless and universal fascination with super-heroes. They have been the stuff of every culture from time immemorial, from Gilgamesh, the ancient Sumerian king whose epic search for immortality is perhaps the oldest written story on earth, to Achilles, the Greek hero of the Trojan wars, to the warriors and nation-founders of ancient and modern history, to the Olympians of every age and nation, to the Supermen and Wonderwomen (real and imaginary) of contemporary warfare, sport, and entertainment. They are always with us, and we love them. We can't get enough of them. So we keep manufacturing new ones through TV shows like *American Idol* and *America's Next Top Model*. They relieve our boredom by exciting and inspiring us. By identifying with them we are able to experience, vicariously, the exhilaration of great achievement. Even their scandals and falls from grace fascinate us and give us relief by making our own faults and failings seem small and excusable by comparison.

The Bible, too, has its superheroes: Samson, who kills a lion with his bare hands; David, who kills Goliath with a slingshot; Daniel and his friends, who brave hungry lions and a fiery furnace rather than sell their souls to pagan Babylon; Esther, whose brave and risky intercession saved her fellow Jews; and the martyrs and giants of faith whose deeds are recalled in Hebrews 11:4–38. The Bible is perhaps more willing than most ancient texts to acknowledge the flawed nature of its heroes, but it still values them as figures who can inspire and warn us and point us beyond themselves to Jesus who in both the perfection of his person and the greatness of his achievement surpasses them all.

But what of Barak? His name, which means "lightning" in Hebrew, suggests he has superhero potential. More seriously, he is the first judge of the book of Judges to be ranked with such heroes of faith as David, Samuel, and the prophets in the book of Hebrews:

> And what more shall I say? For time would fail me to tell of Gideon, *Barak*, Samson, Jephthah, of David and Samuel and the prophets—who through faith conquered kingdoms, enforced justice, obtained promises, stopped the mouths of lions, quenched the power of fire, escaped the edge of the sword, were made strong out of weakness, became mighty in war, put foreign armies to flight. (Hebrews 11:32–34)

Gideon, for reasons unknown, may be named first in Hebrews, but Barak precedes him chronologically and prevailed against overwhelming odds just as surely as Gideon, Samson, or Jephthah. He certainly "put foreign armies to flight" (v. 34) and for this alone deserves to be regarded as a hero. But a *super*hero? As we will see, the account of Barak's career in Judges 4 is too ambivalent about him to justify placing him in *that* lofty category.

The Need for a Champion (vv. 1–3)

Shamgar had saved Israel by repelling a band of Philistines who threatened to disturb the peace Ehud had won for them (3:31). But after Ehud's death (4:1) bigger problems emerged, requiring more complex solutions. Israel lapsed back into apostasy (v. 1) and was handed over, for discipline, to someone who didn't just threaten their well-being but destroyed it completely for twenty long years (vv. 2, 3).

As his impressive title suggests, "Jabin king of Canaan, who reigned in Hazor" (v. 2) was a formidable enemy. "Hazor" was a fortified city in the territory of Naphtali, approximately ten miles (fifteen kilometers) north of the Sea of Galilee, close to what is now the Israel-Lebanon border. It was at one time the most powerful city in northern Canaan. Its imposing ruins can still be seen today on the high ground overlooking Lake Hula (the ancient "waters of Merom") (Joshua 11:5, 7). The site is visible from miles away, and the remains of Hazor are the largest ancient ruin in modern Israel. "Jabin" was probably a royal title, like Pharaoh for the kings of Egypt. Joshua had defeated another Jabin at Hazor almost one hundred years earlier.[1] But now Hazor had recovered, and from his stronghold there this Jabin dominated the whole of northern Canaan from the Jezreel Valley, southwest of the Sea of Galilee, to the upper reaches of the Jordan River in what is now the Lebanon Ranges.

Like his predecessor, Jabin's strength lay largely in a network of alliances he had formed with the rulers of other Canaanite cities in the area.[2] But his real enforcer, and the secret of his military dominance, was his general, "Sisera," who had "900 chariots of iron" at his command (vv. 2, 3). Sisera's name is non-Canaanite and suggests that he may have been a leader of the so-called Sea People who arrived in Canaan from the region around the Adriatic Sea in the early Iron Age. He had established himself in "Harosheth-hagoyim" ("Harosheth of the Nations") (v. 2), much as the Philistines had established themselves in Ashkelon and other coastal cities in the south. The exact location of Harosheth-hagoyim is uncertain, but as a staging post for chariotry it was presumably on level ground rather than in the hills, and the details of the battle given later suggest that it was at the western (Mt. Carmel) end of the Jezreel Valley. Jabin's alliance with Sisera squeezed Israel's northern tribes between the two, on their north and south respectively. Sisera was someone who could not be ignored, but he seemed invincible. So after twenty years of suffering, Israel "cried out to the LORD" (v. 3). They were helpless and knew it. Israel needed someone who could take on Sisera and win.

The Commissioning of a Champion

For the first time in Judges we are shown *how* God raised up a deliverer for his people. He used Deborah, "a prophetess" who "was judging Israel at that time" (v. 4). We will not spend time on Deborah here as we will be considering her in some detail when we get to Judges 5. Suffice it to say that she summoned Barak and commissioned him in the name of the LORD (v. 6).

His Background (vv. 4–6)

Barak ("lightning") is a very suitable name for a warrior in the Canaanite environment in which Israel found itself. In Canaanite mythology Baal was pictured as riding on the storm clouds, wielding a club (thunder) in one hand and a spear (lightning) in the other, doing battle with Yam, the chaos monster of the sea. It was quite a name for Barak to live up to. The comparison with Baal is interesting in view of the fact that the Lord (Yahweh), in whose name Barak is commissioned here, is described in storm imagery in the victory song that follows, where what turns the tide in the battle with Sisera is a divinely sent cloudburst that turns the river Kishon into a torrent that sweeps the enemy away (5:4, 5, 19–21). Barak's destiny is to be the agent of Yahweh, the *true* rider "on the clouds" (Psalm 68:4).[3] More mundanely,

Barak is "the son of *Abinoam*" ("father of pleasantness") (v. 6), which has no particular significance except that it contrasts nicely with Barak's own name, suggesting that his family background did not prepare him for being a warrior. Barak will need divine aid, which is exactly what Deborah promises he will be given (v. 7).

"Kedesh-naphtali" (v. 6), from which Barak is summoned, was a town seventeen miles (twenty-seven kilometers) north of the Sea of Galilee in the tribal territory of Naphtali, at the extreme northern limits of Israelite settlement. Why Deborah summoned him and not someone else is not explained, except by the words she speaks to him when he arrives: "Has not the LORD, the God of Israel, commanded you . . ." She is a woman with prophetic insight and acts on orders from above. Barak is not *her* recruit but God's. The reason for his being chosen lies with God, not with Deborah; she is just the Lord's agent and mouthpiece. However, Barak must have already developed into a man of some influence because he is told, "Go, gather *your men* at Mount Tabor, taking 10,000 from the people of Naphtali and the people of Zebulun" (v. 6). Barak was probably the leader of a band of volunteer fighters—a local militia—known and respected in Zebulun as well as in Naphtali. He was the kind of man whose summons would be taken seriously, a man whom other men would follow. In that sense Barak was a logical choice. But even if he could muster ten thousand men, what could such a bunch of amateurs do against Sisera's professionals with their state-of-the-art military hardware? At the very least they would need the kind of strategy that would give them a significant tactical advantage.

His Marching Orders (vv. 6, 7)

As it turns out, Barak is not left to his own devices but is given a ready-made battle plan. "Mount Tabor," where he is told to assemble his men, was on the Naphtali-Issachar border, at the head of a valley leading down into the broad Jezreel plain where the battle would take place. Sisera could be expected to approach from his base in Harosheth-hagoyim in the west; so from Mount Tabor in the east, Barak and his men would be well-positioned to see before they were seen. They would also be ideally located to make a swift descent using the contours of the mountain itself for cover and so take the enemy by surprise. But as foot soldiers (if they could be called that) they would still be at a huge disadvantage against Sisera's chariots on the flat country at the base of the mountain. At this point Barak would have exhausted all that mere strategy could do to help him. He would need a miracle.

His Faith Challenge (v. 7)

Thankfully, Deborah gave him more than strategy; she gave him a divine promise. She told Barak that when he did what God had commanded him to do ("gather," or literally "draw," his men to Mount Tabor, v. 6), the Lord would "draw" (same word) Sisera and his forces to meet him at the river Kishon and "give" them into Barak's hand (v. 7). In other words, the meeting at that particular place would be choreographed by God and would issue in divinely-given success for Barak. Barak is told nothing about the "how" of this victory, nor why the river Kishon is the place where it will happen. On the face of it, the Kishon is a very unpromising site for a miracle. It is nothing like the Red Sea or even the Jordan River, where Israel had experienced previous miracles. In the eastern part of the Jezreel Valley closest to Mount Tabor the Kishon is nothing but a small, shallow stream. We ourselves will not find out why it was so strategic until chapter 5. For the moment we, like Barak himself, have just the bare command and promise that he was given: in essence, "Go there, and I will give you victory." The challenge for Barak is to decide whether that is enough for him. Does he have faith strong enough to go forward against overwhelming odds with nothing but the promise of God to rely on? If he can, he will indeed be a hero, but of a rather different kind from that of popular imagination. He will be "given" victory rather than achieve it; and the real battle will be won before he goes to face Sisera, in his decision to stake everything on God's being faithful to his promise.

His Equivocation (vv. 8–10)

Barak's response to Deborah's command is neither a definite yes nor a definite no. In the one sentence he says both "I will go" and "I will not go" (v. 8). In other words, he equivocates, shifting the responsibility of determining his response back onto Deborah: if she goes with him he will go; otherwise he will not. What are we to make of this? It could be seen as an act of piety on Barak's part. Barak has such high regard for Deborah as God's spokesperson that he wants her at his side so that he can always be directed by God's word through her. This is in fact what happens. She accompanies Barak to the battlefield and at the crucial moment speaks the word that spurs him into action: "Up! For this is the day in which the Lord has given Sisera into your hand. Does not the Lord go out before you?" (v. 14). Clearly though, Deborah herself does not think this is how things should have been. For her, Barak's equivocation did not reflect well on him. She went with him, but only reluctantly, and after issuing a warning that was effectively a rebuke: "I will surely go with you. *Nevertheless, the road on which you are going will not lead to your glory,* for the LORD will sell Sisera into the hand of a woman" (v. 9). Fighting was men's business, and Barak should have been willing to go at God's command and fulfill his manly responsibilities, trusting in the promise he had already been given. He should not have needed any further word from Deborah. But if that is the case, why is he mentioned in Hebrews 11 as a hero of faith? We will have to ponder this further, but at the very least we must conclude that in the faith department Barak is at best a rather flawed hero. Barak's luster as a potential superhero is fading and is destined to fade further because there will be no glory for him on this campaign. Sisera will now be handed over to a woman rather than to Barak himself. We naturally think this woman is Deborah herself, but we are in for a surprise!

His Victory (vv. 10–17a)

Now the talking is over. Barak swings into action, and the pace of the narrative quickens. The "Kedesh" where Barak's men assemble in verse 10 can hardly be the Kedesh-naphtali from which Barak was called, as that is far too remote to be a feasible mustering point for the battle. It is probably another town of the same name, known to archeologists as Khirbet Qadisa, just twelve miles (nineteen kilometers) from Mount Tabor.[4] From there Barak's men followed him up Mount Tabor, with Deborah accompanying them (v. 10b). Sisera, whose intelligence gatherers have apparently been at work, gets news of this and immediately summons his entire force, including his nine hundred iron chariots, from their base at Harosheth-hagoyim to the river Kishon (v. 13), not knowing that he is being drawn there by Yahweh. This time Barak does not hesitate when Deborah gives him the command to act. He immediately makes a lightning strike before Sisera's forces can get properly set. Down he comes from Mount Tabor with ten thousand at his heels (v. 14), and against all odds victory is achieved with astonishing ease. Sisera's formidable forces almost immediately break ranks and flee. It's a complete rout for which no explanation is given except that the LORD made it happen: "the LORD routed Sisera and all his chariots and all his army before Barak by the edge of the sword" (v. 15). Barak's men had nothing to do but pursue and cut down their demoralized enemies. They chased them all the way back to their base in Harotheth-hagoyim, until "not a man was left" (v. 16).

Of course, this leaves us with many questions. *How* did the Lord produce such a sudden reversal? *Why* were Sisera's much-touted iron chariots suddenly so ineffective against Barak's volunteers after twenty years of complete dominance over Israel? *Why* did the river Kishon prove such a propitious site for the battle to be fought? Again we will have to wait until Judges 5 for the answers. The one thing that is blindingly obvious at this point is that God made good the promises he had made to Barak. When Barak went at God's command, God gave him an overwhelming victory, just as he said he would (vv. 7, 14, 15). But there is a complication: "Sisera got down from his chariot and fled away on foot" (v. 15b). The biggest prize of all has escaped! Or has he?

His Embarrassment (vv. 17b–22)

This complication shifts the focus of the story from the victory at the river Kishon, which we expected to be the climax, to the fate of Sisera, and especially the fulfillment of Deborah's prediction that he would be given into the hand of a woman (v. 9). And this sets the stage for the entrance of someone we haven't heard of until this point: "Jael, the wife of Heber the Kenite" (v. 17b). As with Deborah, we will reserve most of what we are going to say about Jael until we move on to Judges 5. However, some background to her sudden appearance is needed here.

According to verses 11 and 17, Jael's husband Heber had broken away from the Kenites who had settled in the south with the tribe of Judah (1:16) and aligned himself with Jabin, Israel's enemy. "The oak in Zaanannim," where he set up camp (v. 11), is mentioned in Joshua 19:33 as a boundary marker on the edge of the tribe of Naphtali's allotment and was "near Kedesh" (v. 11), where Barak had mustered his men back in verse 10. Heber was ideally positioned to observe Barak's preparations for battle and may well have been the person who alerted Sisera to what was happening (v. 12). The point is that, given Heber's alliance with Jabin, his encampment was a logical place for Sisera to flee to when things went against him in the battle (v. 17). Meanwhile, Barak had continued pursuing Sisera's men westward toward Harosheth-hagoyim, not realizing that Sisera was no longer among them (v. 15). When he realized his mistake, he too headed east. But he'd lost valuable time. When Barak finally arrived at Heber's camp, Jael came out and called to him, "Come, I will show you the man whom you are seeking" (v. 22). And there at last Barak found his quarry, already dead in Jael's tent (v. 22).

Seeing the way things were going, Jael had decided to save her own skin by joining the winners. She enticed the exhausted Sisera into her tent and killed him before Barak arrived. So the warning of Deborah was fulfilled in a way that none of us could have guessed. Sisera is handed over to a woman—not to Deborah, though, but to Jael!—and Barak, as surprised as we are, can only stand and stare (v. 22b). And behind all this was the sovereign hand of

God. The same God who "routed" Sisera's army at the Kishon (v. 15) also sold him "into the hand of a woman" (v. 9). Sisera is shamed by being killed by a woman,[5] and Barak is shamed by having the honor of slaying him man-to-man taken from him. Heber is nowhere to be seen. Jael alone stands tall; she has eclipsed all the supposedly powerful men around her. If Barak is a hero at all in this story, he is a very red-faced one. He has won a victory, but no glory.

His God (vv. 23, 24)

The story ends by reminding us how it began and points out what a mighty reversal has taken place. "Jabin the king of Canaan" has been so much in the background that we might almost have forgotten he exists. But the story has never been fundamentally about Barak and Sisera; it has been about Jabin and Israel—and God. When Israel sinned, the Lord "sold them into the hand of Jabin king of Canaan" (v. 2). Jabin, not Sisera, was the real oppressor of Israel. But now without Sisera his power is broken, and his eventual subjugation by Israel follows as a matter of course: "And the hand of the people of Israel pressed harder and harder against Jabin the king of Canaan, until they destroyed Jabin king of Canaan" (v. 24). None of this would have been possible without God: "*God* subdued Jabin the king of Canaan before Israel" (v. 23).

His Faith

We haven't finished with Barak yet. Judges 5 will revisit his story and elaborate on some of the details we have passed over here. But even then we won't have heard all that Scripture has to say about him. A further reference to him occurs in Samuel's farewell address to Israel in 1 Samuel 12:11: "And the LORD sent Jerubbaal and *Barak* and Jephthah . . . and delivered you out of the hand of your enemies on every side." And the final comment on Barak comes, as we have seen, in Hebrews 11:32–34:

> And what more shall I say? For time would fail me to tell of Gideon, *Barak*, Samson, Jephthah, of David and Samuel and the prophets—who *through faith* conquered kingdoms, enforced justice, obtained promises, stopped the mouths of lions, quenched the power of fire, escaped the edge of the sword, were made strong out of weakness, became mighty in war, *put foreign armies to flight.*

Which brings us back to the question we posed at the beginning of this chapter: was Barak a superhero? Now, looking back, we can see that the whole way Barak's story is told in Judges 4 tends to downplay his hero status. He equivocated. He refused to go with nothing but the promise of God. By insisting that Deborah go with him he forfeited the glory that could have been his. He arrived too late at Jael's tent and found that Jael had already done what he should have had the honor of doing. God sold Sisera into the hand of a woman.

However, the references in 1 Samuel and Hebrews highlight three important things about Barak that we would do well to note:

First, the LORD "sent" Barak, and used him to "deliver" Israel (1 Samuel 12:11). In other words, Barak was God's man—called and commissioned by him and used mightily by him for Israel's good. That's no small honor! He may have forfeited the lesser honor of being the one to kill Sisera, but not the far greater honor of being God's agent to rescue his people. That places Barak despite his shortcomings in an elite category of servants of God, from Moses through Joshua and the judges to David and beyond.

Second, he won a major battle. The next chapter of Judges has much more to say about this, but even here in chapter 4 the few details that *are* given are impressive. This was no minor skirmish. A militia force of ten thousand footmen fought against a professional army equipped with nine hundred war chariots reinforced with iron. And the result was not just a decisive win, with the enemy left to fight another day, but a rout, all the way back to Harosheth-hagoyim. Every enemy soldier was slain, including their general. Jabin's hold over Israel was broken, and he himself was eventually destroyed. It's the only battle in Judges celebrated with a victory song (Judges 5). Barak certainly ranks with those who "put foreign armies to flight" (Hebrews 11:34).

Third, and most important of all, he did what he did "through faith" (Hebrews 11:33). Barak's faith was a cautious, qualified one at first, but when the command to "go" came a second time he did not hesitate. Down from Tabor he went, with ten thousand men following him. That is true, manly leadership, the kind of leadership that inspires others and rouses them to action. The biggest challenge faced them, though, when they reached the valley floor. At that point they had to break cover and advance twelve miles or more across open country to the river Kishon to confront Sisera's seemingly invincible chariotry in open battle. That took nerves of steel, a leader who would not falter, and men who would follow him into the very jaws of death. But most of all it took *faith*—an unwavering trust in God who had promised them victory. This is where we see Barak at his very best, a man of faith indeed, faith that acts, faith that stakes everything on God and gives a man tremendous courage, and faith that God honored by giving Barak a victory he could not have achieved without God's help. That is why Barak deserves the honorable mention he gets in Hebrews 11. Barak was certainly a hero, but a hero with a difference. He was not a professional soldier or mighty warrior in the traditional sense. He did not prevail by raw strength or prowess in battle. His victory was a gift rather than a personal achievement. Nor was he naturally a man of great faith. His faith was faltering at first, but matured under testing to become the kind of faith that God honors.

Barak is by no means the greatest of Biblical heroes. Much, much more space is given in the Old Testament to Abraham, for example, or Moses, Joshua, or David. And the passing reference to him in Hebrews 11:32 does not begin to compare with the eight whole verses in that chapter devoted to Abraham or the six to Moses. Like us, Barak was no superhero. That title, if it is appropriate to use it at all in this context, belongs to God alone. Judges 5 will make this very clear. And among human beings there is only One whose faith was perfect (Hebrews 12:2, 3). Nevertheless, Barak is among a great "cloud of witnesses" (Hebrews 12:1) whose courageous faith can and should inspire us to trust in God too, whatever our misgivings and whatever challenges obedience to him requires us to face.

9

Singing

JUDGES 5:1–31

FIRST REFLECTION

NOW FOR SOMETHING COMPLETELY DIFFERENT! Unlike the rest of Judges, chapter 5 is poetry rather than prose, and song rather than narrative. The story of Deborah and Barak, Sisera and Jael has already been told in chapter 4. Now it's time for reflection and celebration, and what better way to do that than in song? There's no other chapter like this in Judges; so rather than treat it like the others we're going to take a different approach. Instead of working though it consecutively we're going to look at three aspects of it in succession, beginning here with singing. Let's join in the celebration by singing along with Deborah and Barak (v. 1)!

Surprised by the Song

Judges is a rather grim book, to put it mildly. There are a lot of dark and depressing things in it. It's a difficult read. Things go from bad to worse. You keep hoping they'll get better, but they never do—at least not for long. Israel was in deep trouble in the days of the judges, partly because of their own wrongdoing and partly because of what others did to them. Judges is a collection of unhappy stories, and when you're unhappy you're not much inclined to sing. Judges is a book that quenches singing rather than evoking it. So why a song here in chapter 5—and not just a song, a whole 31 verses of exuberant praise and celebration? It's one of the most surprising things in the whole book.

The Reason for the Song

The reason is that something had happened on the "day" mentioned in verse 1: "Then sang Deborah and Barak . . . *on that day,*" and the previous chapter has told us what that something was. For twenty years Israel had been cruelly oppressed by an enemy that had a stranglehold on them and was squeezing the life out of them (4:3). And verses 6–8 of the present chapter tell us what life had been like during that time. "The highways were abandoned" because people were too afraid to travel on them. They kept to byways. Village life ceased. Normal life was impossible. War was at the gates. The enemy had nine hundred chariots, and Israel had nothing—not a shield or spear was to be seen among forty thousand in Israel (v. 8). The enemy was invincible, and Israel had no hope. Fear was in everyone's eyes. Then one day something happened that changed everything. After twenty long years their bonds were suddenly broken, and they were free again. That's why they sang this song. It was what their ancestors had done when the Lord delivered them from slavery in Egypt (Exodus 15:1). It's what a later generation would do when God rescued them from exile in Babylon (Isaiah 26:1), and it's what *all* God's redeemed people will do one day in Heaven (Revelation 5:9, 10). Singing is a natural and proper response to deliverance. It's something people do when God saves them and they are glad and grateful to him. Judges 5 is the natural accompaniment of Judges 4.

The Themes of the Song

Leaders and Willing Volunteers

The first theme taken up by the singers is leaders who led and people (ordinary people like you and me) who responded to their leadership.

> That the leaders took the lead in Israel,
>   that the people offered themselves willingly,
>   bless the LORD! (v. 2)

> My heart goes out to the commanders of Israel
>   who offered themselves willingly among the people.
>   Bless the LORD. (v. 9)

Among other things, this tells us that the victory celebrated here did not come easily. A battle had to be fought, and battles are never nice. For twenty years people had been avoiding this necessity—keeping their heads down, staying off the highways, taking bypaths, suffering quietly. But one day there were leaders—people of strength and character like Deborah and

Barak—who knew that the issue couldn't be avoided any longer. The battle had to be fought, and they were willing to take a stand and face whatever came. And there were men and women like you and me who were willing to answer their call, stand with them, and see the struggle through. And against all odds the battle was won.

That's the way it was for Israel, it's what it was like at the time of the Reformation, and it's how it has always been and always will be for the Church of Jesus Christ. The environment is hostile. The enemy seems overwhelmingly powerful. There's a battle that cannot be avoided. It's not physical as it was in Barak's day, but it's a real battle nonetheless, and if the church is not to die, it needs leaders who will take a stand and people who will stand with them and support them. And when you have leaders like that and ordinary people like that, you have something to sing about, because people like that are precious. They are God's gifts to the church, and if you have people of sterling character like that in your church, don't leave them to fight the battle alone, and don't destroy them with criticism. Stand with them, support them, and see what God will do.

God the Warrior

Good leaders are great and are indispensable to the life of God's people. So are willing volunteers who support them. That's part of what this song is about. But it's not the main focus of it, because no matter how courageous Israel's leaders were and how willing their supporters were, they wouldn't have won this battle unless God had shown up and given them victory. Barak was reluctant at first, but did eventually accept the commission God gave him through Deborah and began to make preparations for battle. Then when the critical moment came and the battle had to be fought, Deborah gave him another word from God: "Up! For this is the day in which *the Lord* has given Sisera into your hand. Does not the LORD *go out* before you?" (4:14). It was a word about the Lord, who had already "gone out" before Barak; and when Barak obeyed, he found it was true. Notice how this is recalled in verses 4 and 5 of chapter 5:

> LORD, when you *went out* from Seir,
> when you *marched* from the region of Edom,
> the earth trembled
> and the heavens dropped,
> yes, the clouds dropped water.
> The mountains quaked before the LORD,
> even Sinai before the LORD, the God of Israel.

God came like a mighty warrior marching into battle. Israel had seen him do this before, when they were fleeing from slavery in Egypt and he destroyed Pharaoh's chariots and their riders by drowning them in the Red Sea.

> The Lord is a man of war;
>   the LORD is his name.
> Pharaoh's chariots and his host he cast into the sea,
>   and his chosen officers were sunk in the Red Sea.
> The floods covered them;
>   they went down into the depths like a stone.
> Your right hand, O LORD, glorious in power,
>   your right hand, O LORD, shatters the enemy. (Exodus 15:3–6)

"The LORD is a man of war" (Exodus 15:3). How do you feel about that description of God? Christians of a former generation felt no embarrassment about it at all. One of the most sung hymns in Sunday school when I was a child began with the words, "Onward, Christian soldiers, marching as to war." It went on to speak of "Christ, the royal Master," *going before us* and of the Church of God moving "like a mighty army." Billy Graham, arguably the greatest gospel preacher of the twentieth century, used to call his evangelistic campaigns "crusades." I and many others of my generation were converted at those meetings. With hindsight "crusades" may have been an unfortunate title for them, but at least we knew that a battle was being fought and that commitment to Christ entailed a willingness to participate in it. We were not ignorant of the fact that we lived in a very different world from the Old Testament people of God, and that the church of Jesus Christ should not try to defend itself or advance its cause by acts of war as it had in the past. There was no incitement to violence at Billy Graham's meetings. But he and we understood that Old Testament passages about God going before his people to fight for them and give them victory still had something to teach us. We knew that in some sense it was still right to think of God as a warrior, and we were not embarrassed about doing so. In these days of violent jihads and religious pluralism we've largely given up using militaristic language for God. Talk of God our heavenly Father is still acceptable among all but the most extreme left-wing fringe of Christianity, and so is Jesus the Good Shepherd. But God as warrior has almost entirely disappeared from Christian discourse.

More is involved here, though, than Christian jargon. What is at stake is Biblical truth. We need *everything* the Bible has to teach us about God, not just the things we feel comfortable with. Why is it important that God is a man of war? It is important because there are some battles that you and I can't win. When we step forward to follow Jesus, we step into a battle zone. The Christian life has to be lived in a world that is hostile to the gospel and is becoming more hostile every day. And behind the people who oppose us are spiritual powers that are far beyond our capacity to deal with. We can't overcome them by just trying hard. The enemy is too strong for us. If we are to have the victory, God must win it for us and give it to us. The good news is that the critical battle has already been won, and the Person who won that battle for us has promised to be with us in all the battles we will have to face as his followers this side of Heaven (Colossians 2:13, 14; Matthew 28:16–20).

That's how it was for Deborah and Barak. The enemy was too strong. They had no hope against Sisera and his nine hundred iron chariots unless God went before them and fought for them. But he did. That's what they sing about in Judges 5.

God the Lord of Nature

How did God fight for them? Look at verses 4, 19–21:

> LORD, when you went out from Seir,
> when you marched from the region of Edom,
> the earth trembled
> and the heavens dropped,
> yes, the clouds dropped water. . . .
>
> The kings came, they fought;
> then fought the kings of Canaan,
> at Taanach, by the waters of Megiddo;
> they got no spoils of silver.
> From heaven the stars fought,
> from their courses they fought against Sisera.
> The torrent Kishon swept them away,
> the ancient torrent, the torrent Kishon.
> March on, my soul, with might!

What would you have seen if you had been there? The enemy was advancing eastward along the Jezreel plain, following the course of the Kishon River. At the eastern end Barak and his men had rushed down from Mount Tabor and were moving westward across the plain to engage them. As they did so the skies began to darken—quickly. A storm approached from the south, from the direction of Edom. It swept across the Dead Sea, gathering moisture and increasing in intensity as it came up the Jordan Valley into the central highlands. Then, with the precision of a smart bomb, its mighty clouds broke open and dropped their payload of flooding rain right at the source of the Kishon River. Suddenly all the small streams and dry wadis leading down to the valley floor became raging torrents. By the time Barak and his men reached the banks of the Kishon where the battle was to take place the enemy was already defeated. Sisera's fancy chariots had all bogged down, and their drivers were all scrambling down from them and beginning to run.

You can always explain things like that in natural terms—a freak storm, an amazing stroke of luck, and so on. Ah, but the timing! What were the chances that such a "freak" of nature would happen at the precise moment when Barak and his men would otherwise have faced certain death? And how likely was it that such a thing should happen on the very day that Deborah had declared that this was the day the Lord had gone before them to give Sisera into their hands (4:14)? This was no accident. This was the hand of God who'd literally moved heaven and earth to save them. When you've cried out to God for deliverance, as Israel did (4:3), and something like that happens, the only right thing to do is to acknowledge it as a gracious act of God and give him praise for it, or even better, give God the glory by telling *others* what he has done for you, which is what Israel does here.

> Hear, O kings; give ear, O princes;
>   to the LORD I will sing;
>   I will make melody to the LORD, the God of Israel. (v. 3)

Notice how they refer to God here as "the LORD [Yahweh], the God of Israel." This is covenant language, language that recalls God's special relationship with Israel. Verse 5 makes this especially clear, with its reference to mountains quaking, "even [like] *Sinai* before the LORD, the God of Israel." Mount Sinai was where God made a covenant with the people of Israel after saving them from slavery in Egypt. On the way to Sinai, he had rescued them from Pharaoh and his fearsome chariots, as we saw above. Then, too, the Israelites had sung a mighty song of praise to God (Exodus 15). So the outburst of praise in Judges 5 marks what has just happened as another great God-moment in the history of the Lord's covenant relationship with his people. The God who saved Israel from slavery in Egypt has saved them again—from slavery to Sisera and Jabin. This tells us, among other things, that God remains committed to his covenant relationship with his people, and at this moment at least they recognize this and are full of thankfulness to him for it. Judges 5 is arguably Israel's finest moment in the whole book of Judges.

But then, just when we least expect it, like a cloud crossing the sun on an otherwise perfect day, a shadow suddenly falls over the song. Some did not play their part.

Disappointment

For more than thirty years I was a lecturer in a theological college. Since I also doubled up as a chaplain, part of my responsibility was to meet with a group of students once a week to discuss issues relating to their studies and Christian ministry and to provide pastoral support. Each week one of the students would lead a discussion on a topic of their own choice. Students gave careful thought to what they would share with the group, and the discussion normally concluded with prayer for the person who had led us and for others in the group who requested it.

One week when it was time for a particular student to introduce his topic, he simply said, "I haven't prepared anything for today." He gave no explanation and offered no apology and did not look in the least embarrassed. He simply made the bare statement and stopped talking. There was a long awkward silence. None of us knew what to do or how to respond. Then when he saw that we were sufficiently confused and embarrassed to be sure that what he said next would have maximum impact, the student himself broke the silence. "Why don't we discuss how we feel and react when someone lets us down, especially in ministry?" It was not a pleasant topic, and it was not what we were expecting, but what followed was one of the best discussions we ever had!

In Judges 5 the reality of letdown and the sense of disappointment and betrayal it brings is reflected in verses 13–17 and 23. Verse 13 takes us back to the moment when the volunteers went down with Barak to engage the enemy. Chapter 4 has spoken only of men from Naphtali, Barak's own tribe, and Zebulun, its immediate neighbor (4:6, 10). But now a broader picture begins to emerge. The roll call of those who did and did not participate begins with Ephraim, the southernmost of the northern tribes. It was in Ephraim's territory that Deborah was "judging Israel" before hostilities began (4:4, 5). At that time Ephraim was the "root" (v. 14) or heartland of Israel; so we would expect Ephraim to come first and to receive creditable mention, as it does in verse 14a. They were followed by men from Benjamin, further south (v. 14b). Next comes "Machir," a leading clan of Manasseh from east of the Jordan River, then Zebulun and Issachar (vv. 14b, 15a). In verse 15b, however, the language of unity and resolution begins to give way to expressions of equivocation and division, and the tone of the song begins to darken. The clans of Reuben deliberated what course of action to take and in the end stayed with their sheep (vv. 15b, 16). The people of Gilead[1] stayed where they were, on the other side of the Jordan River (v. 17a). The Danites, in the far north, stayed with their ships (v. 17b). They had apparently entered into some kind of arrangement (perhaps as hired workers) with the Phoenicians, who specialized in sea trade. The tribe of Asher, right on the coast, also was too wedded to the sea to leave it (v. 17c). Their failure to pull their weight is made all the more blameworthy by the contrast in verse 18 with the heroism and self-sacrifice of Zebulun and Naphtali (Barak's own tribe), who "risked their lives to the death . . . on the heights of the field." The bitterest reproach, however, is reserved for "Meroz," in verse 23:

> Curse Meroz, says the angel of the LORD,
>   curse its inhabitants thoroughly,
> because they did not come to the help of the LORD,
>   to the help of the LORD against the mighty.

The location of Meroz is unknown, but the reference to its "inhabitants" suggests it was a town rather than a clan. Given that it is mentioned immediately after the description of the rout of Sisera's forces in verses 19–22, it may have been a town well-situated to help Barak's men by cutting off the fugitives, as in the seizing of the fords of the Jordan in 3:28 and 7:24. If so, the fact that they did nothing was particularly reprehensible. "They did not come to the help of *the LORD*, to the help of *the LORD* against the mighty" (v. 23). It was not just God's people they failed, but God himself, to whom they owed covenant loyalty. Hence the appearance of "the angel of the LORD" (v. 23), God's special messenger, at this point in the song to utter a solemn curse on Meroz and its people.[2] It is the darkest moment in the song and marks in a particularly striking way the serious nature of the offense. In some circumstances doing nothing can be the worst of all sins!

Everyone had cause to praise God that day because the whole of Israel had been delivered. But not everyone could sing as Deborah and Barak did. Those who had failed to play their part probably stayed away from the celebrations. If they were there, they must have hung their heads in shame as their unfaithfulness was recalled, and even those who sang must have had very mixed emotions. The victory at the river Kishon was a great deliverance, but not a perfect one. The foreign oppressor was gone, but Israel was still far from well. God had a lot of work to do with his people yet.

Singing in the Life of the People of God

Have you ever considered how important singing is in the Bible? Both the Old and New Testaments are punctuated with songs. The singing starts in Exodus 15 after God saved Israel from the pursuing army of Pharaoh at the Red Sea, and it goes right through to the "new song" of the book of Revelation that goes on "forever and ever" (Revelation 5:9–14). And right in the middle, in the largest book of the whole Bible, there are no fewer than 150 songs! The book of Psalms is the hymn book of the Old Testament people of God; so singing is central to Biblical religion.

It is has also been one of the most outstanding characteristics of Christianity for more than two thousand years. The singing of psalms was a distinguishing feature of Christian worship from the beginning (Matthew 26:30; Mark 14:26; Ephesians 5:19; Colossians 3:16), and the book of Psalms has provided the inspiration for countless Christian hymns. Singing God's praises is a sign of being filled with the Holy Spirit (Ephesians 5:18, 19), and every outpouring of the Spirit in revival blessing has been accompanied by a flood of new songs. Such singing is not the cotton candy of the Christian life; it is the steak and vegetables, or at least the vegetables—a standard part of the main course! Of all the major world religions, only Christianity has congregational singing at its heart.

The particular song we've been looking at in Judges 5 has several things to teach us about the nature of Biblical song. First, it is a natural and proper response to salvation. "Then sang Deborah and Barak the son of Abinoam *on that day*" (v. 1)—the day they were delivered from twenty years of oppression (4:3). Deliverance is a joyful thing; it sets people singing, and so it should! Second, such singing is God-centered: "to the LORD I will sing; I will make melody to the LORD" (v. 3). Deborah and Barak's song has a number of subthemes, as we have seen, but it is essentially God-directed and God-focused. Above everything else, it is *about* God—who he is and what he has done for his people. He is the God of war who fought for them, the God of creation who moved heaven and earth to save them, and the God of the covenant, who speaks to them and holds them accountable for their actions.

Third, this song thanks God for his servants—leaders who lead and volunteers who stand with them. "My heart goes out to *the commanders* . . . who offered themselves willingly among *the people.* Bless the LORD" (v. 9). Fourth, it acknowledges the reality of human failure: "Meroz . . . did not come to the help of the LORD" (v. 23). Finally, it gives expression to the full range of human emotions, from jubilation to disappointment and questioning to righteous anger, but it never descends into mere sentimentality. The strong feelings are theologically grounded and directed to God as the primary audience and witness of the song: "*to the* LORD I will sing" (v. 3). All these qualities are also found in the Psalms and in the best traditional hymns and contemporary Christian songs.[3] We need such strong singing in the church today. It is God's gift to his people, inspired by his Spirit, inviting us to engage with our great God with our hearts, minds, and spirits.

Among other things, the song of Judges 5 reminds us that things are never so grim that there can't be victory with God. This is a song of people who had been hopeless for twenty years. But it also reminds us that such singing is not just a gift, it is also a choice: "to the LORD I *will* sing" (v. 3, my emphasis). So choose to sing. Sing *this* kind of song. It glorifies God and edifies those with whom you sing it. And if Israel had reason to praise God for delivering them, how much more do we who are the beneficiaries of the great victory God has won for us in Jesus Christ! If that doesn't start us singing, what will?

10

Mothers

JUDGES 5:1–31

SECOND REFLECTION

MY MOTHER DIED ON JULY 29, 2009 at the age of one hundred years and ten days. Holding my mother's hand as she slowly sank toward death is an experience I will never forget. Sitting there with her in her last two days was very painful, but as time went by I realized it was also a gift, one I will treasure for the rest of my life. My mother gave me many good things, but I think the greatest of them were her faith in God and her love for my father and for me. I realized as I sat there holding her hand, watching her face change, and hearing her breathing become shorter and shorter, that I was truly a blessed man. I loved her then more than ever, and I knew God better too. Life's deepest lessons are learned through suffering. That is just one of the lessons that the cross of Jesus teaches us (Hebrews 5:8).

Mother was not a great thinker. Her faith was uncomplicated and straightforward. She knew she was a sinner like the rest of us, but she was not crippled by guilt because she also knew that God loved her and forgave her. And she was completely sure that she would go to Heaven one day because Jesus had taken full responsibility for her sins and died in her place.

I remember on one occasion reading her the story about Jesus going to visit Mary and Martha after their brother Lazarus had died (John 11:1–44). Martha was quite cross with him for not coming sooner. "Lord," she said, "if you had been here, my brother would not have died" (v. 21). Jesus replied, "I am the resurrection and the life. Whoever believes in me, though he die, yet shall he live, and everyone who lives and believes in me shall never die" (vv. 25, 26). Mum said to me, "Barry, do you think that's true?" "Yes," I said,

"I *do* think it's true." She was quiet for quite a while. Then she just said, "So do I." It was one of the shortest and best sermons I ever heard! Notice, she didn't ask me whether I found these words *comforting*, but whether they were *true*. Christians believe certain things about Jesus, and these things comfort us in situations like the one I was going through. But that's not why we believe them. We believe them because they are *true*.

Mum's favorite verse of Scripture was Deuteronomy 33:27: "The eternal God is your dwelling place, and underneath are the everlasting arms." It hung on the kitchen wall at home. When she had to move to a nursing home she took it with her and set it on the windowsill beside her. It was still there when she died. I only had to say the first couple of words, and she would complete it in a strong, clear voice. This was the God she knew—her dwelling place and her loving Father, whose strong arms always supported her. To know God this way is not an achievement but a gift. None of us deserve it, and we cannot earn it. Our part is simply to reach out and take it in simple, childlike faith. The price for it has already been paid in full; that is the *greatest* lesson the cross of Jesus teaches us. God so loved sinners like you and me that he gave up the most precious treasure he had to save us. My mother knew that. That is why death had no terror for her. She was going home, and she knew it.

Her other favorite passage of Scripture was Psalm 23. Again I only had to say the first few words, and she would recite it all, almost word perfect, even when she couldn't remember what day of the week it was or what she'd just had for breakfast.

> The LORD is my shepherd; I shall not want.
>   He makes me lie down in green pastures.
> He leads me beside still waters.
>   He restores my soul.
> He leads me in paths of righteousness
>   for his name's sake.
>
> Even though I walk through the valley of the shadow of death,
>   I will fear no evil,
> for you are with me;
>   your rod and your staff,
>   they comfort me.
>
> You prepare a table before me
>   in the presence of my enemies;
> you anoint my head with oil;
>   my cup overflows.

Surely goodness and mercy shall follow me
     all the days of my life,
and I shall dwell in the house of the LORD forever.

It's words like that that convince me beyond all doubt that the Bible is inspired. Such words come from the very heart of God and tell us what life *is*
like and *can* be like for all of us. Darkness and death, evil and enemies—yes.
The Bible does not gloss over these things. But it also shows us green pas-
tures, quiet waters, a table spread, and a cup overflowing. And most of all
a God who will be with us, even through the valley of the shadow of death
itself, and will be there at journey's end to welcome us home.

If we walk with God, suffering will not destroy us or make us bitter.
It will humble us and free us from the terrible burden of our pride until we
rest again, like little children, in his arms. Through my many times with
her, I watched my mother slowly approach this second childhood again and
remembered the words of Jesus: "Unless you turn and become like children,
you will never enter the kingdom of heaven" (Matthew 18:3). Before I left
Mum at night on those last few days we had together we would say her favorite verse again, "The eternal God is your dwelling place," and then the
good-night prayer she used to say over me:

Now I lay me down to sleep,
I pray the Lord my soul to keep;
If I should die before I wake,
I pray the Lord my soul to take.

We are made for God, and only knowing him can make us whole. My
mother knew him. She did not live a perfect life, but she lived a good life,
and she died well. She, too, was a gift from God—another blessing I did not
earn, but am grateful to have had.

Mothers are very important to all of us. We all have one, whether our
relationship with her is a happy or unhappy one, even if we have been separated from her by abandonment, tragic circumstances, or death. We owe our
very existence to our biological mothers, and most of us owe much, much
more. Mother's Day provides us with a special opportunity to acknowledge
this. It is a celebration of mothers and motherhood, maternal bonds, and the
role of mothers in society. It is celebrated at different times and in different
ways in different places, but its observance, in one form or another, is virtually universal. Motherhood extends through generations, from great grandmother to grandmother to mother, and their influence is immense.

We have already noted the striking fact that there is a song at all in Judges 5. A second remarkable fact about this chapter is how prominently women feature in it, and not just women but mothers. There is one mother, Deborah, at the beginning (we will see what kind of mother shortly) and another at the end—"the mother of Sisera," Israel's enemy (v. 28). This is noteworthy to say the least and contributes significantly to the way the song works and makes its impact on us. Let us consider each of them in turn and see what further riches this part of Judges has in store for us.

Deborah

We have already seen how the phrase "on that day" in verse 1 refers back to the previous chapter, and that's particularly important for how we understand Deborah. The circumstances in which Deborah rose to prominence were desperate ones. The Israelites had been oppressed by Jabin king of Canaan and his general Sisera for twenty long years, and hope had begun to fade that they would ever be delivered (4:2, 3). Chapter 5 gives us more detail. The roads were abandoned because people were afraid to use them. When they did have to travel, they made themselves as invisible as possible by keeping to obscure bypaths. Village life ceased because normal community activities were impossible. It was every man and his family for themselves. "War was in the gates," directly threatening every town (vv. 6–8).

In that situation Deborah exercised the kind of leadership described for us back in 4:4, 5. She was "the wife of Lappidoth." She was womanly in that sense; she had a private, domestic existence. We are told virtually nothing about it, however. Was her marriage a happy one? Did she have children (none are mentioned)? Was she therefore a mother at all in the normal sense? Such matters are intriguing, and we'd like to know more about them. But we are not told, because the focus is not on her domestic existence but on her public life. We *are* told at the outset, though, what she *was* ("a prophetess") and what she was *doing* ("judging," 4:4).

That she was a prophetess is clearly the most important thing about her. It was through her as his spokesperson that God spoke his word into Israel's situation and began to change it. It was through her that God raised up Barak the deliverer and broke Israel's bondage to Jabin and Sisera. She was a figure like Samuel—not herself a warrior, but nevertheless a critical agent of change. She was a female Samuel; or perhaps more accurately, Samuel was a male Deborah since Deborah came first! Deborah was a prophetess. However, it was in what she was *doing* that her motherliness was most apparent. She "was judging Israel at that time" (4:4). We are not told that God raised her up or that the Spirit came upon her or even that she was a judge in the way that term is most commonly used in the book. It is Barak, not Deborah, who is remembered as a judge like Gideon, Samson, and Jephthah in Hebrews 11:32. Deborah just quietly did something that needed doing: "She used to sit under the palm of Deborah between Ramah and Bethel in the hill country of Ephraim, and the people of Israel came up to her for judgment" (4:5). Under the stress of the times cracks had opened up in the fabric of Israelite society. There was disunity and brokenness, and Israel was not able to defend itself against the external enemy until these internal divisions were healed, at least to some extent. And it was by judging Israel as she did that Deborah contributed significantly to the healing process. Where circumstances permitted, lesser matters were settled at the town gates (Ruth 4:1–12). But more serious matters required someone of greater stature and more wisdom, and Deborah was somehow recognized as such a person. She had presence. She was a woman of character and authority. She was not just domestic or tribal. She was bigger than that—a woman of larger vision and greater leadership qualities. So the people came to her, and she helped settle their differences. She was a kind of Judge Judy of ancient Israel, but without professional qualifications or celebrity glamor. She held court under a palm tree (4:5). In her own words, she was "a *mother* in Israel" (5:7).

The fact is that in these hard times the Israelites needed mothering, and Deborah met that need; and she had a very clear sense of the importance of what she was doing. "The villagers ceased in Israel; they ceased to be *until I arose; I, Deborah*, arose as a mother in Israel" (5:7). We may find this somewhat jarring. Shouldn't she have been more self-effacing? Perhaps.[1] But remember, this comes in the middle of an exuberant victory song. And what if she does get a bit carried away in the headiness of the moment? No one else in Judges is perfect,[2] so why should we expect Deborah to be unblemished? She is a real woman, and real women are not perfect. The essential point is that she speaks truth here: she *was* a mother in Israel, and her role was critical. We are clearly meant to admire her.

But now let us turn our attention to the mother who is featured at the end of the song.

Sisera's Mother

This mother is shown to us at one frozen moment in her life.

Out of the window she peered,
the mother of Sisera wailed through the lattice:

> "Why is his chariot so long in coming?
>   Why tarry the hoofbeats of his chariots?"
> Her wisest princesses answer,
>   indeed, she answers herself,
> "Have they not found and divided the spoil?—
>   A womb or two for every man;
> spoil of dyed materials for Sisera,
>   spoil of dyed materials embroidered,
>   two pieces of dyed work embroidered for my neck[3] as spoil?"
>   (vv. 28–30)

We can't help but feel some connection with this woman, even sympathy. She's an ordinary mother behaving as any mother would in the circumstances in which she finds herself. She's on the losing side, and her loss is terrible. The gap in her life will be long and very painful. She waits for a son who will never return. She tries to hope, but even as she does so the last shred of hope is slipping away. Her maids try to comfort her, and she tries to believe what they say, but she knows it's not true. She's on the other side of the line that divides the saved from the lost, the people of God from the enemies of God. If Deborah is a mother *in* Israel, this woman is a mother *not* in Israel. She is a mother in pain. We understand her and feel for her. She engages us at the level of our common humanity.

But we also become aware as we watch and listen that there's something deeply wrong with her. The words she speaks open a window for us into her mind, and what we find there is disturbing. Listen to verse 30 again:

> Have they not found and divided the spoil?—
>   A *womb or two for every man;*
> spoil of dyed materials for Sisera,
>   spoil of dyed materials embroidered,
> two pieces of dyed work embroidered for *my* neck as spoil?

This woman is not bighearted as Deborah is. She wants her son for what he'll bring her. Women who don't serve her needs are so much stuff to be divided up like property. "A womb or two" depersonalizes them. They exist only for reproduction and the sexual pleasure of men. It is chilling to hear a woman speak of other women in this way. Even more so when we remember that Deborah could have been one of them.

This woman is not only bereaved but corrupt in her mind, lost inwardly as well as outwardly. This does not mean that she is necessarily a worse sinner than Deborah or Barak or anyone else. Who knows what we might find inside *their* heads if we were able to go there? Nevertheless, the description we have of her presents a striking contrast to Deborah. This mother looks through a lattice (v. 28); Deborah sits under a palm tree. She is attended by princesses (v. 29); Deborah is surrounded by the needy. She is served *by* others; Deborah *serves* others. She is consumed by her own pain; Deborah heals the pain of others. But the biggest difference is simply and awfully this: Deborah sings; this woman weeps. Deborah is a mother saved; this woman is a mother lost. Which brings us to the final verse of the song.

Two Kinds of Mothers

"So may all *your enemies* perish, O Lord!
But *your friends* be like the sun as he rises in his might."
And the land had *rest* for forty years. (v. 31)

I don't know whether or not you can align yourself with the sentiment in that verse. I find difficulty in doing so because I don't want *any* mother to be lost. Of course, as the last verse of the whole song it doesn't refer exclusively to Sisera's mother. It refers to Sisera himself and Jabin and all who had participated with them in the oppression of Israel for the last twenty years, as well as all future enemies of God and his people. Nevertheless, it confronts us with two stark truths. First, in the end there are only two kinds of people in this world—friends of God and enemies of God. And within that broad framework there are only two kinds of mothers—mothers who are among God's people and *rejoice* in his righteous judgment and mothers who are among God's enemies and will *face* his righteous judgment. It's the difference between being like "the sun as he rises in his might" and perishing in utter darkness.

The second stark truth is this: there is only one way to enter into the *rest* of God—the *rest* of salvation—and that is by being God's friends. In Old Testament times this privilege belonged especially to Israel, but with two important qualifications. Outsiders could come in by abandoning their past and seeking refuge in Israel's God. Two outstanding examples were Rahab the harlot and Ruth the Moabitess (Joshua 6:25; Ruth 2:12), but they were not alone. The door was always open to the stranger and the needy (Exodus 12:48, 49; Leviticus 19:34; Numbers 35:15). So being a non-Israelite did not automatically entail exclusion. Furthermore, being an Israelite did not guarantee permanent inclusion. The Law of Moses provided for willful sinners to be "cut off" (banished) from the community,[4] and the prophet Malachi made it clear that on the last day only those who truly feared the Lord would be acknowledged by him as his people (Malachi 3:16–18). Even in

Old Testament times, to be a friend or enemy of God was not an accident of birth but a choice. And it is a choice that still confronts every man and woman, including every mother (John 1:11, 12; 3:16–19). In essence the last verse of Judges 5 is a prayer that what God did for Israel in the days of Deborah and Barak he would finally do for *all* his true people: end their oppression by executing perfect justice and bringing about rest, not just for forty years but forever.

Valuing Mothers

We will have more to say about Deborah in the next chapter of this book. Before we go on, though, let's pause here to reflect again on the priceless value of mothers.

Let's thank God for "mother[s] in Israel" (v. 7)—women of character who have stepped in and provided the care that we needed as members of God's family. In the early eighties my wife and I and our two small children arrived in Sheffield, England on a chilly, damp autumn day to begin three years of residence there while I studied for a PhD at the University of Sheffield. On our first Sunday we attended a small church on the housing estate where we had found rental accommodation. We had arrived as complete strangers and felt the normal awkwardness of visitors at a church we had never attended before and where things were different from what we were accustomed to. Afterward an elderly woman named Marjory approached us, introduced herself and her husband, and invited us to come home with them for Sunday lunch. In the course of the conversation that ensued she asked our eldest daughter, Miriam, just three years of age, if she had a grandma. "No," said Miriam, "my grandma is in Australia." "Well," said Marjory, "would you like me to be your grandma in England?" A shy nod was all Marjory needed. From then on, for the whole of our time in England, we were part of her family. She already had three married sons and several grandchildren, but from that moment on I was treated like one of them and my family as part of hers. We spent countless Sunday lunches at her home and celebrated Christmases and Easters with her as well as many birthdays and other family events. She often healed our hurts, spoke God's word into our lives, and helped us fight our battles. Her support and care were invaluable. For the next thirty years whenever we visited England we would make sure we went to Sheffield to visit her, and even as adults our daughters still called her Grandma Marjory. She has now gone to be with the Lord, but we still remember her and thank God for her. Let us thank God for such mothers. And if you are a mother or hope to be, pray that you too will be a source of healing love not just to your own children but to God's needy children as well.

Let us also pray for the mothers who carried us in their wombs and suffered to give us life. Let us pray that God will help us honor them as we should all the days of their lives and to prepare now to provide for them, as best we can, in their old age. This is a solemn duty specifically spelled out in the law God gave to Israel (Exodus 20:12; Deuteronomy 5:16) and beautifully exemplified by Jesus himself as he gave his life for us on the cross (John 19:26, 27).

Finally, let us pray for all the mothers we know and feel for, who have many admirable qualities but in their thinking are still far from God. Let us pray that they will not remain so, but will have the humility to acknowledge their need of God and faith to entrust themselves to him, so that on the last day they may not perish with his enemies, but "like the sun" (v. 31) rise with us to share in his eternal glory.

11

Mavericks

JUDGES 5:1–31

THIRD REFLECTION

WE'VE CONSIDERED the remarkable fact that there's a song here in Judges 5 and the prominent role that mothers play in it. This time we will focus on mavericks. This final reflection will be somewhat briefer than the previous two because we'll be revisiting characters we've met before but we'll look at them from a slightly different angle. But before we rush in we need to be clear what we are talking about. Singing we know, and mothers, but what is a maverick?

Samuel Augustus Maverick (July 23, 1803–September 2, 1870) was a Texas lawyer, politician, land baron, and signer of the Texas Declaration of Independence. His name is the source of the term *maverick*. Maverick annoyed his fellow ranchers by refusing to brand his cattle. In time *maverick* became a term for unbranded cattle and eventually a way of referring to someone who refuses to conform to others' expectations.[1] The *Merriam-Webster's Collegiate Dictionary* defines a maverick as "an independent individual who does not go along with a group or party."[2] The *Cambridge Advanced Learner's Dictionary* is more general: "A person who thinks and acts in an independent way, often behaving differently from the expected or usual way."[3] Mavericks are irritating people and may be considered either outsiders or insiders depending on the level of annoyance they cause. In extreme cases they may be rejected by the in-group altogether. But this can be a serious mistake, because mavericks are sometimes the most creative, innovative thinkers in the group. They can think outside the box and see possibilities to which others are blind. Every company, committee, and enterprise needs people like this to stop it from becoming so set in its ways that it can't adapt and change when that is exactly what is needed. In this respect churches are no different. An inability to tolerate mavericks and appreciate the contribution they can make can be a recipe for disaster. Mavericks may be annoying, but we need them.

There are at least three mavericks in the song Deborah and Barak sing in Judges 5. The first is Deborah herself. We have already considered her as a mother, but let's now take another look at her from this new angle.

Deborah, the Maverick Leader

As we've seen, the background to Deborah's rise to prominence is given back in 4:1–7. In desperate times she "was judging Israel" by settling internal disputes, and as "a prophetess" she summoned Barak and charged him with the responsibility of delivering Israel. There's no doubt that she's on the side of God and his people, but she doesn't operate in the way things are normally done. She lives in a patriarchal society, where everyone *knows* that God has given the responsibility of headship in the family and the nation to men. But Deborah judges the nation and gives orders to a man in God's name. What are we to make of this? At least three things, the first of which we've already alluded to.

She's Exceptional

Deborah is the only woman to exercise public leadership in the book of Judges and one of the few to do so in the Bible as a whole. Furthermore, this is what we would expect if we pay careful attention to the way the Bible opens. Adam is created first, then Eve to be his companion and helper (Genesis 2:5–7, 18–22; cf. 1 Timothy 2:12–15). When the woman sins, it is her husband who is first called to account, because as the leader in the relationship he is the one who bears ultimate responsibility (Genesis 3:9–12, 17). And from that point on all those who exercise leadership are men—Noah, Abraham, Joseph, Moses, Aaron, Joshua, Othniel, Ehud, and Shamgar. Nor has there been a female prophet before Deborah. Abraham is the first person to be called a prophet (Genesis 20:7), then Moses (Deuteronomy 34:10), and the expectation for the future is that God would raise up more male prophets, like Moses, to succeed him: "I will raise up for them a prophet like *you* from among their *brothers*. And I will put my words in *his* mouth, and *he* shall speak to them all that I command *him*" (Deuteronomy 18:18). Miriam, the sister of Aaron, is called a "prophetess" in Exodus 15:20, but only in her role of leading the women in a song of praise to God. There is simply no precedent for what Deborah does in Judges 4. Nor does the situation change after her. No other judge or prophet in the book of Judges is a woman. In the rest of the Old Testament Athaliah briefly rules as queen in her own right in 2 Kings 11:1–3, Huldah the prophetess features in 2 Kings 22:14–20,[4] and an obscure prophetess, Noadiah, is mentioned in Nehemiah 6:14. But like Deborah these are the exception rather than the rule, and even among them Deborah stands alone by both judging and prophesying. Deborah is not just exceptional, she is *very* exceptional.

She Emerges in Chaotic Times

Deborah leads Israel in a disordered situation. The book of Judges is about the kind of chaos that happens when Israel abandons covenant faithfulness and everyone does what is right in his own eyes (2:11, 12; 17:6). In these circumstances it should hardly surprise us if exceptional things happen, and that most of them are bad. Could Deborah's leadership simply be symptomatic of the general chaos of the times? Perhaps, except for one final, very important consideration.

She Is Praised

The whole way the story of Deborah is told in Judges 4 and 5 tells us that she is not an agent of disorder. In fact, she's the very opposite. She's the healer of Israel's brokenness. She's not part of the problem, but a key part of the solution to it. Furthermore, she herself seems to recognize the limits of what is appropriate for her to do, even in these exceptional circumstances. She calls and commissions Barak, who is recognized elsewhere in Scripture as a man God used to deliver Israel militarily (Hebrews 11:32). Leading Israel in battle is men's work, and Deborah is content to support Barak in this role rather than assume it herself. In other words, she's no proto-feminist with an ideological objection to male headship or any distinction between male and female roles. The song in Judges 5 celebrates her rather than criticizes her and makes it clear that if she is a maverick, she's a godly one, worthy of praise.

However, in terms of the attention given to her and the language applied to her, there is another woman who surpasses Deborah in Judges 5.

Jael, the Maverick Mother

Jael is a more complex and ambiguous figure than Deborah. We have already met her and made some reference to her, so we will focus here on aspects of Jael that justify seeing her as a maverick.

First, she has a rather murky background. She was a Kenite (5:24), a clan whose connections with Israel had a rather checkered history. They were the descendants of Moses' father-in-law, Jethro. They had accompanied the tribe of Judah in its battles to possess and occupy their allotted territory in Canaan and had eventually settled among them in the dry Negeb region in the south (1:16). But Jael's husband, Heber, separated from the other Kenites, presumably taking his extended family with him, and settled in the north, close to the place where the battle described in Judges 4, 5 was later fought (4:11). There Heber's clan attached itself to Jabin, king of Hazor, who was Israel's enemy (4:17). That's probably why Sisera fled there after his forces were routed, expecting to find refuge (4:17). As far as Israel was concerned, Jael was an outsider, a member of a splinter group that had deserted them.

Second, she's a rebel. She is her own person and, like Rahab the harlot, chooses to break with her own people and side with Israel. She's either a traitor or the opposite, depending on your point of view. In the patriarchal world to which she belonged it took tremendous courage to defy one's husband. But that is what Jael did. She refused to follow Heber in his betrayal of Israel. To the singers in Judges 5, she was a hero.

Third, she's unconventional. In a world where men exercised power, she outpowers them all. She draws two powerful men into her tent—Sisera, the general of Jabin's army, and Barak, the commander of Israel's resistance fighters. And there she single-handedly unmakes them both—Sisera by killing him and Barak by denying him the honor of killing his enemy man-to-man. This is expressed very cleverly in Judges 4 by the use of the Hebrew words *'ish* ("man") and *'ayin* ("nothing").

> And he [Sisera] said to her [Jael], "Stand at the opening of the tent, and if any man [*'ish*] comes and asks you, 'Is any man [*'ish*] here?' say, 'No [*'ayin*].'" (4:20)

The *'ish* who comes to the door of Jael's tent is Barak, and the *'ish* who is inside is Sisera, but they are both doomed to become *'ayin* ("nothing") at Jael's hands. There will be no "man" in Jael's tent when she has completed her work! Both will be unmanned by this woman. Yet she is not a usurper of male power and therefore no radical feminist. She takes only what is given her, for it is the Lord who takes away Barak's glory in this story by "selling" Sisera into the hand of a woman (4:9). And since it is *God* who honors Jael in that way in chapter 4, it is fitting that Israel should honor her too in the song of chapter 5. She is unconventional but praiseworthy.

Finally, though, she is not nice. In our second reflection on Judges 5 we considered mothers—Deborah, "a mother in Israel" (v. 7), and Sisera's mother, a woman in pain. But Jael, too, is a kind of mother. Notice how she treats Sisera in verses 24–27:

> Most blessed of women be Jael,
>   the wife of Heber the Kenite,
>   of tent-dwelling women most blessed.
> He asked for water and she gave him milk;
>   she brought him curds in a noble's bowl.
> She sent her hand to the tent peg
>   and her right hand to the workmen's mallet;
> she struck Sisera;
>   she crushed his head;
>   she shattered and pierced his temple.
> Between her feet
>   he sank, he fell, he lay still;
> between her feet
>   he sank, he fell;
> where he sank,
>   there he fell—dead.

Jael behaves like a mother—up to a point. She calms Sisera's fears, she tucks him into bed, she gives him milk, she hushes him to sleep. *Then she takes a tent peg and hammers it through his skull!* That's not nice. Jael may be "most blessed of women" (v. 24), but would you like to be married to her? Would you be able to sleep at night? If she was my wife I think I'd work very hard at sleeping with my eyes open and hide all sharp objects, because Jael is not safe and respectable. She's a seriously dangerous woman. She's a maverick, to be sure; she even turns motherhood on its head. But she is "most blessed" because she chose to stand with God and his people. She took risks for them, and it was to her that God gave the honor of striking the blow that ended once for all Jabin's and Sisera's oppression of Israel.

One more maverick remains for us to consider, and we could easily miss him because he's mentioned only in passing.

Shamgar, the Maverick Savior

In a chapter on mavericks we can hardly omit Shamgar, but since we've already considered him at length, our comments here will be quite brief. This is appropriate anyway, since he receives only passing mention in the song. Notice carefully, however, how Shamgar and Jael are linked in verse 6:

In the days of Shamgar, son of Anath,
    in the days of Jael, the highways were abandoned,
    and travelers kept to the byways.

The writer could easily have left Shamgar out altogether, but he clearly wants us to remember him when we think of Jael. They are linked by time and circumstances. "The days of Shamgar" and "the days of Jael" had similar characteristics: Israel was in desperate circumstances. But Shamgar and Jael have much more in common than this. Both have murky backgrounds—Jael because she belonged to a clan that betrayed Israel, and Shamgar because he was probably not even an Israelite at all (3:31). As we have already seen, his name, "Shamgar, son of Anath," suggests that his family was Canaanite or at least tainted in some way with Canaanite religion.[5] As far as their backgrounds were concerned, neither Jael nor Shamgar was respectable. They were not the sort of people we'd want our sons or daughters to marry. They were similar, too, in the improvised nature of their weapons. Jael nailed Sisera with a tent peg, and Shamgar dispatched the Philistines with an ox goad. Both take us by surprise. Neither of them is the type of person we would expect to take violent action. Jael is a woman; Shamgar is a farmer. But in Jael's case there is at least some preparation for her appearance in the narrative: God will sell Sisera into the hand of a woman. In Shamgar's case there is no such preparation. There is something quite shocking about Shamgar—the background he comes from, the suddenness of his appearance, and the scale and violence of his actions. He was a maverick if ever there was one. But the writer is clear that he, too, was part of God's way with his people, a man God used to "save" them (3:31; 10:11).

Mavericks All

There are in fact a lot of mavericks in Judges. Ehud was a left-handed assassin. Shamgar was probably a Canaanite. Deborah was a woman. Barak was reluctant. Jael was from a Kenite splinter group. Gideon was fearful. Jephthah was an outcast and gang leader. Samson was a womanizer. In fact, with the exception of Othniel all the judges were mavericks in one way or another. None of them were mainstream in terms of their background or social acceptability. But if those mentioned in Hebrews 11:32 can be taken as representative, all of them, at their best, accomplished great things for God by faith. None of them were too warped or tainted for God to use to save his people. And there are several important lessons for us there.

First, something about God. God can and does at times use people with whom we don't feel entirely comfortable. This is irritating, but we have to be humble enough to accept and respond to such people as our brothers and sisters in Christ and be open to what God has to teach us through them. For some years I attended a church where the preaching was shared by a number of people. There was always something encouraging or challenging to be gleaned from the sermons. One preacher, though, used to make me cringe. His manner, I thought, was inappropriately flippant. His sermons, regardless of the text, all seemed to be basically the same. Because of his personal experience, certain aspects of Christian teaching were very meaningful to him, and he returned to them again and again, sermon after sermon, regardless of the passage he was supposed to be expounding. His sermons were often poorly structured and unclear. He often seemed to me to have given little thought to what he was going to say beforehand, trusting too much, in my opinion, that the Spirit would make up for his lack of diligence by giving him at the time of delivery whatever God wanted to say through him. I found it all very frustrating and annoying. But I have to say that some of the most profound experiences of God speaking to me with deeply convicting power came under that man's preaching. Many a time after he preached I had to go and seek God's forgiveness for something that needed to change in my attitude or behavior. It was humbling but very good for me. And when I went through a period of deep depression and was really struggling, it was that man who came to my home to sit with me and pray for me. So many things about him annoyed me, but God used him to help me as few others have done.

Many others, some of whom have been mightily used of God, can testify to similar experiences. In the mid-1940s John Stott was reading theology at Cambridge in preparation for Anglican ministry. He had been confirmed in 1936, but was not converted until 1938 when he heard the Rev. Eric Nash present an evangelistic address to the Christian Union at Rugby School, where Stott was a boarder. From that time on Stott was a convinced evangelical and went on to become a prolific author and preacher and one of the most influential leaders of the worldwide evangelical movement. But his years at Cambridge were a time of severe testing for him. He was exposed to liberal theology as taught by some of the most distinguished scholars of his day. This put him under considerable stress. To quote from his biographer Timothy Dudley-Smith, "Faced with emotional isolation from his home and intellectual isolation in his studies, there were few people in Cambridge to whom John Stott could turn with confidence in his desire to combine intellectual integrity with faithfulness to revelation."[6]

In these circumstances, help came from an unexpected quarter. Dr. Basil Atkinson, Senior Under-Librarian at the university library, was a distinguished scholar in ancient languages, but a very unusual man. Eccentric to a degree few other dons achieved, he used to ride through Cambridge on an old upright bicycle, dressed in a blue pinstriped suit and a green pork-pie hat, and his voice, strong and with extraordinary emphasis placed on every word, was often mimicked by his many friends.[7]

Friendship with Basil Atkinson could be costly because not only was he eccentric, he was also a very convinced and outspoken evangelical. Even within the CICCU (the Cambridge Inter-Collegiate Christian Union), loyalty to him was fickle. When the CICCU was strongly evangelical, Basil Atkinson was admired, but when its evangelical zeal wavered, he was disowned. Basil used to tell, with good humor, of an occasion when he spoke for the LIFCU, the London equivalent of CICCU:

> I had been asked to address a weekday evangelistic meeting, and I turned up and did so. There was an undergraduate in the chair and, when I had finished, he got up and announced, "We thank Dr Atkinson very much for coming to speak to us this evening. Tomorrow we are to have two undergraduates from Oxford who are perfectly normal human beings."[8]

It was hard to think of a man with Basil's eccentricities as a "perfectly normal human being," nor, we might add, a man like Shamgar who killed six hundred Philistines with an ox goad, or a woman like Jael who killed someone by hammering a tent peg though his head. But there was no doubting whose side they were on or that God chose to use them to save his people. So it was with Basil Atkinson. This unusual man was there for John Stott when he needed him and understood his struggles as few others did. He was one of John's most stalwart supporters and counselors. We all owe a tremendous debt to Basil for John Stott's emergence from that time of trial as the great evangelical scholar and teacher he proved to be. So thank God for mavericks.

Second, there is a warning here about absolutizing our Christian culture, including our theological systems, so that what is generally true becomes the whole truth. That would leave us with no capacity to grow and no capacity to deal with exceptions to our norms. Deborah's leadership as judge and prophet was exceptional, but right in the circumstances. If we were to condemn her for exercising headship as a woman we would be completely out of step with what Judges 4 and 5 are telling us to do. Exceptional circumstances need exceptional solutions, and God reserves to himself the freedom to act in ways that are outside the norm and confound our expectations. Communities that are unable to cope with this eventually become sects, who will always reject mavericks as enemies. The Pharisees are a classic case. They believed they had the beginning and end of the matter when it came to keeping the Law. So when Jesus healed on the Sabbath and declared all foods clean, they couldn't learn from that. The only response they were capable of was to attack Jesus as a lawbreaker. Job's friends fell into the same error. Their theology of reward and punishment was right as far as it went, but they simply couldn't see that Job was an exception. So instead of being Job's comforters, they became his judges and tormentors.

This can be very hard for us as evangelical Christians because we are committed to being faithful to what the Bible teaches. What we sometimes fail to see is that the Bible itself allows for exceptions to what should ideally be the case and refuses to let us put God into a box. We must always be prepared to acknowledge the blind spots in our Christian cultures and the limits of our theological systems. We must be able to sing, rather than mutter, when God does something extraordinary.

Finally, there's a warning here against confusing godliness with respectability. Deborah may have been respectable even though she broke certain norms. Jael and Shamgar certainly weren't. Respectability has never been a reliable indicator of which side people are on, in either the Bible or in the history of Christianity. The more respectable the church becomes, the less real, the less salty (Matthew 5:13; Luke 14:34), the less authentically Christian it will be. Jesus was not respectable (Luke 7:34). Nor were his disciples (Mark 2:18; 7:2–5). In the end a church that has no place for mavericks will have no place for Jesus and no place for the gospel.

12

Gideon: The Making of a Leader

JUDGES 6:1—8:3

GREAT MEN AND WOMEN OF GOD are not made in a moment. None of us is born one; we start with a gene package inherited from our parents, who were deeply flawed human beings like ourselves. We also inherit an inborn sinfulness from them that has its ultimate source in Adam and Eve's rebellion against God at the dawn of human history. This does not mean that we are absolved of responsibility for our own wrongdoing. When King David, struggling to come to terms with the enormity of his own moral failure, said, "Behold, I was brought forth in iniquity, and in sin did my mother conceive me" (Psalm 51:5), he was not trying to shift the blame to his mother. His particular sin was his own, but his vulnerability to it was something he shared with all other human beings. It was a characteristic of the whole environment he was born into, where "death reigned . . . even over those whose sinning was not like the transgression of Adam" (Romans 5:14). This was the world, and the Israel, that Gideon was part of. And as we will see, there is nothing in either his family's conduct or circumstances to suggest they were any better than others. How can a man of God be fashioned from such beginnings? Not easily, is the short answer, and not without a great deal of patient, persevering work on God's part. But let us begin by noticing carefully the particular environment of sin and death that was Gideon's world.

The Israel Gideon Knew (6:1–10)

The Gideon story begins much the same as those of Ehud and Barak: "The people of Israel did what was evil in the sight of the LORD" (v. 1; cf. 3:12;

4:1). There are a couple of differences, though, that provide an important clue to the context in which Gideon grew up. The first is the backdrop provided by the great song of praise in chapter 5 and the last statement of that chapter: "And the land had rest for forty years." If, as what follows will suggest, Gideon was called to leadership as a young man, he must have been born into good times rather than bad. Israel had been delivered from twenty years of oppression, and as their praise shows in chapter 5, they knew they owed their freedom to God. They were God's "friends" and were strong, like the rising sun (5:31). The second difference is the absence, this time, of the word "again." Here we do not read that "the Israelites *again* did what was evil," as in 3:12 and 4:1, as though there was something inevitable about it (this is what they *always* did), but simply that they *did* what was evil. It's a subtle change, but if we are attuned to the context there is a hint here that things might have been different this time. The exuberant praise of chapter 5 might have ushered in a new era in Israel's life. The cycle of sin and misery caused by Israel's repeated failure might have been broken and the "forty years" lengthened to eighty or one hundred or an entirely new future different from Israel's recent past. The book of Judges could have ended with chapter 5. Sadly, it was not to be. The pull of Canaanite worship was too strong and Israel's resistance to it already too weakened by past lapses. Israel reverted to its old ways, and a dark shadow fell over the land once again. "The LORD gave them into the hand of Midian seven years" (v. 1). These years of Gideon's life were to be very different from the good times he had known until then.

This time the invaders are "Midianites," "Amalekites," and "the people of the East," desert people occupying the marginal lands east and south of Israel. The Amalekites were ancient enemies of Israel and have already appeared as part of an enemy coalition in the Ehud story (Exodus 17:8–16; Judges 3:13). There had been trouble between Israel and the Midianites, too, in the time of Moses (Numbers 25:1–18; 31:1–12). Old animosities still smoldered in the background. Unlike previous invaders, however, the enemy did not come on this occasion to conquer and occupy Israelite territory, but to plunder. Like the other desert dwellers they led, the Midianites were hungry for the riches that fertile, arable land could produce. So they would sweep in like a locust plague, year after year, when the crops were ripe for harvest and strip the land bare. They would also carry off sheep, oxen, and donkeys, the sum total of economically valuable animals, leaving the people without food or the means to produce it (vv. 3–5). The Israelites were reduced to living like animals, in dens and caves, to survive (v. 2), until they could bear it no longer and cried out to the Lord to save them (v. 6). Under these harsh conditions Gideon left his carefree youth behind and matured into the resourceful and angry young man he is when we meet him in verse 11. Before that, however, something else happens that seems to cast into doubt any hope of relief. The Lord sends a prophet to confront the Israelites with their unfaithfulness to him and tell them, by implication, that they have forfeited all right to deliverance (vv. 7–10). In view of this, just what, if anything, God will do next is unclear.

Gideon's Unexpected Visitor (6:11–25)

The day that Gideon had his unexpected visitor was just like any other day in the last seven years. Gideon was threshing wheat—what little he had—on his father's farm. And not in the open, as he had done in better times, but in a winepress, to make what he was doing less obvious to the enemy (v. 11). He was in hiding, like everyone else, and certainly not expecting deliverance. He was just trying to stay alive.

Then Gideon senses that someone is watching him, and has been for some time. "The angel of the LORD came and sat" under a nearby oak (v. 11) and just watched for a while before "appearing" to Gideon in verse 12. This is the third time this mysterious messenger has appeared in Judges,[1] but the first time he has done so to a single person. It is a moment of great significance for Gideon. Given the circumstances and the suddenness of the visitor's appearance, we might expect Gideon to be alarmed. But for some reason he is not. His visitor sits like an ordinary man. His gaze is somehow penetrating, but not threatening. And his words, when he speaks, astonish Gideon: "The LORD is with you, O mighty man of valor" (v. 12). This makes no sense to Gideon; it just brings all his frustration to the surface in a rush of angry, accusing words.

> Please, sir, if the LORD is with us, why then has all this happened to us? And where are all his wonderful deeds that our fathers recounted to us, saying, "Did not the LORD bring us up from Egypt?" But now the LORD has forsaken us and given us into the hand of Midian. (v. 13)

Who is this person? A prophet? Well, let him go back to his Master and give him a piece of Gideon's mind! But the visitor will not be put off so easily. On the contrary, he "turn[s]" to face Gideon and gives him a direct command: "Go in this might of yours and save Israel from the hand of Midian; do not I send you?" (v. 14). Now Gideon is shaken (perhaps his visitor really *is* a prophet), so he drops his bluster and begins instead to make excuses. "What is this 'might' you speak of? 'Behold, my clan is the weakest in Manasseh, and I am the least in my father's house'" (v. 15). But the visitor is relentless; he's no more moved by Gideon's excuses than he was by his anger. "But I will be with you, and you shall strike the Midianites as one man" (v. 16). Like Moses at the burning bush (Exodus 3:1–12), Gideon is being backed into a corner. How can he possibly accept such a commission? If the visitor really is from God, though, how can he refuse him? *But he must be sure.* So Gideon asks for a sign that will settle once and for all who his visitor is. And his request is granted. The visitor waits patiently while Gideon prepares a meal for him, but when it is brought he treats it like an offering instead of a meal. He touches it with the tip of his staff, sends it up in flames, then vanishes (vv. 17–21)! Gideon is past anger now, and uncertainty too. He's scared witless because he knows at last that he's dealing with God. "Alas, O Lord GOD! For now I have seen the angel of the LORD face to face" (v. 22). How foolish all his anger seems now, and how dangerous. If only he could retract his outburst about everything being God's fault (v. 13). But it's too late for that now. All he can do is blurt out his fear, like a condemned man. And then somehow Gideon hears the God he fears, who is still strangely present, speak his pardon: "Peace be to you. Do not fear; you shall not die" (v. 23). Now God is everything and Gideon is nothing—except a profoundly grateful human being. In the midst of war and devastation, anger, frustration, self-doubt, and the threatening future—which is still there—he has peace. So he builds an altar and calls it Yahweh Shalom, "the LORD Is Peace" (v. 24). It's his first act of faith, a kind of concrete testimony to what he has learned from his encounter with God: God himself is his peace.

Gideon Takes a Stand (6:25–32)

Gideon has had a great experience, but he has hardly had a chance to draw breath before the awful reality of what God is asking of him is hammered home to him with one terrible command. "*That night* the LORD said to him, 'Take your father's bull . . . and pull down the altar of Baal that your father has'" (v. 25). Israel's root problem was not the Midianites, but their addiction to evil, and in particular the worship of Baal. The Lord would not deliver them from the Midianites until they renounced that. There could be no having the Lord as their deliverer while they had Baal as their god. The problem for Gideon, and it was a big one, was that Baal-worship was enshrined in his own village and sanctioned by his own father. Gideon has built an altar to the Lord (v. 24), but his father already has an altar to Baal. Gideon's new commitment to the Lord has set him at odds with his own family and his own community. At the moment the conflict is only symbolic, but God has made it clear what he requires of him: to take a stand, and to do it *now*. If the Lord is to be his peace, he cannot put peace with his family above his commitment to God. The altar to Baal must be pulled down, whatever the cost. It's a story that's been repeated countless times in the history of God's people and still faces believers in homes and families and communities on every continent. And it was no easier for Gideon than it is for any of them. In fact it was harder for Gideon than for many today, because of the authority that fathers had in Gideon's world. To go against your father was to risk disinheritance, shame, and even death. God had said to Gideon, *"Do not fear; you shall not die"* (v. 23). Those words had settled his fears and brought him peace at that moment. But it's not so easy to rest in that peace now. Gideon is very much afraid, too afraid to do what he had to do by day. To his immense credit, however, he didn't let his fear paralyze him. What he couldn't do that *day* he did the following *night*, with the help of ten servants (v. 27).

In the morning Baal's altar is gone and a new altar to Yahweh stands in its place, and all Gideon's worst fears begin to materialize. The men of the town are incensed and demand to know who had done it. When they find out it was Gideon, they begin baying for his blood. They demand that his father Joash bring him out and hand him over to them, and Gideon finds his life literally hanging in the balance, with his father on one side and an angry mob on the other. Then, to Gideon's astonishment and relief, Baal's hold over his community begins to weaken. What has already happened symbolically, in the tearing down of his altar, begins to happen actually in the way people behave. Faced with having to choose between Baal and his son, Gideon's father Joash chooses to save his son and let Baal take his chances. "Will you contend for Baal? Or will you save him?" he says to the mob. "Whoever contends for him shall be put to death by morning. *If he is a god, let him contend for himself*, because his altar has been broken down" (v. 31). It's an extraordinary turnabout by Joash and an astonishing act of courage.

Joash speaks as head man of the town, with the power of life and death over its citizens. It's likely that the mystique surrounding his person, and his authority, has largely been based on his claim to be a priest of Baal with charge of his altar. But realizing now that the game is up, he chooses to use the last vestiges of his fading power to save his son. And it works! The mob proves fickle. Apparently fearing the wrath of Joash more than the wrath of Baal, they abandon their attack on Gideon and instead hail him as a hero! So the man who was as good as dead moments before is suddenly reborn as

"Jerubbaal," the man who fought against Baal and won![2] It was only a small victory. Ophrah was only one town, and a small, relatively obscure one at that. But it was a good start. Gideon had pushed through his fears and proven God faithful. Nevertheless, he is not yet the superhero his new name suggests he is. The Midianites still have to be faced, and that will take tremendous courage. Gideon will be tested severely and will have to confront his fears again.

Gideon Seeks Reassurance (6:33–40)

The Midianites have begun a fresh assault on Israel's heartland. "The Valley of Jezreel" (v. 33) is where Barak had fought Sisera and his force of nine hundred chariots. It stretched right across northern Israel from just south of the Sea of Galilee to Mount Carmel on the Mediterranean coast. It was and still is the richest agricultural land in the whole of Palestine. In the period of the judges this area was critically important for Israel's economy and the feeding of its people. Barak's victory here had broken Jabin's stranglehold on Israel and freed them from twenty years of oppression. But now the same valley has become contested territory again. By their repeated raids on this area the Midianites were impoverishing Israel by effectively stealing the food out of their mouths. By this point in the Gideon story they have arrived again and are encamped in the Jezreel valley ready for a fresh raid (v. 33). It's time for Gideon to act, and at this critical moment God intervenes to *enable* him to do so by "cloth[ing]" him with his Spirit (v. 34). It's not literal armor Gideon needs at this moment, but God's Spirit to envelop and empower him, and that is what he is given.

Whether or not Gideon is conscious of the Spirit coming upon him, the effect is seen immediately in the remarkable decisiveness and boldness with which he acts and in the electrifying effect he has on those around him. He blows a trumpet, summoning the Abiezrites (his own clan) to follow him, then sends messengers throughout Manasseh, calling them to arms, and also to Asher, Zebulun, and Naphtali, and they too go up to meet him (vv. 34, 35). The Spirit has transformed him from a local hero into a commander of men. He has been *authorized* to act (v. 14). He has been *empowered* to act (v. 34). He had already been given the *promise* of God's presence (v. 12). Now he has the *reality* of it, and the people seem to sense it. With the rise of Gideon, hope has sprung up again in Israel. Gideon is in a position of great strength at this moment; everything is going his way.

How odd it is, then, that Gideon does what he does next. He asks for *further* evidence that God is with him!

> Then Gideon said to God, "*If you will save Israel by my hand, as you have said*, behold, I am laying a fleece of wool on the threshing floor. If there is dew on the fleece alone, and it is dry on all the ground, *then I shall know that you will save Israel by my hand, as you have said*." (vv. 36, 37)

Why the word "if"?—"*If* you will save Israel by my hand, as you have said" (v. 36)? Where did that come from? It arose from something deep inside Gideon that no one else saw, something quite different from how he appeared on the outside. It's fear again, and insecurity, and it's very understandable. Consider again what Gideon is going to have to face the next day. All the Midianites and the Amalekites and the people of the East have come together, crossed the Jordan, and encamped in the Valley of Jezreel (v. 33). For seven years Gideon and his friends have been hiding in caves for fear of their lives while this lot came through, killing and pillaging. These enemies came on camels without number, like a locust plague, destroying everything and leaving Israel with nothing—no crops, sheep, or donkeys (vv. 4, 5). For seven years they've been invincible. Israel has been powerless to do anything to stop them. But tomorrow Gideon has to go out and face them, on foot, with a hastily assembled bunch of untrained amateurs at his heels. Suddenly, after all the excitement of the last few days, the full reality of his situation has kicked in, and Gideon is scared. He wants something *more*—a sign, something to confirm what God has said so he can believe it enough to do what he has to do tomorrow morning. So he lays out a "fleece of wool" on the threshing floor (v. 37). There's something rather pitiful and touching about that. Gideon used to have sheep; now all he has is a skin with some wool on it. But he lays it out and says, "Please, God, do something powerful with *that*, and I'll *know* that you can use me to save Israel."

It's entirely understandable, but at the same time it's surely insulting to God for Gideon to ask him for proof that he can trust him to do as he has said he will! Shouldn't God's word be enough for him? And if not, shouldn't all that God has already done for him have been all the confirmation Gideon needed? Yes, it should have been, but it wasn't. We should be careful, though, of being too hard on Gideon, not just because of our own failings, but because of the way God himself responds to Gideon's request. He doesn't lecture him on the weakness of his faith but gives him the sign he has asked for. And when even that is not enough for Gideon, he gives him another one (vv. 38–40)! In other words, what is really amazing here is God's grace to his struggling servant. What Gideon did was not a model of piety or an example of how to seek guidance from God. This was not about guidance at all. Gideon already knew what he had to do. It was about his fearfulness and need for reassurance. Gideon was struggling, but God did not condemn him for it, but rather gave him what he needed. Surely there's great comfort in that for all of us!

Gideon's Three Hundred (7:1–8a)

Gideon looks strong again as this scene opens. He gets up early in the morning (v. 1). That's a good sign. People who are crippled by fear don't do that; they lie in bed as long as possible because they can't face what the day holds for them. Not Gideon; at least no longer. The signs God has given him have settled his fears and nerved him for action again. He's ready now to do what God has asked of him, and he's not alone. It has been said that the only thing necessary for someone to be a leader is to have someone following them. Gideon has thirty-two thousand (v. 3), and they've all risen early with him (v. 1)! And Gideon seems to know what he's doing. He has a plan, and it's a good one. He moves his men to a forward position "beside the spring of Harod" (v. 1). The exact location of this is unknown, but it must have been high, because from there they could see the Midianite camp "below" them (v. 8). The Midianites were near another hill, "the hill of Moreh," but not on it. So Gideon and his men had the advantage of height and presumably invisibility. In short, they were well situated to take the enemy by surprise. Gideon has given them a significant tactical advantage.

But this story is *full* of surprises! The next one comes in verse 2, just as Gideon is set to strike:

The Lord said to Gideon, "The people with you are too many for me to give the Midianites into their hand, lest Israel boast over me, saying, 'My own hand has saved me.' Now therefore proclaim in the ears of the people, saying, 'Whoever is fearful and trembling, let him return home and hurry away from Mount Gilead.'" Then 22,000 of the people returned, and 10,000 remained.

And the Lord said to Gideon, "The people are still too many. Take them down to the water, and I will test them for you there, and anyone of whom I say to you, 'This one shall go with you,' shall go with you, and anyone of whom I say to you, 'This one shall not go with you,' shall not go." So he brought the people down to the water. And the Lord said to Gideon, "Every one who laps the water with his tongue, as a dog laps, you shall set by himself. Likewise, every one who kneels down to drink." And the number of those who lapped, putting their hands to their mouths, was 300 men, but all the rest of the people knelt down to drink water. And the Lord said to Gideon, "With the 300 men who lapped I will save you and give the Midianites into your hand, and let all the others go every man to his home." So the people took provisions in their hands, and their trumpets. And he sent all the rest of Israel every man to his tent, but retained the 300 men. And the camp of Midian was below him in the valley. (vv. 2–8)

Poor Gideon. He's dealt a number of heavy blows here. First he's shown that his army is not what it appears to be. What's the good of having thirty-two thousand men if twenty-two thousand of them are trembling with fear? So God says, "Tell those men to go home." And they don't need to be told twice. Off they go, and Gideon has to watch as nearly 70 percent of his men walk away (v. 3). But God isn't through with his culling program yet. He tells Gideon there are *still* too many! "Take them down to the water, and I will test them for you there" (v. 4). What happens next is very peculiar; in fact it's so confusing that most scholars think the text has suffered some damage in transmission. So if you feel confused about the lapping and kneeling and who was doing what, you're in good company! The original distinction must have been between those who knelt down and scooped the water up to their mouths with their hands and those who put their faces right down to the water and lapped like dogs. Only the latter were chosen. It's not clear whether the three hundred were chosen because they showed less fear or less aptitude (the Lord would get more glory by saving Israel by the least able men). Or maybe they were just chosen because they were the smaller group (the Lord would be more glorified by saving by few rather than many). The bottom line is that it was *God's* test, and he did it to take away everything that Gideon could possibly trust in except God himself and to make sure that Israel would give the glory for what was about to happen to God alone (v. 2).

Nevertheless, Gideon has had his confidence badly shaken—again. It's one thing to face the Midianites with thirty-two thousand men and quite another to face them with three hundred. The common and decisive factor, of course, is God, who is just as able to save with few as with many (1 Samuel 14:6). But the battle between faith and fear is harder with only three hundred, and now Gideon's faith is being tested to the extreme, and night is closing in again.

A Dream in the Night (7:8b–15)

Nights before a battle are notoriously nerve-racking. The wait seems endless, and the buildup of tension brings men almost to the breaking point. That is the situation Gideon is in at the beginning of this passage. The Midianite camp is down in the valley, but he can't see it because it's still dark (vv. 8b,

9). And notice carefully the wording of the text at this point. It does not say that the enemy camp was below *them* (plural) but "below *him*" (singular). Can't you sense a great loneliness there? Like the loneliness of an airline pilot over the Atlantic in the middle of the night, staring at a warning light on his instrument panel with three hundred sleeping passengers in the cabin behind him. Like a parish minister in his study late at night, thinking about a pastoral problem he's going to have to deal with tomorrow and wondering what the outcome will be. Nights were Gideon's worst times, and on this one he was not only lonely, he was afraid—*very* afraid.

Last time Gideon felt like this he asked for a sign. But this time he doesn't do anything, because God sees his need and meets it even before he asks.

> That same night the LORD said to him, "Arise, go down against the camp, for I have given it into your hand. But if you are afraid to go down, go down to the camp with Purah your servant. And you shall hear what they say, and afterward your hands shall be strengthened to go down against the camp." Then he went down with Purah his servant to the outposts of the armed men who were in the camp. And the Midianites and the Amalekites and all the people of the East lay along the valley like locusts in abundance, and their camels were without number, as the sand that is on the seashore in abundance. (vv. 9–12)

Notice how, in verse 10, God acknowledges both Gideon's fear and his loneliness: "if you are afraid to go down, go down to the camp with Purah your servant." Gideon doesn't have to say, "Lord, I'm afraid, and I feel alone." God knows that already and in a sense asks Gideon to confront the very thing he's afraid of—the Midianite camp in the valley below him. But he puts Purah at his side to support him. Purah doesn't have to say anything; he just has to *be* there.

So down they go into the valley of death, where the enemy is everywhere and uncountable, like a locust plague, filling the valley floor. And they are armed and have camels! Camels were a frightening thing to men on foot. Gideon had none, and the Midianites had thousands of them, like the sand on the seashore for multitude, like devil spawn come to mock the afflicted seed of Abraham (v. 12).[3] Can you imagine what Gideon felt as he went down into that valley? This was everything he had dreaded and more. But God had promised that when he got down there he would hear something to strengthen him. And so he pressed on, his heart in his mouth, with the faithful Purah at his side. At last they reach the outskirts of the Midianite camp, creep into it under cover of darkness, and hear a hushed conversation coming from one of the tents. They edge closer to try to hear what is being said. And sure enough, in the pre-dawn stillness the conversation in the tent becomes clearly audible.

> A man was telling a dream to his comrade. And he said, "Behold, I dreamed a dream, and behold, a cake of barley bread tumbled into the camp of Midian and came to the tent and struck it so that it fell and turned it upside down, so that the tent lay flat." And his comrade answered, "This is no other than the sword of Gideon the son of Joash, a man of Israel; God has given into his hand Midian and all the camp." (vv. 13, 14)

What Gideon finds out, of course, is that things are not as they seem, because the Midianites, too, are frightened. In fact they seem to believe the very thing that Gideon himself has been finding it so *hard* to believe: God has given the whole Midianite camp into his hand (v. 14). Why the two men in the tent identify the barley cake of their dream as Gideon is not entirely clear. They would certainly not have done so unless they hadn't already heard of him and feared him. Otherwise they would have simply dismissed the dream as absurd. It's ridiculous, isn't it? An out-of-control barley cake "tumbles" into the camp, hits their tent, and *bam!* they're destroyed! But it's precisely the whole eerie uncanniness of the dream that unnerves them. And in that state of heightened anxiety they read it as an omen telling them they cannot win because the rules of the game have been changed. They are doomed because their strength has become irrelevant. God is with Gideon and not with them. They cannot beat him. And of course they're right.

The little barley cake *must* be Gideon. When we first met him he was threshing grain. By his own admission he was weak, and so was his clan. And isn't it *he* who has just come tumbling down, in all his weakness, to the Midianite camp, to the very tent in which these two men were sleeping? So Gideon has heard exactly what he needed to "strengthen [his] . . . hands," just as God had promised (v. 11). God has again been gracious to him in his weakness, and it's another turning point in his struggle to be the man God has called him to be.

Victory at Last (7:15—8:3)

We begin this final, climactic part of the story with Gideon on his knees. It's arguably his greatest moment—certainly one of them. It's taken him a long time to get to this point. He's challenged God ("If you're with us, why has all this happened to us?"), he's made excuses ("I'm a weak man from a weak clan"), he's doubted that God will keep his promises to him, and he's tested God by asking for signs. He's been paralyzed with fear. But now he's done with all that. He worships God before going out to do, at last, what God has had in mind from the beginning. It's his Gethsemane moment. He's a man completely surrendered to the will of God. But it's a Gethsemane moment with a difference. There's no struggle here, or even resignation. Instead there's sheer amazement at what God has just done. Gideon is simply in awe of God and so grateful to him. So he falls on his knees and worships.

When he rises from his knees he's a new man, and in what follows there are several things about him that are very impressive. First, he gives all the glory to God. He goes back to his men with a message: "the LORD has given the host of Midian into your hand" (v. 15b). Notice "*your* hand" and the past tense, "*has* given." This is Gideon's gospel: God has done something that makes all the difference to our situation—God has gone before us—he's won the battle even before we begin to fight. He doesn't mention himself. This is not out of false modesty, but because he wants his men's confidence to be grounded where his own is, in God alone. This is God's battle, and Gideon is determined, even before it has begun, to give God all the glory. Second, Gideon acts as a leader. "Look at me . . . When I come to the outskirts of the camp, do as I do" (v. 17). He gathers and leads the people for whom he's responsible. He doesn't drive them with threats or mere commands but by his personal example. He goes with them and before them, just as God has gone with and before *him*. That's the mark of a true leader.

Third, he shows great resourcefulness. He's vastly outnumbered. He has only three hundred men against a vast enemy host. He's not daunted by that anymore, but it does present certain difficulties. The question is how best to deploy the three hundred men he still has, how to make the most of them. It's a very down-to-earth question, and Gideon hits on a brilliant solution to it. Make them seem like a much larger force. Take advantage of the night. Make the most of the uneasiness of the enemy. Come upon them when they least expect it. Stampede them by waking them suddenly with blinding light and deafening sound. Attack while they are still in disarray. Chase them and cut them down before they have a chance to regroup. "Jars" and "torches" are strange pieces of equipment to take into battle, but the willingness of Gideon's men to do so shows they share their leader's radical trust in God, as does their battle cry: "For the LORD and for Gideon" (v. 18). As far as we know, none of this is a revealed strategy; it's just Gideon's natural leadership ability being put at God's disposal and used in dependence on him and for his glory.

When God commissioned him back in 6:14, he told him to "Go in this might of yours." Even then some of his resourcefulness was apparent in his threshing of wheat in a winepress to hide it from the enemy. But he didn't see himself as a leader, nor did we. His considerable capabilities were largely hidden, behind anger, fear, a sense of personal inadequacy, and doubts that God could or would do anything about his situation. Now that faith rather than fear has become the controlling principle of his life, however, all that was strong and good and capable about him has been freed up to flourish. Even this would not have been enough to save Israel, though, if God had not intervened at the critical moment to tip the balance in Gideon's favor. "When they blew the 300 trumpets, *the LORD* set every man's sword against his comrade and against all the army. And the army fled as far as Beth-shittah toward Zererah, as far as the border of Abel-meholah, by Tabbath" (v. 22). In the end it wasn't Gideon's cleverness or even his faith that saved Israel, but God's commitment to his promise to be with him and give him victory (6:16).

Fourth, Gideon shows leadership in pressing home his advantage. The battle was won from the moment God intervened, but Gideon knows that one battle does not make a war and that God's intervention does not release him from responsibility to make the most of what God has given him. There is nothing unusual about Gideon's strategy now. The place names in verse 22 indicate that the Midianites were fleeing in a southeasterly direction, toward the Jordan River.[4] So Gideon does the commonsense thing: he calls for reinforcements and orders them to cut off the Midianites at "the waters," where they would be trying to cross over (vv. 23, 24). Ehud had used the same tactic successfully back in 3:28, 29. This time, though, it is not quite as effective—some did escape, as chapter 8 will show. Nevertheless, the enemy has been decisively beaten and driven out of Israel's heartland, and the impressive victory is sealed by the capture and execution of "Oreb and Zeeb," the two Midianite princes, and the presentation of their heads to Gideon (v. 25). Gideon received his call at one winepress (6:11) and is given these tokens of his victory near another (v. 25). It is a moment of closure fit for a conqueror.

The final leadership quality Gideon displays here is the wisdom to know when to fight and when to conciliate. A great victory has been won, but the men of Ephraim are angry because they were not included in the initial call-up (8:1). And as the description of that call-up in 6:34, 35 shows, they are apparently right; they were not summoned until the crucial nighttime attack on the Midianite camp was over, when the enemy was in headlong flight toward the Jordan. It's not clear whether this was an oversight on Gideon's part, a deliberate snub, or a decision made for strategic purposes. Because of their position (to the south of Manasseh, on the flank of the retreating enemy) they were ideally situated to make just the kind of contribution that Gideon did eventually call on them to make. But they have clearly *taken* it as a snub, and their extreme sensitivity to it ("they accused him fiercely," 8:1) reflects a rivalry between Ephraim and Manasseh,[5] the two leading tribes of northern Israel, that went right back to the time of their father Joseph (Genesis 48:8–20) and, like tinder, needed only a spark to ignite it. But this is a grubby little squabble about who came out looking best, you or us? And Gideon knows it's not worth fighting about. After all, it was the Ephraimites who had the honor of capturing and killing the two enemy princes (8:3), and they had acknowledged Gideon's leadership by bringing their heads to him (7:24, 25). So Gideon chooses the path of conciliation. He talks the Ephraimites down and lets the matter pass (8:2, 3). Handled well, a situation like this can enhance rather than detract from a leader's stature, and Gideon has the wisdom to know this.

In all these ways Gideon is very impressive in this passage. What we are seeing, though, is not the product of self-belief and determination to succeed. Gideon is not a self-made man, but a testimony to God's perseverance with someone who knew himself to be inadequate, who doubted again and again that God could or would do what he had promised to do through him, but whose recognition, at last, of the greatness and goodness of God released all his potential and allowed him to blossom into the leader God always intended him to be.

Resonances

We have watched the emergence of a leader in this story. But reading a Biblical narrative is like playing a violin. As the bow is drawn across one string, others begin to vibrate with it. And the body of the instrument is designed to capture and blend the resonances of the strings to produce the rich sound that we hear. In the same way the canon of Scripture captures and blends the resonances of each of its parts, so that when we read it there is a richness of meaning greater than that of any one part read in isolation.

One passage that clearly resonates with the story we have just read is Hebrews 11:32–34, where Gideon is explicitly referred to. What we see in Gideon at his best is the faith that Hebrews 11 is all about—the confidence in God that makes a man sure of what he hopes for and certain of what he cannot see (Hebrews 11:1). When Gideon rises from his knees after hearing the dream in the enemy camp he hasn't yet seen Midian defeated. But he's seen the awesome power of God, and he's not afraid anymore. He's free to attempt the impossible relying on the promises that God has made to him. Out of weakness he was "made strong . . . became mighty in war, put foreign armies to flight" (Hebrews 11:34). And he did it, the writer to the Hebrews tells us, "through faith" (Hebrews 11:33). The story we have read may be about leadership, but more fundamentally and more importantly it is about faith.

Another string that vibrates for me is 2 Corinthians 4:5–7:

> What we proclaim is not ourselves, but Jesus Christ as Lord, with ourselves as your servants for Jesus' sake. For God, who said, "Let light shine out of darkness," has shone in our hearts to give the light of the knowledge of the glory of God in the face of Jesus Christ. *But we have this treasure in jars of clay, to show that the surpassing power belongs to God and not to us.*

I don't know whether Paul had Judges 7 in mind when he wrote that, but I do know that his words resonate with it at several levels. Second Corinthians is about a fight we're all involved in, a fight in which we are sure to fail unless God helps us. The strategy in this battle, too, is strength in weakness, breakable clay jars with something precious inside, and light shining out of darkness. And God works this way so that when victories happen it is apparent to all that "the surpassing power belongs to God and not to us" (2 Corinthians 4:7). A godly leader is someone who is aware of his weakness but knows that it is no impediment to God's working through him. And what is the treasure hidden in our jars of clay? ". . . the light of the knowledge of the glory of God in the face of Jesus Christ" (v. 6). All that is needed for it to shine forth is for us to be willing to be broken in his service, to become nothing that he may be everything (John 3:27–30).

13

Gideon: Self-Destruction

JUDGES 8:4–35

ALL OF US HAVE SEEN PEOPLE who started well finish badly. It's always sad, and it rarely leaves others unaffected, especially if they have been leaders. The Old Testament has several examples, most notably King Saul and King Solomon. Saul crossed a fateful line when he moved into presumption and disobedience and thought that sacrifice and offering could make up for it (1 Samuel 13:8–15a; 15:17–26). Solomon did likewise when he thought that making marriage alliances with surrounding nations was the way to long-term peace and prosperity for Israel instead of a heart that remained true to the Lord his God (1 Kings 11:1–5). Gideon perhaps comes less readily to mind in this connection, but unfortunately his life follows a similar pattern. In the previous chapter of this book we began with Gideon hiding from the enemy and threshing grain in a winepress and watched as his career unfolded step by step like a flower bursting into bloom as confidence in God rather than fear took hold and became the controlling principle of his life. As that development reached its climax, what we saw was Gideon at his best—the phase of his life that made it most understandable why he turns up in Hebrews 11 as a hero of faith. In this chapter, however, what develops is something rather different, as we are about to see.

A Different Crossing (8:4)

Crossing a river is not normally something of great significance. Some of us who commute to work cross a river twice every day and never give it more than a passing thought. We would hardly record it in our diaries as something worthy of note. Some of us have had the exciting experience of crossing national boundaries and experiencing different cultures. These crossings certainly are noteworthy, and we normally mark them with diary entries, photographs, and souvenirs. But they have no moral significance; they are simply indications of our increasing capacity to expand our horizons and perhaps engage in business or ministry on a wider front. Some crossings, though, have much greater significance. Many of us can remember the tremendous moment when we heard and believed the gospel and crossed over from death to life, from the power of Satan to God (Acts 26:18). For me that moment came on the afternoon of Sunday, May 24, 1959, when I was converted under the ministry of Billy Graham at a huge evangelistic rally in Brisbane, Australia. I still have the Bible my parents gave me soon afterward to mark the event, with the Scriptures that meant so much to me at that time underlined and marked with colored pencil. For Israel the crossing of the Jordan into Canaan was a moment like that. They'd had some significant victories east of the Jordan under Moses. But it was not until they crossed the Jordan that they circumcised a new generation at Gilgal and celebrated their first Passover in the land (Joshua 5:1–12). Like the crossing of the Red Sea, the crossing of the Jordan was a rite of passage into a whole new situation and the beginning of a new chapter in their lives. So important was that crossing that they set up twelve large stones to mark the spot where it had happened, so that they would always be reminded of it and would remember to tell their children about it (Joshua 4:1–24).

The passage we are looking at in this chapter begins with Gideon crossing the Jordan in the opposite direction, *out of* the land of Canaan (8:4),[1] and as the story develops from this point a very different Gideon begins to emerge. On the face of it, there was no need for Gideon to cross the Jordan. The current troubles began when the Midianites and their allies crossed the Jordan *into* Israel's heartland back in 6:33, and now none of them are still there. Those who aren't dead have fled, and Gideon has the heads of their two "princes" in his hands (7:25). Surely he's won, hasn't he? Well, yes, that's beyond question. But something still drives him on. Some have escaped, among them Zebah and Zalmunna, the two "kings of Midian" mentioned in 8:5, and Gideon cannot rest until he has them as well. They are the really big prize as far as Gideon is concerned, and perhaps with good reason. They probably represented the highest level of authority in the enemy coalition and still had a force of about fifteen thousand men with them (v. 10). If they are allowed to escape, the Midianites and their allies may be able to regroup and mount another attack in the foreseeable future. In Gideon's mind the job is not done until they are accounted for, so he crosses the Jordan and continues the pursuit. At one level his actions here make perfect sense. But there are some causes for concern. Things are not quite as straightforward as they seem.

A Different Gideon (8:21)

The first ominous sign of change is that Gideon no longer has the same following he did before he crossed the Jordan. The men from Naphtali, Asher, and Ephraim who had supported him west of the Jordan are no longer with him; only the initial three hundred are with him now, and they are "exhausted" (v. 4). And when he calls on the men of Succoth and Penuel to support him they refuse to do so (vv. 5–9). Second, Gideon is no longer conciliatory. Previously when faced with opposition from his fellow Israelites he had reasoned with them and avoided conflict (8:1–3). Now he seems to have lost either the will or the ability to do this. His request that the leaders of Succoth and Penuel give his exhausted men food was reasonable, but so was their refusal. They had doubts about what Gideon was now doing. He had only a small following, and the two towns in question were the most eastern Israelite settlements; so if Gideon failed they would be in a very exposed position. To support Gideon on this campaign was risky; they had the welfare of their own citizens to consider. But Gideon is furious and immediately threatens retaliation (vv. 7, 9). His new style of leadership is beginning to fracture Israel rather than heal it.

Third, God now seems marginal rather than central to what is happening. Gideon refers to him twice, but in both cases it's to justify his own actions (vv. 7, 19). The author himself doesn't attribute anything that happens in this phase of Gideon's life to God. Even at the climax, in which Gideon comes upon the remaining enemy unawares, it is he, not God, who throws them into a panic (vv. 11, 12). In contrast to what happened earlier, this victory is Gideon's own achievement rather than God's gift. Finally, in verses 20 and 21 we see the man that Gideon has become. Gideon now has the two kings of Midian at his mercy. But instead of killing them himself he orders his firstborn son Jether to do it (v. 20). In the warrior culture of the times this was an honor and effectively marked Jether as Gideon's favorite and potential successor. But Jether hesitates, and in the way the author describes him at this critical moment we are suddenly reminded of the man *his father* used to be: "the young man did not draw his sword, for *he was afraid*" (v. 20). Now Gideon's own honor is at stake, as his two captors quickly realize. They taunt him with being weak and challenge him to kill them himself: "Rise yourself and fall on us, for *as the man is, so is his strength*" (v. 21). It is their final act of defiance, and Gideon answers it at once by slaughtering and stripping them (v. 22). He has proved himself to be a man in contrast to his son. His son hesitates; Gideon does not. His son is afraid; Gideon is not. His son is weak; Gideon is strong. His son is what Gideon used to be; Gideon is the man he has now become, someone different not only from how he began, but from how he was in the whole of chapters 6 and 7. God made him what he was then; Gideon has made himself what he is now. And Jether, who refuses to be remade in his father's image, acts as a silent witness to the change that has taken place.

A Different Ending (8:22–28)

All that Gideon has been doing since he crossed the Jordan in verse 4 leads naturally to what happens in verse 22: "Then the men of Israel said to Gideon, 'Rule over us, you and your son and your grandson also, *for you have saved us* from the hand of Midian.*" In other words, *assume the authority you are entitled to because of what you have accomplished! Become a king! Establish a dynasty! You have shown yourself to be kinglike by slaying Zebah and Zalmunna. What could be more appropriate than for you to take their royal title? Let the king-slayer become king! You have saved us!* Not everyone thought this way, of course. Not the men of Succoth; but they were too intimidated by now to protest (vv. 15, 16). And not the men of Penuel; they were all dead (v. 17). What a travesty this is of all that Gideon had been called to be and do! This is exactly what God's dealings with him in chapters 6 and 7 had been intended to prevent. And how different this is from the great song of praise that had been sung in chapter 5 after Deborah and Barak's victory. There the Lord had been praised; here only Gideon is praised, a man who has become godlike in the eyes of his followers.

To his credit Gideon recognizes that things have gotten out of hand and tries to deflect their misguided adulation: "I will not rule over you, and my son will not rule over you; *the LORD* will rule over you" (v. 23). But it's too late. The damage has been done. His actions have set Israel on a fundamentally different course from the one God intended, and increasingly Gideon himself becomes mired in their drift back into idolatry. He asks them to give him the gold they've taken from the Midianites so he can make an ephod, ostensibly so he can inquire of the Lord, Israel's *true* ruler (v. 24).[2] But the ephod he makes is much more like an idol than a priestly garment,[3] and the whole episode turns into a virtual repeat of Aaron's manufacture of a golden calf (Exodus 32:2–8), with the same tragic outcome. Instead of it being a means of honoring God as Israel's ruler, it becomes an idolatrous object that leads them even further away from him. And most tragic of all, Gideon himself and his family become ensnared by it (vv. 27, 28). So the man who began his career in Ophrah by leading Israel out of idolatry ends his career by leading them back into it. Baal has answered Gideon's challenge[4] and apparently prevailed. It is a sad ending indeed to a career that began so well. The fact that "the land had rest forty years" was a pure gift of God's grace (v. 28), not something that Gideon or Israel deserved.

A Different Agenda

What was the underlying cause of this tragic end to Gideon's career? What can account for his behaving so differently after he crossed the Jordan in 8:4? The answer lies in something very revealing that he says to his two captives before he kills them, back in verses 18 and 19:

> Then he said to Zebah and Zalmunna, "Where are the men whom you killed at Tabor?" They answered, "As you are, so were they. Every one of them resembled the son of a king." And he said, *"They were my brothers, the sons of my mother.* As the LORD lives, if you had saved them alive, I would not kill you."

Gideon had a score to settle with these men and couldn't rest until he'd done so. In the preceding verses Gideon has referred to Zebah and Zalmunna by name five times, and the narrator has done the same two additional times. They had killed Gideon's brothers in an earlier clash at Mount Tabor, and he was determined to make them pay for it. This has been his agenda ever since he crossed the Jordan, and in a sense it is quite understandable and even justifiable. The trouble is, it was not part of the mission he was given. He has been pursuing his own agenda, not God's, and by letting that take over and determine his actions he damaged the very Israel he was sent to save.

Beware!

There are warnings here for all of us, but especially those called to leadership of God's people. First, this story is a reminder of how easy it is for a good man to go wrong. I remember how shocked and confused I felt as a young man when a very respected leader in the church I belonged to suddenly left his wife of thirty or more years and went off with another woman. He was a very gifted man, and I had seen God use him powerfully in gospel ministry. I myself had been blessed by his preaching and his example of service to God and others. Then suddenly, in a way that took us all completely by surprise, he seemed to turn into a completely different person and to this day has never repented of the wrong that he did. How can such a thing happen?

As I was struggling with this, an older friend spoke some wise words to me that I will never forget. He said that by the time a man like the one I have referred to reaches midlife he has learned to do a lot of things. He can lead services, he can pray publicly, he can preach, he can counsel people, and so on. And because he can do all these things he appears to be a strong Christian. Furthermore, he keeps getting feedback from others that *tell* him he is a strong Christian, and so he begins to think of himself as one. However, if he has neglected the basic disciplines of daily meditation on the Word, prayer, confession of his sins, and accountability to others, he is in reality a very weak Christian, and when a big temptation hits him, as it often does in midlife, he can be gone in a moment. And everyone is shocked because they thought he was a strong Christian, when in reality he was not. What they are witnessing is the final outcome of a deterioration in the person's relationship with God that has been progressing in small steps over a long period of time. There's great wisdom there, and a warning for all of us, especially for those in leadership. "Let anyone who thinks that he stands take heed lest he fall" (1 Corinthians 10:12).

Second, there is a reminder here that some boundaries should never be crossed. Most of these are moral boundaries, and we all have a pretty good idea of what they are. But the reality is that we are never very far from crossing them. I remember a speaker at an ordination service I attended some years ago turning to the young man about to be ordained and saying to him, "When you get up in the morning, realize that before you go to bed that night you could do something that will ruin your integrity and your ministry." Sins can be forgiven, but there are some sins that are very hard to recover from, the effects are so damaging and so long-lasting. There are moral boundaries that should never be crossed, and the safest way to avoid crossing them is always to stay well away from them. Flirting with danger is the first step toward being overcome by it. However, there are also other, more subtle kinds of boundaries that should never be crossed, and these are the ones more obviously seen in the story we have just considered—the boundary between exhorting people and threatening them, between taking a stand and just being authoritarian, between using God's name to honor him and using it to justify your own actions, between pulling people into line and just pushing them out of your way, between being justly angry and just being angry, between tackling hard issues and just settling old scores, and between being a servant ruler and just being a ruler. You can cross these boundaries and still have victories, but not ones that glorify God. And whatever you achieve, you'll leave a lot of wreckage behind you.

Finally, there's a warning here against idolizing leaders. We all have people we admire and would like to be like. But all of them will cross boundaries at times that they shouldn't, and if we've idolized them they'll take us with them. So if you're going to draw inspiration from Gideon, as Hebrews 11 encourages us to do (Hebrews 11:32–34), make sure you draw it from the first phase of his career, not the second. Better still, fix your eyes on Jesus. The true climax of Hebrews 11 is Hebrews 12:1–3:

> Therefore, since we are surrounded by so great a cloud of witnesses, let us also lay aside every weight, and sin which clings so closely, and let us run with endurance the race that is set before us, *looking to Jesus, the founder and perfecter of our faith*, who for the joy that was set before him endured the cross, despising the shame, and is seated at the right hand of the throne of God.

Jesus not only started well, he also finished well. He never crossed any of the boundaries we have mentioned, and he's the only leader we can follow absolutely. May God help us do that, so that if he entrusts us with leadership we may truly bless those we lead and not damage them.

14

Abimelech:
The Son from Hell

JUDGES 8:29—9:57

SADLY, it is not an uncommon thing for a good father to have a bad son. Jesus' Parable of the Prodigal Son is a classic example (Luke 15:11–32). Everything we are told about the father suggests he was generous, humble, loving, and forgiving. But the son was ungrateful, disrespectful, selfish, willful, and dissolute. In the Old Testament Adam had Cain, Eli had sons that shamed him, and so did Samuel. David had Amnon and Absalom, Hezekiah had Manasseh, and Josiah had Jehoahaz (Genesis 4:1–8; 1 Samuel 2:22–25; 8:1–3; 2 Samuel 13—15; 2 Kings 21:1–6; 23:28–32). In some of these cases the fathers can be held partly to blame for the way their sons turned out. But can Samuel really be held responsible for sons who "did not walk in his ways" (1 Samuel 8:3), and did Hezekiah deserve to have Manasseh? In the end nothing can absolve the sons of responsibility for their own choices, and in some cases those choices, and the actions that followed from them, were so evil that only the term *hellish* seems adequate for them. The Apostle James invoked such language to describe the devastating evil that can be unleashed by an unbridled tongue:

> The tongue is a small member, yet it boasts of great things. How great a forest is set ablaze by such a small fire! And the tongue is a fire, a world of unrighteousness. The tongue is set among our members, staining the whole body, setting on fire the entire course of life, *and set on fire by hell.* (James 3:5, 6)

That's figurative language, of course, intended to make a point in a particularly forceful way. Some human words are so devastatingly harmful as to produce a virtual hell on earth. And so are some sons. They pursue such an evil agenda and wreak such havoc on all around them that they can fittingly be called sons from Hell. Such was Gideon's son, Abimelech.

The Seeds of Disaster (8:29–35)

Sadly, Gideon is one of those fathers who must be held partly to blame for the way his son behaved. Abimelech's name, which means "my father is king," provides the first clue to the roots of the problem. According to verse 31, Gideon himself gave him this name and so sowed something into Abimelech's consciousness that was bound to cause trouble sooner or later. And unfortunately the likelihood that it would *indeed* produce trouble was increased by Gideon's own behavior in his later years. After publicly declining the offer of kingship (8:22, 23) he "went and lived in his own house" (v. 29), apparently retiring into private life. Paradoxically, though, Gideon's lifestyle as described in the following verses looks far more like that of a ruler than of a private citizen. He had "many wives" and a "concubine" (vv. 30, 31). In the Canaan of those days this was typically kinglike behavior, but something that would-be kings of Israel were not to emulate (Deuteronomy 17:17). Unlike his seventy brothers, Abimelech was the son of the concubine and a native of Shechem rather than Ophrah (v. 31). By birth and background he was different, making conflict with his brothers almost inevitable.[1] And his name made it virtually certain that the flash point would be the issue of succession. Abimelech's name was the clearest possible indication that his father had secretly fancied himself a king, even if he publicly disavowed it. It also gave Abimelech grounds for thinking he would be justified in claiming to be his father's rightful successor and the founder of a dynasty his father had tacitly endorsed. Gideon had flirted with kingship; his son would claim it directly and prove to be someone with far fewer scruples about the acquisition and exercise of power than his father had had. The following story is to be one of unfaithfulness, in which people forsake the Lord who saved them, worship the Baals (vv. 33, 34), and forget the good things Gideon had done and embrace only the bad (v. 35). Gideon's mixed legacy is about to turn into a nightmare.

Abimelech's Bid for Power (9:1–6)

Knowing that his seventy brothers are unlikely to acquiesce in his plans, Abimelech goes to Shechem to appeal to his mother's family (v. 1). They are his blood relatives and have the ears of the "leaders" (rulers) of Shechem (v. 2); so if he can persuade them to support him, he will already have a strong power base in the city. His message, through them, to the rulers of Shechem is that a power struggle is already under way and that they are going to have to choose between him and his seventy brothers. His own relatives are going to have to do the same, but Abimelech puts it to them that in their case at least the choice should be clear, because he alone is their "bone and . . . flesh" (v. 2). It was a telling argument in a society where faithfulness to God was on the wane and tribalism in the worst sense was on the rise. Abimelech's family do not hesitate; they immediately take up his cause, and the rulers of Shechem follow suit. They adopt him as *their* brother too (v. 3). If there is to be a power struggle, they will stand with Abimelech (v. 3), and they immediately put their money where their mouth is by giving him "seventy pieces of silver" to finance his bid for power (v. 4). But it was bad money in every way. Its origin was tainted, sourced as it was from "the house of Baal-berith," a local shrine where Baal was worshiped instead of Yahweh (8:33). And its *purpose* was evil. It was blood money. The correspondence between the number of the silver pieces and the number of Gideon's other sons hints that its givers clearly understood, and condoned, what Abimelech would use it for. It was not a large sum,[2] but enough for Abimelech to hire a bunch of "worthless and reckless fellows" (v. 4) to follow him and do his bidding.

Abimelech wastes no time. He hurries to Ophrah with his hired help and kills his seventy brothers on "one stone." But paradoxically one of the seventy escapes and goes into hiding (v. 5). It's the first sign that not quite everything is going according to plan for Abimelech. Both the "one stone" and the one brother will come back to haunt Abimelech later in the story. But his backers in Shechem are impressed. Convinced that in Abimelech they have a strong leader who is one of them and will further their own interests, they formally install him as their king (v. 6).[3] It's one thing to be crowned, though, and quite another to rule, as Abimelech is about to find out.

Jotham Speaks Up (9:7–21)

It takes a lot of courage to be a lone voice crying "foul" and stand out against the crowd, especially when the crowd has a strong and ruthless leader at their head. But that is exactly what Jotham does here. He had escaped by hiding when Abimelech came to Ophrah (v. 5), but when he hears what Abimelech has done to his brothers, instead of fleeing he goes to Shechem and raises his voice in protest (v. 7). It was an incredibly brave act. "Mount Gerizim" overlooks the modern town of Nablus, just two and a half miles (four kilometers) northwest of ancient Shechem. It provided a superb vantage point from which Jotham could be seen and heard but not easily reached before he had a chance to escape. It was called the mount of blessing because here the blessings for obedience were pronounced in a solemn covenant renewal ceremony in the time of Joshua, after Israel's arrival in Canaan (Joshua 8:30–35). Ironically, for the rulers of Shechem it is about to became a mountain of curse.

Jotham captures the attention of his hearers by telling them a fable about trees trying to find one of their own to rule over them. Given what the rulers of Shechem have just done, the relevance of Jotham's tale is obvious, but it is a story with a moral, and the moral will not be easy for the men of Shechem to hear. All the trees with obviously good qualities—the olive, the fig, and the vine—reject the offer of kingship, until only the bramble is left (vv. 8–13). This is generally reckoned to be the buckthorn, a thorny bush or small tree with black berries. Some varieties are edible, but that is irrelevant to its significance here. Unlike the olive, fig, and vine, it is a wild rather than cultivated tree, and the things specifically associated with it in Jotham's story are "shade" and "fire" (v. 15). But how can the bramble provide much shade, and why is it prone to burst into flame? Whatever the answer to these questions may be, the essential point is that the bramble is a dangerous plant for human beings to associate with because it is unpredictable: it can provide shelter of sorts, but it can also destroy. Unlike the other, more worthy trees, however, the bramble does not demur when kingship is offered to it. On the contrary, it responds at once with a command and a threat: if you really mean it, shelter in my shade at once, or I will destroy you (v. 15)! The "cedars of Lebanon" (famously tall) at the end of verse 15 are probably symbolic here for the proud rulers of Shechem whom Jotham is addressing.[4]

By now it must have been obvious to Jotham's audience that his fable is about them, and that Abimelech is the "bramble" they have chosen as their king. Jotham's point, though, is not merely that they have acted foolishly in choosing Abimelech, but that they have acted *unfaithfully*. In the fable the bramble itself uses the expression "in good faith" in a hypothetical sense: "*If in good faith* [really, genuinely] you are anointing me king . . ." (v. 15). But in the moral he draws from the story Jotham turns this same expression *against* the rulers of Shechem. They have *not* acted "in good faith," but have conspired with Abimelech against Gideon, who had risked his life to save them from the Midianites (vv. 16–19). Gideon had not deserved this, and to make the murderer of his sons their king was an act of sheerest treachery and utter unfaithfulness, and it will have the most dire consequences. Jotham predicts that fire will come from Abimelech and destroy the rulers of Shechem, and vice versa, and (by implication) that it will be nothing less than they deserve for their unfaithfulness (v. 20). Then, having done his job, and with his audience probably still in shock, Jotham makes his escape across the Jordon to Beer (v. 21).[5] The rest of the chapter will show how true his words were. What follows will be no fable but a *true-life story* of terrible retribution on unfaithful people.

Trouble in Shechem (9:22–41)

The normal practice in Judges is for the length of a person's rule to be specified only at the end, and usually in terms of the land having rest for an extended period of time.[6] But with Abimelech it is different. The length of his rule, "three years," is stated at the outset (v. 22), and then the story moves immediately to an account of his downfall. And all we are told about those three years is that Abimelech "ruled over Israel." Given the way he had come to power and the fact that he was made king only in Shechem, he probably had to enforce his authority over the rest of Israel, ruling much more as a warlord than a judge. But all that is passed over in silence. The significant thing about Abimelech is that his rule did not last because the dire prediction of retribution that Jotham had spoken against him and the rulers of Shechem soon began to take effect.

The Breakdown of Trust (vv. 23–25)

Things started to go wrong for Abimelech when "God sent an evil spirit between Abimelech and the leaders of Shechem" (v. 23). This is significant for a number of reasons. It shows that the story Jotham had spoken against Abimelech and his supporters did not have any power of itself to bring retribution on them. His words had no magical power, as curses are sometimes thought to have. Rather they were words that depended for their efficacy on God's acting to put them into effect. They left the evil that Abimelech had done in God's hands, for him to deal with in his own time and his own way. The fact that he did so by "sen[ding] an evil spirit" between Abimelech and Shechem's leaders is disturbing, however, in more ways than one. It disturbs, and fatally weakens, Abimelech's fragile power base. But it also raises for us the unsettling question of God's relationship to evil. Is God the source of evil? And does his sending of such a spirit absolve the persons involved of responsibility for their own actions? The latter cannot possibly be the case, as that would undermine the theme of retribution that runs right though the story. This is not about people being absolved of responsibility for what they do but of being held to account for it. Nor does God's intervention in this way mean that he himself is tainted with evil. He did not *make* this spirit evil, but made this evil spirit *serve his own good purpose* of punishing evil men for the evil they had done (v. 24).[7]

The first effect of the evil spirit sent by God is that Abimelech's supporters begin to act "against" Abimelech instead of for him (v. 25). Shechem lay just east of a narrow pass between Mount Gerizim and Mount Ebal; so the tops of these mountains provided excellent vantage points from which defenders could see and intercept any potential enemies. Given the precariousness of his hold on power, Abimelech may have originally set men in ambush there for this very purpose. But from the moment the evil spirit begins to exert its influence, Abimelech's men start to act like brigands, robbing everyone who passes by (v. 25). Perhaps they had hoped that Abimelech's rule would bring them prosperity, and when it failed to do so they decided to use their position to get rich their own way. For whatever reason it was a serious breach of trust and if left unchecked would destabilize Abimelech's fledgling kingdom and create a situation like the one that had existed in the dark days of Shamgar and Jael (5:6, 7). Someone still loyal to Abimelech told him of it (v. 25b). It was bad news; he could no longer trust those who had put him in power. But worse, much worse, was to come.

Outright Betrayal (vv. 26–33)

The state of disorder created by the behavior just described provides the climate for another opportunist to make a bid for power. "Gaal the son of Ebed" arrives in Shechem, and its leaders quickly change sides and align themselves with him (v. 26). He bolsters his right to rule by claiming to be a descendant of Hamor, the founder of the city (v. 28). He may have been one of the rulers of Shechem who had not supported the move to make Abimelech king and had fled into exile. If so, his return now "with his relatives" (v. 26) is doubly ominous for Abimelech. Abimelech had come to power with the support of *his* relatives (v. 1); now Gaal comes with relatives of his own. Abimelech had claimed to be a true Shechemite. Gaal, on the face of it, has an even stronger basis for making that claim (v. 28).

Gaal and his supporters don't confront Abimelech immediately, however, but go out "into the field" near the city (v. 27). Gaal has apparently arrived at grape harvest time, which gives him and his allies the opportunity to meet and plan their next move under the guise of attending a harvest festival.[8] It's more a drunken orgy, though, than an occasion for thanksgiving, and this is ideal for Gaal's purpose. Dissatisfaction with Abimelech has apparently been developing for some time, and Gaal seizes the opportunity to stir up the crowd against him and present himself as their liberator (vv. 27, 28).

Zebul, the city governor, is also maligned, though, and becomes incensed (vv. 28, 30). He may have even been in the crowd that Gaal was addressing. Realizing that things are getting out of hand, he quickly sends messengers to Abimelech (who is apparently absent), urging him to set ambushes against Shechem and prepare for battle at first light the next morning before Gaal can fortify the city against him (vv. 31–33). The situation is dire, and open conflict is now inevitable.

The Battle for the City (vv. 34–41)

Abimelech takes Zebul's warning seriously and acts on it. Like his father Gideon,[9] he divides his men into "companies" (v. 34)—in this case four—to maximize the surprise factor and confuse the enemy about the real size of his forces. The strategy works perfectly. Expecting an attack just before dawn, Gaal goes and stands just outside the city gate. Taking this as their cue, Abimelech and his men begin to show themselves. They are immediately spotted by Gaal, and a curious conversation ensues between him and, of all people, Zebul (vv. 36–38)! Zebul has obviously survived the seizure of the city by Gaal and his followers, possibly by surrendering it to them without a fight. So from Gaal's point of view he is a collaborator and therefore an ally. But Zebul's speech is in fact full of guile and clearly intended to delay, as long as possible, Gaal's recognition of the real situation he is facing. Gaal thinks he sees "people . . . coming down from the mountaintops," most likely Mt. Gerazim and Mt. Ebal. Zebul replies that his eyes are deceiving him; all that's really there is the shifting shadows cast by the mountains in the first light of dawn (v. 36). But Gaal says he can now see two more groups of people approaching, from different directions (v. 37).[10] Gaal has realized that some kind of carefully planned maneuver is taking place, doubtless by Abimelech. But what is Abimelech's intention? To lay siege to the city? If so, should Gaal and his followers stay where they are and risk being trapped or go out and try to break through the enemy lines before the encirclement is complete? Sensing his indecision and vulnerability, Zebul casts aside his pretense. He openly taunts Gaal and urges him to do the very thing that Abimelech's tactics are intended to induce him to do: "Go out now and fight with them" (v. 38).

Few details are given about the battle itself, but the very terseness of the account is telling. There was no real contest. Gaal realizes too late that he has been outmaneuvered and tries to beat a hasty retreat, losing most of his men in the process. Gaal and his brothers, the instigators of the rebellion, do make it back into Shechem, but are unable to remain there or cause any further trouble. Zebul, now in full control of the city again, drives them out, and we never hear of them again (vv. 39–41). Surprisingly, Abimelech himself does not take up residence in Shechem again either, but "lived at Arumah," a few miles to the southwest (v. 41).[11] At the very least it suggests that Abimelech still has some unsettled business with the residents of Shechem. They are yet to feel the full force of his rage against them for betraying him.

Revenge—and Abimelech's Downfall (vv. 42–51)

It is the way of arrogant men to fly into a rage when they are crossed. Not satisfied with victory, they must have revenge and cannot rest until they have utterly crushed and destroyed all they believe have betrayed them. That was the way of Hitler and Stalin and despots and tyrants from the beginning of time. It is exemplified Biblically in the boast of Lamech in Genesis 4:23, 24:

> Lamech said to his wives:
>
> > "Adah and Zillah, hear my voice;
> >   you wives of Lamech, listen to what I say:
> > I have killed a man for wounding me,
> >   a young man for striking me.
> > If Cain's revenge is sevenfold,
> >   then Lamech's is seventy-sevenfold."

But such uncontrolled rage is dangerous. It makes people lose perspective, trust no one, see enemies everywhere, kill innocent people, and in the end overreach themselves and bring about their own destruction. We saw it to some extent in Gideon's vendetta against Zebah and Zalmunna in Judges 8; now we see it again in a more terrible form in Abimelech.

Slaughter in Shechem (vv. 42–49)

The battle fought here is a virtual repeat of the one in verses 22–41, but this time it is fought against unarmed civilians and is carried to a far more extreme end. In reality it is no battle at all, but a massacre carried out with ruthless efficiency. With the crisis apparently over, the people of Shechem "went out into the field" near the city (v. 42), perhaps to see how much it had been damaged or to try to start working it again. The last time they "went out into the field," though, it was to conspire with Gaal against Abimelelch (v. 27). Now someone still loyal to Abimelech suspects that mischief is afoot again and tells Abimelech (v. 42). It is more paranoia than a sober assessment of the situation, hinting that the "evil spirit" of verse 23 is still at work. But it gives Abimelech the only excuse he needs to attack them. A rout ensues, as before. This time, however, it is not just the people who are destroyed, but their whole city. Shechem is razed to the ground and symbolically "sowed . . . with salt" as a way of cursing it and consigning it to perpetual desolation (v. 45).[12] But Abimelech is not finished yet. Some of the rulers, "all the leaders of the Tower of Shechem," have escaped. Seeing that the end was near, they had somehow got out before the city was destroyed and have taken refuge in "the stronghold of the house of El-berith" (v. 46).[13] This was probably a fortified temple complex outside the city walls, with a tower that was designed to be a last place of refuge if the city itself fell. The "leaders" in question may have been a group of men with special responsibility for the defense of this fortress. But when they hear how total the destruction of the city has been, they realize that defending even the fortress will be impossible and retreat into the tower to await their fate (v. 47).

They don't have long to wait. Determined that no one will escape, Abimelech commands his men to help him gather wood and stack it against the tower. When it is torched, the conflagration kills everyone in the tower—not just the leaders, but all who have taken refuge with them, one thousand human souls in all, including women and children (v. 49). It's a literal holocaust, complete immolation. Fire has gone forth from the bramble and destroyed the people of Shechem, just as Jotham said it would (v. 15). And that, surely, should have at last satisfied Abimelech's lust for revenge. But alas, it did not. He's drunk with power now and can't stop. And for him power equals slaughter. That's how it was from the beginning (v. 5) and how it will be until his end. Abimelech knows no other way to live or die.

Death in Thebez (vv. 50–56)

"Thebez" was a few miles northeast of Shechem.[14] But we have not heard of it before, and it is not clear why Abimelelech attacked this town in particular. Was it perhaps a satellite of Shechem, or perhaps just another convenient target for a man whose rage is now out of control? Who knows? There's no need, in any case, to seek a rational explanation. Abimlelech is clearly paranoid, and it's the nature of paranoia to subvert rationality and cause leaders who suffer from it to commit excesses that eventually bring about their own ruin. That is precisely what is about to happen here.

At first, however, there is no sign at all that Abimelech is doomed. On the contrary, he seems to be in total command. He "encamp[s] against Thebez," "capture[s]" it, and goes about destroying its "tower" and its terrified inhabitants with the same callous efficiency with which he had destroyed the one in Shechem (vv. 50–52). But he hasn't reckoned with the resourcefulness of "a certain woman" with "an upper millstone," the small, upper stone of a hand-operated grain grinder—not massive, but heavy enough to do a lot of damage if dropped from a height and well-aimed, as this one will be (v. 53). The woman has positioned herself above the door to the tower, its most vulnerable point, and therefore the place the enemy is most likely to approach to destroy it. Like Jael with her tent peg, this woman is armed and deadly and grimly determined not to waste her one chance to achieve her goal. It's a well-set trap, and Abimelech, who now thinks he is invulnerable, walks right into it. He approaches the door to set fire to it, and at that precise moment the woman "threw" her millstone down to give it maximum impact. And it does its work, crushing Abimelech's skull (v. 53). Abimelech is fatally wounded and knows it, but cannot face the shame of being slain by a woman; so he asks his armor-bearer to draw his sword and kill him, which he does (v. 54). Abimelech dies by assisted suicide, a violent end for a violent man. As for his followers, seeing their leader is dead they simply disperse and go "everyone . . . to his home" to try to resume something like a normal existence, with nothing gained and much lost (v. 55). There are no winners here except God.

> Thus God returned the evil of Abimelech, which he committed against his father in killing his seventy brothers. And God also made all the evil of the men of Shechem return on their heads, and upon them came the curse of Jotham the son of Jerubbaal. (vv. 56, 57)[15]

Retribution

The story of Abimlelech is about retribution. The stories of the judges that preceded and follow it are about God saving people who don't deserve it, because they have done evil in his sight. In short, they are stories of God's grace to sinners. Not so the story of Abimlelech. It is not about God showing grace to the undeserving, but about him giving them *exactly* what they deserve. It is a story of divine judgment carried out with almost mathematical precision. God's sending an evil spirit between Abimelech and the leaders of Shechem sets a series of events in motion that have a relentless, repeating pattern to them. Abimelech's going to Shechem to incite its leaders to conspire against Gideon's sons is answered by Gaal's arrival in Shechem to incite its leaders to conspire with him against Abimelech. The ambush the men of Shechem set against Abimelech in verse 25 is answered by the ambush set by Abimelech against Shechem in verse 34. Abimelech, who killed his brothers on one stone in verse 5, is himself killed by a single stone thrown from a tower in verse 53. As the story unfolds, act answers to act and evil to evil. The evil spirit sent by God to begin the process itself answers to the evil committed by Abimelech and his supporters. This spirit is not exorcised until the chief instigator of the evil is struck down and his followers are scattered to try to pick up the remaining pieces of their shattered lives. It's a sobering story that has at least three important things to teach us.

Lessons Worth Learning

First, God is not obligated to show grace to sinners. He is perfectly within his rights to punish them exactly as they deserve. Judgment is not his preferred option. He takes "no pleasure in the death of the wicked" (Ezekiel 33:11). Rescue, rather than punishment, lies much closer to his heart and is more truly reflective of his essential nature. Judgment is his "strange" or "alien" work (Isaiah 28:21). We cannot say that God *is* judgment in the way that we can say that he is love (1 John 4:8, 16). More often than not his judgments are tempered by grace and intended to discipline and restore people rather than destroy them. His handing of Israel over to foreign oppressors elsewhere in Judges are remedial judgments of this kind. But the story of Abimelech is a reminder that God does have another principle of operation that he can invoke at his discretion, and will do so when circumstances warrant it. It's a warning to Israel what a dangerous thing it is to do what is evil in the eyes of the Lord, and how close they themselves came to destruction every time they did so. Biblical history is punctuated with such warnings, from the great flood and the destruction of Sodom and Gomorrah to the sudden death of Ananias and Sapphira and the solemn warnings of Jesus and the letter to the Hebrews to the seven bowls of God's wrath in the book of Revelation (Genesis 6—8; 19:23–29; Acts 5:1–10; Matthew 5:27–30; 10:28; Hebrews 6:4–8; 10:26–31; Revelation 1). The final expression of divine retribution, of course, is Hell, which is the withdrawal of grace forever (Revelation 14:11; 20:11–15). Retribution is real, and we forget it at our peril.

Second, God is sovereign over evil. Evil is destructive by its very nature, and those who turn to it almost always bring themselves to ruin sooner or later. This happens with such regularity that we can begin to think that God is not involved at all, that evil has a power that operates quite independently of him. But the Bible tells us that this is not the case. Pain, frustration, broken relationships, violence, and death are not in the world by accident and do not mean that the world or any part of it has slipped from God's sovereign control. At one level these are the natural consequences of human beings refusing to submit to God's rightful rule over them. But at a deeper level they are judgments that God himself has placed in the world as continual reminders that all is not well between us and him, that we are not masters of our own fate and cannot rebel against our Maker with impunity. They are also warnings of a greater judgment to come, beyond death, if we do not come back to God. The Bible teaches us all this quite independently of Judges 9.

However, the book of Judges, and the account of Abimelech's downfall in particular, has some more specific things to teach us about God's sovereignty over evil. Judges 9 shows us that apparently commonplace events can be specific judgments of God. Given the general truth that people reap what they sow (Galatians 6:7), it's not surprising that Abimelech came to a bad end, and all the contributing factors, on the face of it, are completely commonplace—jealousy, rivalry, ambition, paranoia, revenge. We would not know, if we were not told, that God was involved at all. But in this particular case he was. "*God sent* an evil spirit between Abimelech and the leaders of Shechem" (v. 23), "*God* returned the evil of Abimelech," and "*God* also made all the evil of the men of Shechem return on their heads" (vv. 56, 57). Evil appears to be running rampant in Judges 9, but the truth is that God is sovereignly directing it to a quite particular and just outcome. Men who have chosen evil are given evil in full measure as their just punishment. However, the wider context of Judges as a whole tells us something else. God can use evil to discipline evildoers (as when he hands Israel over to oppressors) and can intervene to limit evil and *save* sinners from the worst consequences of their wrongdoing (as in his repeated raising up of judges).[16] These are in fact more characteristic of how God acts in Judges than the pure retribution we see in chapter 9. And even *there* something positive is achieved. Ironically, Israel as a whole benefits from the judgment visited on their bramble king. The process of retribution has the precision of a surgical operation that excises a cancer from their body politic, so that normal life can be resumed. However God is related to evil, he is never tainted by it, is always sovereign over it, and causes it to serve, in the end, his own just purposes. There is great comfort for us all in that.

Finally, although Hell itself is beyond the horizon of the book of Judges, Judges shows us that there are definitely foretastes of it in this life. The evil of Abimelech's career is indeed like that of the undisciplined tongue of James 3, a raging blaze "set on fire by hell" (James 3:5, 6). As Jotham predicted, fire breaks out from the bramble king and devours the leaders of Shechem and eventually breaks out from them (via their surrogate in the burning tower) to destroy Abimelech himself. It's as though Hell has for a time burst its gates and released its fire into the world, with devastating effects. Some of us can remember similar things happening in our own lifetimes—the flaming cauldrons caused by carpet bombing of whole cities with incendiary devices in the Second World War, the smoke rising from the incinerators of Nazi concentration camps, the nuclear explosions that vaporized Hiroshima and Nagasaki. Some of these were acts of retaliation for evils already committed; others were acts of pure evil, still awaiting just retribution. All involved terrible suffering, in which the innocent perished along with the guilty. All of them are consequences, in one way or another, of the refusal of the human race to submit to the good and just rule of God. They are the worst manifestations of the kind of world we began to create for ourselves when we turned our backs on God. They are also warnings of a future judgment that will be complete and final. There is no perfect justice in this world. Even in Judges 9 there were innocent victims. But there will be perfect justice on the last day when God "will judge the world in righteousness by a man he has appointed." By raising Jesus from the dead, God has put the world on notice that judgment day is coming (Acts 17:30, 31).

The story of Abimelech does not make pleasant reading, but like all other parts of Scripture it is there for our good. In its own unique way it bears witness to the precision of divine judgment. God will make a full end; there will be no unfinished business with him. It warns us not to test God by choosing evil. It should make us deeply thankful to God for having mercy on us and rouse us to renewed prayer for those we love who continue to defy him, that he may not visit on them the terrible retribution they deserve.

15

First Interlude: Tola and Jair

JUDGES 10:1–5

AN INTERLUDE is normally a welcome break in an activity that is demanding in some way, as in a morning tea break on a busy workday. In musical terms it is a composition inserted between the parts of a longer work.[1] In drama it is "an entertainment between the acts of a play."[2] In medieval times it was normally a short, farcical piece of light relief between the acts of a mystery or morality play.[3] An interlude is transitional—a kind of hinge between the major parts of a performance. As an intermission in a concert or play today it allows for refreshments and conversation, but also provides an opportunity for more thoughtful patrons to reflect on what has happened so far and to prepare themselves for what is to come. The present interlude in the book of Judges shares all these characteristics. It is short, light in tone, bordering on farcical in its second half and acts as a transition between the Abimelech and Jephthah narratives. It gives us some breathing space in a part of the book that is particularly intense and emotionally demanding. It contains reports of the careers of two judges of whom almost nothing is known—Tola, a man of Issachar, and Jair the Gileadite.

An Unspectacular Savior (vv. 1, 2)

The opening two words of this note bring Abimelech's turbulent career into sharp focus as the backdrop to Tola's contribution to Israel's life in the judges period. The statement that "*After Abimelech* there arose to save Israel Tola" (v. 1) can hardly mean that Tola arose to save Israel as Abimelech had done! That would be absurd after what has happened in chapter 9. Rather it simply means that after Abimelech Israel needed saving, and Tola arose to do this. "Shamir," where he lived, is otherwise unknown, but since it has the same three consonants in Hebrew as the better known Samaria it was probably the same place under an earlier name. Certainly the accompanying phrase, "in the hill country of Ephraim," places it in the same general locality. But the fact that we're forced to speculate about it is significant in itself. Of his father, "Puah, son of Dodo," we know nothing at all. Tola is an obscure man from an obscure place and an obscure family. Nor does anything of much significance seem to have happened during his rule. Despite the use of the word "save," no military action is attributed to Tola. There was apparently no military threat during his period of office, and he is not remembered for any acts of heroism. We are just told that he "lived" (literally "sat") in Shamir and "judged Israel twenty-three years" (v. 2). The language is reminiscent of the early career of Deborah, who used to "sit" under her palm tree in the hill country of Ephraim and "judge" Israel (4:4, 5). The details of his activity are few, but those we are given, together with the reference to Abimelech and the similarity to Deborah, all suggest that he saved Israel from the disastrous effects of Abimelech's rule by providing a period of stable administration. He saved it from disintegration by being a steady hand on the tiller to steer it out of troubled waters. He judged Israel for twenty-three years, and then "he died and was buried" (v. 2)—not a spectacular career perhaps, but he left Israel better than he found it, and that is a mighty good thing to be remembered for.

Some years ago I belonged to a church that went through a deep crisis that nearly tore its heart out. The career of a pastor who had served us for fifteen years and achieved great things for the kingdom of God ended in circumstances that left us bewildered and discouraged. Many left the church, and those of us who remained found it hard to see how we could recover. The way ahead, if there was to be one, was very unclear. In those circumstances God gave us a man like Tola. He was a quiet man. He was not a great preacher, and he had no big vision to cast or great ideas to inspire us with except those of the unchanging gospel of grace and the witness of Scripture to the unfailing love of our heavenly Father. He and his wife, his true partner in ministry, gathered us together, healed our wounds, and nursed us through a time of grieving and acceptance until we were ready to lift our heads and start hoping in God again and pulling together in his service. He saved us. He came for a year, but stayed for three or more, and then when we had a new pastor ready to take us on to the next chapter of our life as a church he and his wife quietly withdrew and did the same thing for another hurting congregation elsewhere. People like that are priceless. Their autobiographies may never be written, and there may be no spectacular achievements to record, but their reward will surely be great in Heaven. Such a man was Tola.

And then there was Jair, a judge of a very different kind.

A Man Who Had It All (vv. 3–5)

If the account of Tola's rule alludes back to the reign of Abimelech in chapter 9, this note about "Jair the Gileadite" prepares the way for the story of Jephthah the Gideadite which follows in 10:6—12:7. Jair comes to power after the crisis that Tola faced has passed. What Tola had achieved, Jair received as a gift. He was born into good times, which had been served up to him on a plate. And Gilead was a good place to live. It was the central and northern part of Israel's territory east of the Jordan, spanning the old tribal allotments of Gad and east Manasseh. It was excellent grazing land that the Israelites had acquired on their way to Canaan after defeating the Amorite kings who lived there (Deuteronomy 2:26—3:22). It was so good that the tribes that had this territory allocated to them did not want to go on into Canaan proper and did so only after strong persuasion by Moses. Only after they had helped the other tribes conquer *their* territories west of the Jordan were they allowed to go back to Gilead and occupy what had been given to them there (Numbers 32). Gilead was a place that promised prosperity, and those that received it as their inheritance had good prospects.

The little we are told about Jair suggests that he fully realized the potential that Gilead offered. The reference to his "thirty sons who rode on thirty donkeys, and . . . had thirty cities" (v. 4) suggests the peacefulness of the times and the prosperity and prestige of the judge.[4] The period of the judges was not all crisis and turmoil. We have been told repeatedly in the preceding chapters of times when the land had rest, ranging from forty to eighty years, but virtually no detail of what life was like during these peaceful interludes. Here at last we get a glimpse of how it was for one man living east of the Jordan; the book of Ruth will provide us with a much more extended look at what it was like for a family in Bethlehem, in Canaan proper. In Bethlehem the peace was interrupted for a time by famine, but there is no hint of any such trouble for Jair and his family in Gilead.

There is nothing wrong with peace and prosperity, of course. It is a blessing to be enjoyed with gratitude to God. However, it also has its dangers, and there are hints in what we are told here about Jair that he succumbed to some of them. His "thirty sons" implies that he had many wives, as Gideon did, and perhaps had the same secret desire to be a king, or at least to have the trappings of royalty. And following the account of what followed from

Gideon's straying in that direction, Jair's flirtation with the same thing does not speak well of his character and judgment. Moreover, the fact that his sons rode on thirty donkeys and had thirty cities suggests that they too fancied themselves as at least princes and that Jair had groomed them as his successors—a kind of Jair dynasty—rather than leaving the decision of who should rule after him for others to determine in dependence on God. His placing all thirty of his sons in positions of authority, apparently regardless of their suitability for such high office, smacks too much of nepotism and abuse of power. In short, Jair seems to have used the wealth and prosperity that came his way more to advance the interests of his own family than to promote the welfare of the nation. And the style of his rule hints at the unpreparedness of Israel for the disaster about to fall on them (10:7). Jair's pampered sons will be of little use when the Ammonites invade! Then the Gileadites will find themselves without any effective leadership at all and will seek desperately for a fighter. The places called "Havvoth-jair" ("the villages of Jair") would stand as a testament to Jair's folly rather than to his wisdom.

Opportunities and Dangers

The circumstances of Christian communities and individual believers vary greatly. For some, life is full of crises, and daily life is a struggle to survive. Others have all the necessities of life. They live in a relatively safe environment, and disturbances serious enough to be called crises are relatively infrequent. But no life in this world is completely untroubled. Sickness, stress, relationship problems, aging, bereavement, and death are issues we all face. Thank God, though, for times when the stress is relaxed and life seems manageable again, when our spirits lift and we become aware again of how blessed we are. Such interludes are gifts from God to be enjoyed with gratitude to him.

Some interludes are part of the normal rhythm of life and, circumstances permitting, can be planned for. The weekly Sabbath was a gift of God to his people under the old covenant, but taking full advantage of it required a determination to observe it regularly. The Christian Sunday bears some similarities to this, though it is no longer a legal obligation as the Sabbath was under the old covenant. Vacations, for those who can afford them, are a kind of secular equivalent that recognize the importance of rest for our well-being. Planning for such interludes in our busy working lives is wise and in accord with God's good intentions for us. Of course, such planning is not always possible, and even when plans are made they can easily be overtaken by circumstances. There are other kinds of interludes, however, that have nothing to do with our planning. They come because God intervenes to deliver us in some way, lift our burdens, and give us rest. They are pure gifts of God. These are the kinds of interludes we find in the book of Judges.

The interlude in 10:1–5 is an interlude of this latter kind and illustrates the special opportunities and challenges that such interludes provide. Israel needed respite from the chaos and horrors of Abimelech's rule, and suddenly there it was! It was certainly not a result of wise planning on Abimelech's part! It was something God brought about by bringing Abimelech's disastrous reign to an end. But what was to be done now that relief had come? Tola and Jair illustrate well the kinds of possibilities and dangers that such interludes provide.

They give opportunity for healing. Tola provided this by his wise administration, and I mentioned above how a godly man and his wife did the same thing for a wounded church to which I once belonged. The denomination that church belonged to has recognized the value of such ministry by providing special training for those able and willing to engage in it. These are mainly older pastors with the wisdom of experience, but also others who are suited to it and recognize its importance. This has "saved" many faltering congregations in much the same way that Tola's steady and wise leadership saved Israel. Interludes give opportunity for such healing ministry to take place.

They also give opportunity to plan for the future. In crisis situations immediate and pressing matters claim all our attention; but interludes allow time to reflect on lessons learned and how a better future may be shaped by careful planning. They are an opportunity for a good leader to remind God's people of what they are called to be and do and to prepare them for the time when he will no longer be with them. They are times to equip emerging leaders with the values and skills they will need to take their people forward, more ready to deal successfully with future crises than they were to handle past ones.

Sadly, though, good times often have the opposite effect. Rest and prosperity lull people into self-indulgence and a false sense of security. The bitter lessons of the past are soon forgotten. It is assumed that the good times will last forever and that no preparation for anything different is needed. People become self-focused and forgetful of God. They live in the present, with little thought to either the past or the future. The pursuit of the good life, which is thought of mainly in terms of material and social advancement, becomes an end in itself. Leaders, too, become seduced into a way of life that, if not plainly immoral, is a weak and insipid reflection of the watchfulness and service that should be their hallmarks. And when the next crisis comes it finds them and those they lead woefully unprepared. Good times have their hazards just as bad times do. And the dangers of peace and prosperity are more insidious because they are less obvious and come upon us gradually. Jair may have seen his lifestyle as innocent, the simple enjoyment of God-given prosperity. But it led to an ostentation and excess that was not good for him or those he led. Churches pastored by such men may become large and prosperous, but they will not be spiritually strong and will not be able to stand when hard times come (Matthew 13:1–8; Revelation 3:14–22).

Crises of one kind or another are inevitable in this world. Interludes are gracious gifts of God and foretastes of our final rest in Heaven. In an important sense the whole of this era in which we live is an interlude between the cross and the final manifestation of the kingdom of God on the last day. There are good things to enjoy, opportunities to be taken up, work to be done, challenges to face, and dangers to be avoided. One day we must all stand before the throne of God and answer to him for how we have lived (Romans 14:10; 1 Corinthians 3:10–15; 2 Corinthians 5:10). None of us can avoid that crisis. Jesus himself has given us fair warning of it and of the need to be ready for it (Matthew 24:36–51). May God give us leaders who will live in the light of that day and help us to do the same.

16

Jephthah: The Negotiator

JUDGES 10:6—12:7

GENERALLY SPEAKING, negotiation is a good thing, and it's hard to think of a world that could work without it. It's "a formal discussion between people who are trying to reach an agreement."[1] It's the art of accommodation, compromise, give and take, and the making of concessions. It's the skill of making deals and doing business. In many societies it's impossible to buy or sell anything, including basic grocery items, without negotiation, and there are unspoken rules that govern the process involved. During a visit to Jerusalem in the early eighties I ended up with a shopkeeper pursuing me down the street with loud protestation because I had not bought a pair of shoes from him after bargaining about the price for several minutes. Apparently it was understood that after a certain amount of time there was a tacit understanding that a sale would be made; only the price was in question. I had not understood this, and the shopkeeper took offense when I left without making a purchase.

Negotiation is needed across the whole gamut of human relationships, from marriage and family to politics and international affairs. Newlyweds who can't compromise have little chance of building a lasting marriage, and parents who can't negotiate with their teenage children run the risk of losing them completely through relationship breakdown. Politics is largely the art of compromise, particularly in a multi-party democracy. The time it takes to negotiate free trade agreements between competing economies shows how complex and difficult the issues are. And when it comes to international relations in general, highly trained diplomats struggle to keep their respective governments on speaking terms. Much can be at stake, and when diplomacy fails outright conflict can result. Most wars end in peace negotiations of some kind, which makes us wonder why war can't be avoided entirely. Why not proceed directly to a peace settlement rather than resorting to arms? The answer, of course, is that the combatants believe too much is at stake. The war that ensues is largely about establishing the strongest bargaining position possible before coming to the negotiating table. The peace settlement, when it comes, is often a one-sided affair, with the winner extracting punishing concessions from the loser. The result can leave brooding resentment that at a later time erupts into renewed conflict. This is especially the case when a peace settlement involves the redrawing of national boundaries, sometimes subdividing whole countries into separate states or spheres of influence. It took a whole generation for the Berlin Wall to come down after the Second World War.

This shows very clearly that while negotiation may be necessary, it has severe limitations. And the reason is very easy to understand. It is a way of balancing competing self-interests, and relationships conducted on that basis can never be entirely healthy. There is an inherent distrust and jostling for advantage in such relationships that simply masks differences rather than truly resolving them. The basic problem is the sinful human heart with its instinct for self-protection and self-promotion rather than love and trust. Negotiation might be essential in a fallen world, but it is far from ideal.

But what are the implications of all this for people who acknowledge God as their rightful ruler and whose life together is meant to reflect his character? What place can negotiation have in the life of people who are called to love their neighbors as themselves (Leviticus 19:18; Matthew 5:43–45; 22:34–39; Galatians 5:13, 14)? Does it have a legitimate place in the way they relate to outsiders and with one another? And more importantly, what place is there for negotiation in their relationship with God? This is the issue that lies at the heart of the account of Jephthah's career in 10:6—12:7. His story unfolds in a series of episodes in which we see him interacting with several groups and individuals in succession—the Gileadites, the king of Ammon, his daughter, and the Ephraimites. He does a lot of talking. Of all the judges he is the most skilled at negotiation, and this is the part of the book that has the most to teach us about this important issue. First, though, we are told about the situation that led to his rise to power.

Trouble in Gilead (10:6–16)

By now Israel's relapse into idolatry after deliverance and a period of respite has become all too familiar. It is part of the repeating pattern of this whole central part of the book. But this time the detailing of the gods that

Israel turned to is especially elaborate. It includes not just the gods of the Canaanites (the Baals and Ashtaroth), but those of the surrounding nations as well—Syria and Sidon to the north, Moab and Ammon to the east, and the Philistines to the southwest (v. 6). The effect is to stress the gravity of Israel's waywardness; they turn to any and every god other than the Lord. Their propensity for doing what is evil in his sight is going from bad to worse!

This time they are punished by being given over to the Ammonites, who will feature in the Jephthah story, and the Philistines, who will feature in the Samson story that follows (v. 7). There is a special appropriateness to this. Israel chose to serve the gods of these nations (v. 7); now they will pay for it by being oppressed by these nations. And there will be no quick fix. Jephthah will bring them a brief period of respite by defeating the Ammonites (12:7), but the Philistines will prove a much harder foe to deal with. They will harass Israel, on and off, right through to the time of David. There's always a price to pay for sinning against the Lord, and in this case the cost will be very high indeed. The people of Gilead were the first to feel the impact of Ammonite aggression. The first year was terrible; they were "crushed and oppressed." But then that terrible year lengthened into eighteen without any relief (v. 8), until finally the invaders crossed the Jordan to fight against Judah, Benjamin, and Ephraim as well, bringing the whole of Israel to its knees (vv. 8, 9).

In their extremity the Israelites cry out to God to save them, as they have many times before (v. 10). But this time they are in for a shock. Instead of coming to their aid the Lord rebuffs them in the strongest possible terms. Hasn't he saved them again and again in the past? And haven't they always gone back to their own ways? Let them cry out to the gods they have chosen! Let those gods save them if they can! The Lord has had enough—he will save them no more (vv. 11–15)! This is the disaster we always court when we presume on the grace of God by persisting in sin (Hebrews 10:26–31). How this awful message was delivered is not clear. It may have been by a prophet, as in 6:7–10, or by the angel of the Lord, as in 2:1–3. We are not told, and probably deliberately so. In the stark way the encounter is described, God and Israel seem to have reached an impasse. Their relationship is on the brink of complete breakdown, and no priest, prophet, or any other mediator is in sight. Is reconciliation possible? And if not, does Israel have any future at all?

The Israelites panic, confessing their sin, casting themselves on God's mercy, and pleading with him to save them just once more (v. 15). They even renounce their foreign gods and begin to serve the LORD again (v. 16). It's their most impressive show of repentance in the whole book! But can they be trusted? How real is their change of heart, and how long will it last? The only clue we get is God's response, and it's less than enthusiastic, to say the least. We are not told that he relented and forgave them or raised up a judge to save them,[2] but merely that he "became impatient" over their "misery" (v. 16). In other words, it wasn't their repentance (such as it was) that moved him, but their misery. He became tired of it and couldn't bear to see it continue. It will be some time before we see what he will do to end it, but at least there is a glimmer of hope at the end of this first part of the story that he will do something. That is the astonishing grace of God, and it is the sinner's only hope.

The Search for a Savior (10:17—11:11)

As this scene opens we are transported to the battle zone where the enemy is about to launch a new offensive and the Israelites are taking desperate counsel with one another. Since the Ammonites have encamped in Mizpah in Gilead, that is the part of Israel most directly threatened, and "the leaders of Gilead" feel most responsible to take action (v. 18). But who will fight for them? God has said he will not save them (10:13), and none of them is capable of mustering and leading a militia. They are willing to offer inducement to anyone who will do it for them (they'll make him "head over all the inhabitants of Gilead"), but no one suitable is at hand (10:17, 18). In short, there are leaders here, but no leadership! The scene is set for the entrance of Jephthah at the beginning of chapter 11.

Jephthah is "a mighty warrior" (11:1)—just the man they need! But there is a problem. In fact there are several problems, the main one being that he's not present! Jephthah was a Gileadite through and through,[3] but he had not had a good start in life. He was the son of a prostitute, and his brothers had driven him out so that he would not be able to share in their inheritance (vv. 1, 2). So Jephthah had to survive as best he could and ended up being the leader of a bunch of outlaws in the "the land of Tob" (v. 3), somewhere in the remote northeast, near the Syrian border.[4] It was frontier living, where you had to be strong to survive, and many hired themselves out as mercenaries.[5] So Jephthah became a hardened fighter who knew how to sell his services to the highest bidder.

The elders of Gilead are desperate and eventually decide to go and ask Jephthah to help them (vv. 5, 6). But Jephthah is not an easy catch. He realizes that the tables are now turned; he is now the one with all the bargaining power and is determined to use it to maximum advantage. He accuses the elders of being to blame for what his brothers did to him; after all, they were the leaders of the community and were responsible for managing its affairs

(v. 7). "You hated me and threw me out," Jephthah says in essence. "Why are you coming to me now that you are in trouble?" They want him to fight for them, of course, and tell him so. But they also offer him something—headship over all the people of Gilead (v. 8)! It's strong inducement indeed for an outcast. It's all he ever dreamed of and more—status, power, and a complete reversal of the wrongs that had been done to him. But Jephthah is cautious. He's been betrayed by these people before. Now that he has them at his mercy he wants to make absolutely sure they will deliver what they have promised him. So he spells out his terms very precisely: "If you bring me home again to fight against the Ammonites, and the LORD gives them over to me, I will be your head" (v. 9). By invoking the name of the Lord he effectively puts the elders under oath. They understand this, but have no alternative. So they reply in kind, swearing in the most solemn terms to fulfill their side of the bargain: "The LORD will be witness between us, if we do not do as you say" (v. 10).

Satisfied, Jephthah returns with them, where he is received with such enthusiasm that he is acclaimed "head and leader" on the spot (v. 11). When the excitement is over, however, the deal that Jephthah has struck with the elders is ratified in a solemn ceremony in which Jephthah, like them, vows to keep his part of it (v. 11). However, everything now depends on how Jephthah fares in the coming conflict. A great deal hangs in the balance, and the stakes are very high, not just for the people Jephthah leads, but for Jephthah himself.

Curiously, this scene of apparent reconciliation between Jephthah and the Gileadites reads very much like what has taken place between the Israelites and God in the previous one. The Gileadites reject Jephthah but turn to him for help when they are in trouble, just as the Israelites abandon Yahweh but appeal to him when *they* are in trouble. Jephthah initially rebuffs the Gileadites, as Yahweh had rebuffed Israel. The Gileadites say they have changed their attitude and make Jephthah their leader, just as the Israelites apparently changed their attitude toward Yahweh and began to serve him again. The difference is that Jephthah, in the end, does promise to rescue the Gileadites, on certain conditions, whereas Yahweh makes no such promise. Jephthah strikes a deal; God does not. Jephthah sees an opportunity to advance his own interests; God just can't endure Israel's misery. It leaves us wondering two things. Was Israel's repentance real, or was it (as we suspected) just an attempt to bargain with God as the elders now bargain with Jephthah? Second, what does the contrast between how Jephthah and God behave suggest about how the relationship between them is likely to develop? So far God has been the silent witness of all that has taken place. But what will he do? Will he choose Jephthah, as the Gileadites have done? Is this hardheaded, self-interested negotiator going to be the next judge of Israel?

Jephthah Uses Diplomacy and Moves Beyond It (11:12–28)

By dispatching "messengers" (v. 12) to the king of Ammon, Jephthah begins to exercise his new authority as head and leader of the people of Gilead. He also follows the precedent that Moses had set in dealing with the rulers of the same general area long before him (Numbers 21:21; Deuteronomy 2:26). It is unlikely, though, that he is genuinely seeking peace, since armed conflict has already begun and he has been engaged by the Gileadites specifically to "fight" (vv. 6, 8). From what follows it is more likely that his intention is to seize the moral high ground by establishing the rightness of his cause (v. 27) and buy himself sufficient time to recruit a fighting force large enough to have some chance of success (v. 29). His tone is anything but concilia-tory. At the outset "my land" (v. 12) probably refers to Gilead, Jephthah's homeland, and he challenges his opponent to justify his invasion of it. As the messengers go back and forth a complex argument is played out about who has the strongest claim to the territory in question, first on historical grounds (who won it fairly in battle? vv. 13–22), then on theological grounds (who did the relevant deity give it to? vv. 23, 24),[6] and then on historical grounds (if the Ammonites had a legitimate claim to Gilead, why didn't they assert it before now? vv. 25, 26). The longer the exchange continues, the less and less likely any diplomatic solution appears, and the more and more the proceed-ings sound like a court case, with evidence for the competing claims being presented for adjudication by a judge. This may have been what Jephthah had in mind all along. Certainly it is the conclusion he finally brings the pro-ceedings to by appealing to Yahweh in verse 27: "[Let] the LORD, the Judge, decide this day between the people of Israel and the people of Ammon."[7] It is effectively a declaration of war. But it is also an appeal to Yahweh to rule in Israel's favor and rescue them. Here at last Jephthah's belief in Yahweh's unrivaled supremacy shines though, and his willingness to stake everything on him. This is his finest moment and the one that most justifies his inclu-sion among Israel's heroes of faith in Hebrews 11 (Hebrews 11:32, 33). Here surely is a man God can use. We may have had doubts about that before, but now those doubts seem unjustified. Jephthah has potential for real greatness. But we are in for a shock.

Jephthah's Great Mistake (11:29–40)

Since his angry rebuke to Israel in 10:11–14, God has remained silent. Nor has he *done* anything, as far as we know. Jephthah has spoken *about* him (11:9, 21–24) and *before* him (11:11) and appealed *to* him (11:11). But God has not appeared to Jephthah as he did to Gideon or spoken to him either directly or indirectly as he did to Gideon and Barak. Nor has the writer given us any indication of whether or not God approves of Jephthah. All this changes, however, with the statement in verse 29 that "the Spirit of the LORD was upon [came upon][8] Jephthah." It's an appropriate response to Jephthah's appeal in the previous verses and makes it clear that God has indeed chosen him to save Israel. We can't be sure, though, that this was clear to Jephthah himself. God has still not appeared to him or spoken with him as far as we know. Jephthah may have felt something when the Spirit came upon him, or perhaps not. What is certain is that he knew that he now had a fight on his hands and needed more men. The Israelites had already taken up a forward position at Mizpah (10:17), but morale was low and their numbers inadequate. So in verse 29 Jephthah goes on a recruitment drive. The verbs "passed through . . . passed on . . . passed on" suggest haste (he had no time to lose), but also purposefulness. Jephthah knows what he is about. He visits Gilead, Manasseh,[9] and Mizpah of Gilead (his hometown) and finally advances toward "the Ammonites" (probably near the place in Gilead where they were camped).[10] Energized by the Spirit, Jephthah's natural giftedness as a leader of men is enhanced and directed now to a single purpose. The story is gathering speed, and all seems set for the kind of God-given victory we have come to expect from previous episodes in Judges. But suddenly something completely unexpected happens: Jephthah makes a vow.

> Jephthah made a vow to the LORD and said, "If you will give the Ammonites into my hand, then whatever comes out from the doors of my house to meet me when I return in peace from the Ammonites shall be the LORD's, and I will offer it up for a burnt offering." (vv. 30, 31)

The vow is completely unnecessary. God has chosen to use Jephthah. The Spirit has come upon him. Victory is assured. But what is clear to us was apparently not clear to Jephthah; or if it was, he was not as sure of it as we are. His bold appeal to Yahweh back in verse 27 was public and probably intended (partly at least) to unsettle his enemy. The vow, though, takes us much deeper into Jephthah's psyche and shows us a man still haunted by his past. Publicly he has argued that Israel is the innocent party and expressed confidence that God will rule in their favor. Privately, however, he remembers that he himself has been an innocent party in a dispute and found his rights disregarded by those who should have protected him (vv. 1–3, 7). The opening words of his vow ("*If* you will give the Ammonites into my hand," v. 30)[11] express his deep angst. Will Yahweh, after all, reject him too? Jephthah has everything to lose if the battle goes against him, including his life,[12] but also his position in his clan and tribe, and that clearly means a great deal to him. Formerly an outcast, he is now "head over all the inhabitants of Gilead" (v. 8). But if he loses this battle, the whole cycle of rejection will begin again. If God doesn't come through for him now, Jephthah will be an outcast again. So under intense pressure Jephthah reverts to what is most natural to him—negotiation. He is good at it, and it has worked well for him in the past. The difference is that now he tries it with God rather than with men.

The vow is effectively a bribe. As the elders once offered inducement to Jephthah, Jephthah now offers inducement to Yahweh. Jephthah is now the suppliant, but even in this role his words exhibit all the shrewdness that we have come to expect of him. The vow is quite explicit in pledging a burnt offering (v. 31), but circumspect in nominating the victim. In fact, it does not specify any particular victim at all, only the means by which it will be identified: "whatever [or whoever][13] comes out from the doors of my house to meet me." This immediately generates a high degree of tension in the story. Who or what will the victim turn out to be? The language is ambiguous, but more applicable to a human being than an animal, especially the phrase, "to meet me." The gravity of the situation, too, suggests that a human rather than animal sacrifice is what is being contemplated. The vow puts all the occupants of Jephthah's house at risk, but he will offer only what is forced from him. The vow is not impulsive; it is shrewd and calculating and entirely in keeping with Jephthah's character as we have come to know it.

With the fateful vow made, Jephthah commits his men to battle and wins a great victory (vv. 32, 33). But the way the opening words of verse 32 ("Jephthah crossed over to the Ammonites") resume the closing words of verse 29 ("he passed on to the Ammonites") makes it clear that the making of the vow in the intervening two verses has been an irrelevance. Jephthah would have won anyway. God gave Jephthah victory just as he had already determined to do (v. 32). That outcome was assured from the moment the Spirit came upon him, and the Jephthah story could have concluded with the statement at the end of verse 33, "So the Ammonites were subdued before the people of Israel." But now it cannot finish there because things have been radically complicated by Jephthah's vow. Now the story cannot end until Jephthah returns home and faces the consequences of what he has done.

Verses 34–38 show his homecoming with extraordinary vividness and pathos. Verse 34 changes the point of view, so that we effectively see the events as they unfold through Jephthah's eyes: "And behold, his daughter came out to meet him with tambourines and dances. She was his only child; besides her he had neither son nor daughter." She comes out like Miriam who went out to celebrate Yahweh's victory at the Red Sea (Exodus 15:19–21) and like those who would later go out to celebrate David's victories (1 Samuel 18:6, 7). But unlike them she comes out alone, and it is her aloneness that is stressed: literally, "only she, alone; beside her he had neither son nor daughter." The words underline both the isolation of the child (she alone will be sacrificed) and the plight of the father (he has none but her). They are two, but each is utterly alone.

Of course, the girl does not realize her predicament at once. She must have sensed something was wrong from her father's stricken appearance, but only his words fully disclose it to her: "Alas, my daughter! You have brought me very low, and you have become the cause of great trouble to me. For I have opened my mouth to the LORD, and I cannot take back my vow" (v. 35). We feel for Jephthah, of course. This is his only child, and seeing her now he values her more, much more, than when he made his vow. But his words also reveal the crucial weakness in his character that has brought them both to this terrible moment. He calls her his daughter but offers her only reproach: "You have brought me very low . . . you have become the cause of great trouble to me" (v. 35). In other words, in the moment of their common tragedy Jephthah thinks only of himself. We can give Jephthah only our qualified sympathy.

It is otherwise with the daughter, however. When she speaks, she echoes her father's words. "My father, you have opened your mouth to the LORD" (v. 36). It's clear from what follows that she doesn't say these words in counter-recrimination, but as a way of grasping their significance, coming to terms with them, and steadying herself for a dignified response. What she says next shows that she has fully grasped the terrible logic of the situation: literally, "*Do to me* what has gone forth from your mouth, for Yahweh has *done for you* deliverance from your enemies" (v. 36).[14] She asks only for two months to bewail her virginity with her female friends (v. 37). That is where she will find what comfort she can. Her father has only one word for her: "Go" (v. 38). It is the last word he speaks in this scene.

At the end of the two months she returns to her father, her submission complete. The time has come, and there is no word from Heaven to stay Jephthah's hand.[15] So now, quickly and without judgment, the writer tells the deed. He refers to the vow directly, but even here there is reticence: not, "he offered her up as a burnt offering," but "[he] did with her according to the vow that he had made" (v. 39). The one, of course, implies the other, and given the wording of the vow itself (v. 31) we are clearly meant to understand that Jephthah literally sacrificed his daughter.[16] And with that this nameless girl might have disappeared as though she had never existed. It was her virginity she had wept over: "she had never known a man" (v. 39). That was what was most painful for her; not to die, but to die young, unfulfilled, with no child to remember her. But there *were* those who remembered, which may be why this terrible incident lived on in Israel's consciousness and eventually found its way into Holy Scripture. "The daughters of Israel went year after year to lament the daughter of Jephthah the Gileadite" (v. 40); and "it became a custom in Israel" (v. 39). The vow left Jephthah childless too, but no one wept for him as far as we know. He becomes more and more isolated as his story approaches its end. He, too, was remembered, but for different reasons.

"Jephtha the Gileadite" (12:1–7)

In this final part of the story Jephthah's domestic situation fades into the background as a new crisis erupts and demands his attention. Jephthah's leadership has been confirmed by his victory over the Ammonites, but not everyone is happy. Jephthah is from Gilead, east of the Jordan, but the Ephraimites are from Israel's heartland in Canaan proper. They were one of the two leading tribes of northern Israel[17] and are offended that Jephthah did not acknowledge their importance by involving them in his action against Ammon. And they let him know it in no uncertain terms: "Why did you cross over to fight against the Ammonites and did not call us to go with you? *We will burn your house over you with fire*" (v. 1). Gideon had had similar trouble with the Ephraimites, but his situation was different. He still had unfinished business with the Midianites and couldn't afford to have enemies behind him and in front of him as well; so he chose the path of conciliation (8:1–3). Jephthah has already dealt with the Ammonites and is not in any mood for compromise. Perhaps their reference to his "house" and "fire," whether intentionally or not, touches a particularly raw spot in him after the sacrifice of his daughter. At any rate Jephthah is aroused and determines to settle the Ephraimite question once and for all. He gathers "all the men of Gilead" and goes into battle again—this time against Ephraim—and defeats them, just as he had defeated the Ammonites (v. 4). Perhaps Jephthah had no alternative. The Ephraimites were spoiling for a fight and deserved what they got. Their threat to Jephthah was very violent and personal and was a challenge to his leadership that could not go unanswered. Under pressure Jephthah showed himself to be a strong leader.

However, there's another side to all this that becomes obvious when we compare it with Jephthah's dealings with the king of Ammon in 11:12–28. There he made a strong case for the rightness of his cause. He spoke for all Israel with the authority and dignity of a statesman. When the enemy refused to listen, Jephthah committed his cause to the Lord, the Judge, and when he went into battle the victory he won was God-given. What unfolds here in 12:1–7 could hardly be more different. Jephthah claims to be in the right, but on the face of it there is truth in what the Ephraimites say. There is no mention of him calling them back in 11:29, which may be understandable but hardly wise given the historical importance of Ephraim. He refers to the fact that the Lord gave him victory over the Ammonites (v. 3), but the purpose is purely to underline his own authority. There is no appeal to God, and the victory over the Ephraimites is not God-given; in fact, as far as we know God is not involved at all.

Most tellingly of all, in this final scene Jephthah identifies himself again and again as a Gileadite, and it is his solidarity with his own tribal group rather than his leadership of Israel as a whole that is paramount. Note especially verse 2: "*I and my people* had a great dispute with the Ammonites"; and verse 4, "Jephthah gathered *all the men of Gilead* and fought with Ephraim." Ephraim's hostility toward Jephthah had its roots in a much deeper and long-standing animosity between Ephraim and Gilead. This comes out very clearly in the taunt of verse 4: "You are fugitives of Ephraim, you Gileadites, in the midst of Ephraim and Manasseh." The Gileadites are nobodies—ex-Ephraimites, with no clear tribal identity or title to the lands they occupy. Whether or not this has any truth to it, it's plainly inflammatory and draws a predictable response from Jephthah and his followers. Full-scale war erupts again. This time it is the Ephraimites who are routed, and there is a particular vindictiveness in the way those trying to escape are hunted down. They are cut off at the fords of Jordan, identified by a password they cannot pronounce in the Gileadite way, and struck down there. The slaughter is prodigious (v. 6). So the taunts of the Ephraimites have been answered in full. It is they, not the Gileadites who have been scattered and made fugitives, and Jephthah has shown that he cannot be intimidated. But he has also shown that he is first and foremost a Gileadite. His leadership of the nation as a whole has been put beyond dispute only by a bloodbath in which Israelites have turned on Israelites. It is a fateful step toward the full-scale civil war that will tear Israel apart in chapters 19—21. The note that concludes the account of Jephthah's career in verse 7 nicely captures the two aspects of his character and rule that we have seen in this final passage: "*Jephthah judged Israel* six years. Then *Jephthah the Gileadite* died and was buried in his city in Gilead."

Jephthah and Us

What can we say about Jephthah, given all that this story has shown us about him? Like most Biblical characters he is a complex individual. As I have written elsewhere:

> Jephthah is a capable man—capable with words, capable in battle; he has a strong, decisive personality and is a leader of men. At his best he can exercise exemplary faith. But he has a background, a personal history, which helps us to understand his limitations even if we cannot condone them. He is insecure and self-centered. He can never fully engage with anyone's interests but his own. This is the hardness in the man and the reason he can never be truly great. It is to this insecurity and self-interest that his daughter is sacrificed; Jephthah cannot truly be a father. For the same reason he cannot be a Moses or a Joshua. "Jephthah the Gileadite, head and leader of all the inhabitants of Gilead," is as high as Jephthah can rise. He may judge Israel—even save it—but he can never really *care* about it as God does.[18]

Insecurity and self-interest are serious character flaws. All of us fallen human beings are afflicted with them to some extent. However, they can be exacerbated by experiences of rejection, as they were in Jephthah's case, and become extremely damaging in a leader. They do not absolutely disqualify a person from leadership. God did use Jephthah to save his people, and Jephthah *is* honored in Hebrews 11 for his faith and achievements. But he is also a warning to would-be leaders. Leadership of God's people is a terrible responsibility, with great potential for doing both good and harm. Those of us who are called to it need an acute sense of our own sinfulness and the need of God's sanctifying grace in our lives. We also need the humility to be able to acknowledge when we have damaged others by our poor judgment or by acting out of insecurity and selfishness rather than out of genuine love for those we lead. I was very touched recently when a great Christian leader in our city, in his farewell address, sought forgiveness from those he had hurt by his mistakes. It was hardly necessary; he had done much more good than harm, and all but a very few had already forgiven him for his wrongs. But his apology modeled for us qualities that are the marks of true greatness in the kingdom of God—an awareness of our sinfulness and the harm it can do, and a deep desire to be more like our Lord Jesus Christ in the way we treat those he has entrusted to our care (1 Peter 5:1–5).

Finally, what does the Jephthah story as a whole teach us about negotiation? Jephthah is skillful with words. He knows that the elders of Gilead have no genuine regard for him, but Jephthah uses negotiation to arrive at a deal with them that is good for himself and ultimately for Israel as a whole. He knows that the king of Ammon is set on war, but Jephthah uses negotiation to buy time, claim the moral high ground, enhance his credentials as a national leader, and present his case to Yahweh, the divine Judge. His great mistake at the climax of the story, though, is to "open his mouth to Yahweh" (11:35) *in the same way that he has opened his mouth to men.* That is, he tries to negotiate with God as he has negotiated with human beings, and in so doing overreaches his hand and brings disaster on himself and his daughter. He makes the fundamental error of thinking that God, the divine Judge, can be bribed, that salvation is an arrangement that can be negotiated by offering God incentives instead of casting ourselves utterly on his mercy. He fails to see that salvation is a gift. That is his fatal mistake, and from there he begins to lose his integrity, not just as a man of faith, but as a father and as a judge of Israel. At the end of the story he gives up negotiation altogether and uses words only as a pretext for slaughtering his fellow Israelites. In short, the story of Jephthah shows us two things about negotiation. It has a legitimate place in human affairs in a fallen world but has severe limitations; and in the hands of an insecure man like Jephthah it can end up doing more harm than good. More importantly, it shows us that negotiation is the antithesis of faith and has no place at all in our relationship with God.

There is a great difference between the kind of religion that arises from our own insecurity and desire to get God to meet our needs and that which is based on God's own revelation of himself. The former is a reflection of our own sinful natures; the latter is a gift of the God who made us and has reached out to us in Christ. The former conceives of our relationship with God in terms of negotiation: God gives us what we want from him in return for actions that please him; we get in proportion to what we give. True religion, on the other hand, understands that our relationship with God is based on his generosity and free grace. We bring nothing to the table. We have nothing to offer God that can make him love us more than he already does. Our true need is for his forgiveness and adoption as his children, and all that is necessary to have this need met is faith in God and what he has already done for us in Christ.

Religion that arises from our own fallen natures is essentially idola-trous. It dishonors God by denying his sovereignty and grace and making us little gods ourselves, co-negotiators and co-contributors to our own salvation. Such religion is not pleasing to God and, rather than securing salvation from him, exposes us to his righteous wrath. To try to add anything to faith in God's sovereign grace, as Jephthah did, is to lose the heart of true religion and bring disaster on ourselves (Romans 1:18–25; Isaiah 2:6–22). This aspect of the teaching of the Jephthah story is vitally important in a world where evangelicalism has become so broad and the teaching of Christian doctrine so weak that is has become difficult to distinguish between true and false gospels, and many perish for want of hearing the true one.[19]

17

Second Interlude:
Ibzan, Elon, and Abdon

JUDGES 12:8–15

MARATHONS HAVE CHANGED QUITE A LOT in recent times. Fifty years ago they were twenty-six-mile runs for specialist athletes who trained hard all year to reach their optimum fitness for the event. These days marathons are for everyone. High-quality, ultra-fit athletes still compete, and to win is still an achievement that can bring accolades in the sporting world, and financial rewards. The stars still receive a lion's share of the media attention. But a host of others participate too, runners who have no chance at all of being first across the line. Some run to raise money for charities of various kinds, some to help maintain their fitness and have the satisfaction of achieving a personal best. Others run just for the fun of it and to be part of an enjoyable community event. Many wear outfits designed for amusement rather than speed. The length can vary, and the start of the race is staged so that the slower, less serious runners do not get in the way of the major competitors. A modest amount of training is still recommended for health and safety reasons, but no one is turned away because of their size or shape or apparent level of unfitness. The onus is on the runners themselves not to endanger their health by overdoing it. Generally speaking, the runners can be divided into competitors and non-competitors, fundraisers and people just having a good time. More generally still, they can be divided into serious competitors and also-rans. The also-rans are not losers, even if they don't complete the whole course, because their object is not to win; it is just to participate and, for some, to help a good cause. Judges, too, has its also-rans.

Calling men like Ibzan, Elon, and Abdon also-rans implies that the period of the judges, too, can be thought of as a marathon. Certainly it was a long endurance trial that tested the mettle of those involved in it, especially Israel's leaders. There were definitely outstanding participants who did well and won acclaim, as shown by their inclusion in the roll call of Israel's heroes of faith in Hebrews 11. And there were also many others who did not win acclaim at all, some barely remembered and some forgotten entirely. We might call these the also-rans. But the also-rans in Judges are rather different, to say the least, from those in a modern marathon. There were no fund-raisers, of course, and given the harshness of the times also none who took part just for the fun of it. In fact, there were no voluntary participants at all. They were all drafted into this great endurance trial by birth and circumstances rather than choice. There were also other differences from a literal, modern marathon. What justifies the description of men like Ibzan, Elon, and Abdon as also-rans is simply their participation in a great test of strength and character and their relative lack of distinction compared with others. Whatever else can be said about them must be reserved until we have examined the sparse information we are given in 12:8–15. Then we will also be able to compare them with others we've already met who are in the same general class—Shamgar, Tola, and Jair.[1]

Ibzan the Networker (vv. 8–10)

With Ibzan we appear to have entered another of those peaceful interludes that brought relief from the general chaos of the judges period. Neither Ibzan himself nor the two judges who followed him are said to have saved Israel from an oppressor, probably because there was no need for this kind of deliverance.

The Bethlehem that was Ibzan's hometown is not to be confused with the more famous place of the same name in southern Israel.[2] Its exact location is unknown, but according to Joshua 19:15 it was a town of Zebulun, in what was later known as Galilee.[3] As far as the Old Testament is concerned, Ibzan's judgeship, and the fact that he was buried there, is its only claim to fame, and even that is not sufficiently remarkable to give it any real distinction. Only the most dedicated Bible reader would know that this Bethlehem even existed.

The basic facts of Ibzan's life are all given in sparse formulaic terms: he was from Bethlehem, judged Israel for seven years, and died and was buried in Bethlehem (vv. 8, 9b, 10). Apparently the only thing that distinguished him from others and was sufficiently unusual to be remembered was his success in arranging marriages for his extraordinary number of children: "he had thirty sons, and thirty daughters he gave in marriage outside his clan, and thirty daughters he brought in from outside for his sons" (v. 9a). This is so excessive as to be either grotesque or comical depending on your point of view. How many wives must he have had (and worn out) in fathering so many offspring? How did he get the mathematics of it all so perfect—thirty of each gender? And how did he have time for anything else in his seven years as judge but arranging marriages and weddings? It's hard to take Ibzan seriously. We have to be careful, though, not to let our own reactions as modern readers take over and perhaps skew our reading of the passage in inappropriate ways. After all, Psalm 127 says that having many children is a sign of God's favor: "Like arrows in the hand of a warrior are the children of one's youth. *Blessed is the man who fills his quiver with them!*" (Psalm 127:4, 5). The best clue to the significance we are meant to see in Ibzan's large family is the way this note about him comes immediately after the story of Jephthah and the foolish vow that robbed him of his *only* daughter. After Jephthah's emptiness comes Ibzan's fullness, and with that a restoration to covenant blessing. The themes of emptiness and fullness will surface again, as we will see, in the book of Ruth.

Close attention to the wording of verse 9, however, indicates there is another dimension to Ibzan's success in having children. It was not an end in itself, but something Ibzan used to advantage. He gave his thirty daughters in marriage to men "outside his clan" and brought in thirty daughters "from outside" as wives for his sons. But the phrase "his clan" in the ESV is an interpretive addition. All the text actually says is that he sent his daughters "outside" for marriage and got wives for his sons "from outside." Just how *far* "outside" these marriage arrangements extended is not clear, whether to other clans or tribes or even nations, although the latter is very unlikely given Ibzan's relatively low profile. The point is that Ibzan was a networker; he used marriages to establish relationships, not just between nuclear families, but between clans and most likely tribes. Again we must be careful about our instinctive reaction as modern readers from cultures very different from Ibzan's. Some of our concerns may be valid, of course; others may not. Our safest course is to listen carefully to the text in its context, especially its context in the book of Judges. We have heard of multiplying wives and children before (8:29–31), where it had negative connotations. Gideon sowed the seeds of division in his family and in Israel by fathering one of his children by a concubine and calling him Abimelech ("my father is king"). There is no suggestion that Ibzan's domestic affairs were tainted in this way. In 3:1–6 we were told how the Israelites of the judges period intermarried with

Canaanites and ended up worshiping their gods. But there's no indication that Ibzan did this either. As we have seen, the "outsiders" he married his sons and daughters to were almost certainly Israelites, not Canaanites. Furthermore, since this note about his domestic affairs is immediately followed by the statement that "he judged Israel," we are probably meant to see a connection between the kind of intermarrying Ibzan did and the manner in which he ruled Israel. And again the context is significant. Gideon created hostility and division by his marriage and parenting arrangements. Ibzan used the marriages of his children to bind Israel's clans and tribes together. Jephthah enforced unity by violence and the exercise of raw power. Ibzan promoted unity by a particular form of networking—creating linkages between clans and tribes through marriage.

Of course, Ibzan may not have been as high-minded as this implies. We simply don't know what was going on inside his head. Legitimate questions can be asked, too, about the wisdom or even legitimacy of what he did. The ideal established at creation was marriage as a "one man—one woman" affair, which, if adhered to, would necessarily limit the number of children and therefore the number of marriages that could be arranged for them (Genesis 2:18–25). The stories of the patriarchs illustrate the kinds of family problems that can arise from not adhering to this ideal. The Law of Moses stipulated that any future king of Israel, in particular, should not acquire many wives for himself, lest they "turn away your heart after their gods"—something that clearly happened to Solomon (1 Kings 11:1–4). It would probably be going too far, though, to condemn Ibzan on the basis of these cautionary notes sounded elsewhere in Scripture, since that does not appear to be what the author of Judges intended us to do. While Ibzan's domestic arrangements may not have been ideal, the implication of this note about him occurring where it does is that the marriage arrangements he made for his sons and daughters helped heal the wounds that Jephthah's divisive rule had caused and contributed positively to Ibzan's peaceful administration.

One concern that we naturally have as modern readers, though, does seem to be warranted by what follows in Judges, namely, the commodification of women for political purposes. Ibzan was a man of his times and may have seen nothing wrong with what he did, but the story of the use of the captured daughters of Shiloh to heal a breach in Israel in chapter 21 will expose the dark side of using marriage (and therefore women) for political purposes, however well-meant that may be. Perhaps, the most that we can safely say about Ibzan's conduct is that in the circumstances it probably did Israel more good than harm, at least in the short term. Ibzan was neither a hero or a villain as far as we know. What is certain is that he was relatively undistinguished. He was an also-ran.

Elon the Obscure (vv. 11, 12)

Like Ibzan, Elon was from Zebulun. In Elon's case, however, a particular point is made of his tribal identity; twice he is called "the Zebulunite" (vv. 11a, 12a). Elon seems to have been remembered as the quintessential Zebulunite, but why so is not clear. The two verses about Elon here in chapter 12 give us no data to work with; so we are left to surmise, as best we can, from the references to the Zebulunites elsewhere in Judges. The first reference to Zebulun, in chapter 1, is in the catalog of failures by the northern tribes to fulfill the mandate Joshua had given them: "Zebulun did not drive out the inhabitants of Kitron, or the inhabitants of Nahalol, so the Canaanites lived among them, but became subject to forced labor" (1:30). Note, it does not say they "*could* not" drive out the inhabitants of the territory that had been assigned to them, but they "*did* not." It was a failure of will rather than ability. They did eventually redeem the situation to some extent by achieving dominance over the Canaanites they had allowed to remain among them, but this was at best a compromise and does not speak well of Zebulun as a tribe from which we might expect sterling leadership to emerge.

Their record does improve, though, as the book progresses. In 4:6, 10 we are told that Zebulunites were among the ten thousand men who answered Barak's call to follow him into battle against Sisera. In the victory song of chapter 5 special mention is made of their leaders, "those who bear the commander's staff" (5:14, ESV footnote), and in 5:18 Zebulun in general is commended for the way its fighters acquitted themselves in battle: "Zebulun is a people who risked their lives to the death; Naphtali, too, on the heights of the field." Both Zebulun's leaders and those they led showed themselves to be brave men. And according to 6:35 they also answered Gideon's call to fight the Midianites.

So by the time we reach chapter 12 the negative comment about Zebulun in chapter 1 has faded into the background, and it is the positive connotations that predominate and color the description of Elon as "*the* Zebulunite" in verses 11, 12. The Zebulunites were men of honor who did not shrink back when duty called, and it's reasonable to assume that Elon, as leader of Zebulun and judge of Israel, embodied these same admirable qualities. In spite of this, however, no particular honorable or praiseworthy deeds are attributed to him. Either he didn't perform any or those he did do were not sufficiently notable to be remembered. It's no small thing, to be sure, to judge Israel for "ten years" (v. 11). Elon may have been a good man and an able administrator, but in contrast, say, to "Ehud . . . the Benjaminite" (3:15) or "Jephthah the Gileadite" (12:7) he left barely a trace of his existence on Israel's consciousness. He, too, was an also-ran.

Abdon the Ostentatious (vv. 13–15)

There's little new here. The same standard details are given for Abdon as for the previous two judges—his background, the length of time he judged Israel, his death, and the place where he was buried. We have slightly more information about Abdon than Elon, but again the details are sparse, and it's hard to know what to make of them. First, we are told that he was "the son of Hillel the Pirathonite" (v. 13) and that Pirathon (apparently his hometown) was "in the land of Ephraim, in the hill country of the Amalekites" (v. 15). So Abdon was from Ephraim, the same tribe as Deborah,[4] and we will have cause to reflect on this shortly. But the other details are obscure and virtually impenetrable. Hillel is otherwise unknown. Pirathon was later the home of one of David's mighty men (2 Samuel 23:30), but this gives us no grounds for thinking that Abdon himself was a warrior. Most puzzling of all is the reference to the Amalekites. All previous references to the Amalekites in Judges have been negative. They were ancient enemies of Israel and continued to be so in the judges period, participating with the Ammonites and others in raids on Israelite territory.[5] They used to live in the desert fringe of southern Canaan, but the present verse seems to refer to a time when they had gained a foothold in the central highlands, perhaps in the period of oppression during the time of Gideon.[6] They were almost certainly no longer there in Abdon's day, but they had left a trace of their presence in the place name, "the hill country of the Amalekites" (v. 15). However, this too is of no real help in assessing Abdon's character or achievements.

The one thing that has the potential to do this is the note about his family in verse 14: "He had forty sons and thirty grandsons, who rode on seventy donkeys." This reinforces the impression that Abdon lived in a peaceful interlude in Israel's tortured history in the judges period. Horses were for war,[7] donkeys for either work or (as here) for ceremony. In particular this note about Abdon is reminiscent of the similar one about Jair, who "had thirty sons who rode on thirty donkeys, and . . . had thirty cities" (10:4). Both Jair and Abdon were blessed with peace and plenty. They were also blessed with large families and liked to (quite literally) parade the fact. They were both flamboyant in their lifestyle. There is also some similarity to Ibzan, with his thirty sons and thirty daughters (v. 9). But in Abdon's case it is only sons who are mentioned and (in contrast to Jair) grandsons as well as sons.

Furthermore both his sons and grandsons, seventy of them in all, rode on donkeys (v. 14). In other words, he had more male progeny than either Jair or Ibzan and was more given to drawing attention to the fact. Furthermore, the mention of grandsons as well as sons opens Abdon's family toward the future in a more pronounced way than the notes about Jair and Ibzan do. Of all the so-called minor judges, Abdon is the most ostentatious, and the one who seems most intent on creating a family dynasty.

It is a tendency that began with Gideon, who had seventy sons and named one of them Abimelech, "my father is king." From then on judgeship was always on the verge of turning into kingship, with disastrous results. Abimelech took the hint his father had given him and grasped kingship directly, bringing ruin on himself and on Israel as a whole. But even when he fell, the secret desire to be more than a judge lived on in others, showing itself indirectly in the multiplication of wives and the promotion of sons. Even the godly Samuel erred by trying to perpetuate his rule through his own, unworthy sons (1 Samuel 8:1–3).

Seen in this light, Abdon's promotion of his sons and grandsons is part of a trajectory that leads eventually to the demand that the pretense of judgeship should be given up altogether and that Israel should go the whole way and appoint a king to rule them "like all the nations" (1 Samuel 8:5). Kingship would eventually come in God's time, but secret hankering after it through self-aggrandizement and the creation of pseudo-dynasties through the promotion of one's own sons and grandsons was not the right way to it. Abdon's progeny had no power to prevent Israel from sliding back into apostasy after his death or to save it from the Philistine oppression that followed. In the face of that harsh reality, Abdon's ostentation evaporated like the morning dew, and Israel was left leaderless and helpless until God himself raised up another judge to rescue them.

Valuing the Undistinguished

Ibzan, Elon, and Abdon were all also-rans. So were Tola and Jair (10:1–5). So was Shamgar, whose contribution is noted in a single verse (3:31). These are the so-called minor judges, and it's time to reflect on what their presence in Judges has to teach us.

First, also-rans are people. They have names, accomplishments (however modest), families, failings, larger social networks (clans, tribes) to which they belonged, people who remembered them, places where they lived, died, and were buried. They are not just extras or the masses or statistics or gap-fillers between major episodes. They are real human beings.

Second, also-rans are different from one another. Tola, Jair, Ibzan, Elon, and Abdon are all described in fairly formulaic terms; they fit within a certain mold. But Shamgar breaks the mold; the one verse that describes his career is completely different in both style and content. In one respect Shamgar and Tola belong together and are distinct from the other four. These two "save" Israel (3:31; 10:1); the others do not. But they save Israel differently. Shamgar saved it from an external threat, while Tola saved it from internal disintegration. And Tola both "saved" and "judged" (10:2), while Shamgar only "saved." Then again Jair, Tola, and Abdon all have very large families, but only Abdon is said to have had daughters as well and to have married them to men outside his clan or tribe. Jair and Abdon both have sons who ride on donkeys, but only Abdon had grandsons who did so as well. And so we could go on. They all come from different backgrounds and if they judge Israel at all do so for different periods of time. Of course, all we have to work with are the sparse details we have been given, but even these make it clear that these men are not just human beings—they are very distinct individuals.

Third, also-rans are not necessarily undistinguished. The six minor judges are all *relatively* undistinguished compared to people like Gideon, Barak, Samson, and Jephthah, who are named in Hebrews 11:32 and about whom we know so much more. However, all of them except Shamgar rose to national leadership, judging Israel for from seven to twenty-three years! This lifts them well above the rank of most men. They are all much more distinguished, say, than the host of unnamed individuals, such as the ten thousand men from Zebulun and Naphtali (4:6) who fought bravely in the battle against Sisera but were followers rather than leaders. And among the unnamed, too, some are more distinguished than others. For example, the woman of Thebez who killed Sisera with a millstone (9:53) and Jephthah's daughter whose memory is honored in annual lamentation (11:40) are more distinguished than the daughters of Shiloh, who were simply "snatch[ed]" for forced marriage to the survivors of Benjamin (21:16–21). Beyond these are the multitude of other unnamed men and women who lived, loved, struggled, and died in the judges period and are referred to simply as "the people of Israel" (1:1; 21:24). These too were children of Abraham, heirs of the promises made to him, and contributed in one way or another to the fortunes of Israel in this most troubled of times. The also-rans were the vast bulk of the people of God, none of them outstanding, but some more distinguished than others.

Finally, also-rans are just as capable of being noble or ignoble as anyone else. Shamgar and the woman of Thebez were resourceful and brave.

Gideon's three hundred were daring and loyal and served Israel well. So did Tola, in rescuing Israel from the chaos left by Abimelech. Ibzan's conduct was more questionable. Jair and Abdon were ostentatious and left Israel unprepared for the trouble they were about to face. Elon created barely a ripple on the surface of Israel's history and may have been mediocre; we simply don't know. The point is that also-rans as a class are not uniformly unimpressive or second-rate. Little people can be great too, and God can and does use such people to accomplish his purposes. Jesus' twelve disciples were not impressive by worldly standards, but we owe them an incalculable debt for not giving in to their doubts and fears, and fulfilling the mission Jesus entrusted to them. And the Apostle Paul reminds the Corinthians that most of them were also-rans when God chose them to be his:

> For consider your calling, brothers: not many of you were wise according to worldly standards, not many were powerful, not many were of noble birth. But God chose what is foolish in the world to shame the wise; God chose what is weak in the world to shame the strong; God chose what is low and despised in the world, even things that are not, to bring to nothing things that are, so that no human being might boast in the presence of God. (1 Corinthians 1:26–29)

In the marathon of life there are few stars and many runners. The same is true in the history of God's people in both the Old and New Testaments. Thank God for stars like Othniel, Deborah, Barak, and Gideon who encourage and inspire us by their example. But thank God, too, for also-rans like Ibzan, Elon, and Abdon who remind us, by simply being there with their modest achievements and all too human failures, that little people, too, have a contribution to make to the great sweep of God's saving purposes in the world that reaches its climax in Christ and flows on into our own day and age. Also-rans is what nearly all of us are! But praise God that we, too, have a noble calling and can be used to display his astonishing wisdom to a proud, incredulous world. May it be our joy to do so, with God's help, and to his glory.

18

Samson: The Savior No One Asked For

JUDGES 13:1–25

GIVEN THE HEAVY BLEND of passion, heroism, and tragedy it contains, it is not surprising that the Samson story has attracted the serious attention of great creative artists. No one can view *Samson and Delilah* (Rubens, 1577–1640) or *Samson Killing the Lion* (Léon Bonnet, 1833–1922) or hear Handel's impressive *Samson* oratorio (1740) or read John Milton's epic poem *Samson Agonistes* without being aware of both the creative power of the artists themselves and the greatness of the Biblical narrative that inspired such endeavors. Handel's oratorio was composed in the same year as his *Messiah*, and Milton's poem followed hard on *Paradise Lost*, and the treatment in both cases shows that they did not regard the Samson story as a piece of comic relief after the treatment of nobler themes. They took Samson seriously, and the author of Judges clearly means us to do the same. That is not to say that the story has no humor in it. The sight of Samson bursting out of Gaza at midnight, for example, like a crazed orangutan escaping from a zoo, taking the gates with him, is a moment to be relished—especially since the joke is on the Philistines.

But beneath all the surface chaos and mad careening here and there of the wild-man hero there is a steady building toward a predetermined end of profound theological significance. Samson is God's man, as Israel is his people, and neither he nor they can finally escape their destiny. Samson may be a testosterone-charged male behaving badly, but he is also much, much more. More space is devoted to him than to any other judge.[1] He alone has his birth and destiny announced in advance by a divine messenger, and in his story the whole central section of the book is brought to a resounding climax.

The Samson story as we have it in Judges has two main parts. First, in chapter 13 we have an account of the circumstances leading up to his birth. Then in the next three chapters we are given a fairly detailed account of his adult life, climaxing in his dramatic death at the end of chapter 16. Samson is an enigma, with such contrasting aspects to his role and character that it is impossible to do him justice in just one treatment. So we will consider him from two complementary perspectives—first as savior, focusing mainly on chapter 13, then as saint and sinner, focusing mainly on chapters 14—16.

The Dark Backdrop (vv. 1, 2)

And the people of Israel again did what was evil in the sight of the LORD,
so the LORD gave them into the hand of the Philistines for forty years. (v. 1)

Everything about that is bad—the "evil" (idolatry) that the Israelites did, the fact that they did it "again," the consequences of it (subjection to their enemies), and the length of time the consequences lasted ("forty years") (v. 1). All this had happened before, of course—many times. And every other time when Israel became desperate enough they had appealed to God to save them, and he had done so. But now they don't even cry out to him anymore. It's as though a kind of hopeless resignation has set in. They've accepted that this is how they are and will always be. Even the men of Judah, who were singled out for leadership in chapter 1, accept Philistine dominance as an established fact that it's futile to try to change (15:11). Israel as a nation has almost ceased to exist. It's terrible to find something that's evil so irresistible that you find yourself turning to it again and again, in spite of all that God has done to rescue you from it. It takes away your dignity, saps your strength, and leaves you hopeless. That's how Israel is at this point in Judges.

Then after showing us the big picture—the general situation—the camera zooms in on one man and his wife.

There was a certain man of Zorah, of the tribe of the Danites, whose name was Manoah. And his wife was barren and had no children. (v. 2)

This is the family Samson was born into, and as we can see it's a kind of microcosm of Israel as a whole. This is what the hopelessness of everything looked like at the personal level. Infertility is a tragic and sensitive problem, and those who struggle with it need our understanding and support. But there's no skirting around the issue or softening the terminology used about it here. The woman was "barren," sterile, childless, and she remained so. Manoah and his wife wanted to have children and had probably tried for years to fall pregnant, but they couldn't. The problem was intractable. So there was no future for this family, and they'd given up all hope that there could be. Just as Israel was helpless and hopeless, so were Manoah and his wife. But then something happened.

The Surprise Announcement (vv. 3–5)

And the angel of the LORD appeared to the woman and said to her, "Behold, you are barren and have not borne children, but you shall conceive and bear a son. Therefore be careful and drink no wine or strong drink, and eat nothing unclean, for behold, you shall conceive and bear a son. No razor shall come upon his head, for the child shall be a Nazirite to God from the womb, and he shall begin to save Israel from the hand of the Philistines." (vv. 3–5)

This is pure grace. Manoah and his wife weren't expecting it. They hadn't asked for it, as far as we know. They certainly hadn't earned it. It was just given. Samson is a gift of unmerited, surprising grace. But notice two other things about the baby they will have. First, he will be holy: he will be "a Nazirite" (v. 5). We will have more to say about this in the next chapter, but Nazirites were holy men; that's what the word means. So Samson's mother is not to get drunk or eat anything unclean because what she will carry in her womb will be something sacred. Second, Samson will be "a Nazirite *to God*," belonging to God, set apart as God's. This is going to be hard for Manoah and his wife. This boy will never be completely theirs, in fact not even *essentially* theirs. The woman will carry him; her husband will partner with her in nurturing him and raising him up to manhood. But a day will come when God will claim him, and they will have to let him go—not just to adulthood, but to God. He will be "a Nazirite *to God*"; that's the word that has been spoken over his life. But for the moment he is their baby-to-be, their boy: "you shall conceive and bear a son" (v. 5). The sterile woman will be barren no more.

What follows is this couple trying to get their minds around what has happened and respond to it appropriately. There's excitement here, there's confusion, and there's a comical side to the process of Manoah and his wife preparing to become parents. It's one of those man-woman, male-female things.

The Struggle to Understand (vv. 6–23)

Then the woman came and told her husband, "A man of God came to me, and his appearance was like the appearance of the angel of God, very awesome. I did not ask him where he was from, and he did not tell me his name, but he said to me, 'Behold, you shall conceive and bear a son. So then drink no wine or strong drink, and eat nothing unclean, for the child shall be a Nazirite to God from the womb to the day of his death.'"

Then Manoah prayed to the LORD and said, "O Lord, please let the man of God whom you sent come again to us and teach us what we are to do with the child who will be born." And God listened to the voice of Manoah, and the angel of God came again to the woman as she sat in the field. But Manoah her husband was not with her. So the woman ran quickly and told her husband, "Behold, the man who came to me the other day has appeared to me." And Manoah arose and went after his wife and came to the man and said to him, "Are you the man who spoke to this woman?" And he said, "I am." And Manoah said, "Now when your words come true, what is to be the child's manner of life, and what is his mission?" And the angel of the LORD said to Manoah, "Of all that I said to the woman let her be careful. She may not eat of anything that comes from the vine, neither let her drink wine or strong drink, or eat any unclean thing. All that I commanded her let her observe."

Manoah said to the angel of the LORD, "Please let us detain you and prepare a young goat for you." And the angel of the LORD said to Manoah, "If you detain me, I will not eat of your food. But if you prepare a burnt offering, then offer it to the LORD." (For Manoah did not know that he was the angel of the LORD.) And Manoah said to the angel of the LORD, "What is your name, so that, when your words come true, we may honor you?" And the angel of the LORD said to him, "Why do you ask my name, seeing it is wonderful?" So Manoah took the young goat with the grain offering, and offered it on the rock to the LORD, to the one who works wonders, and Manoah and his wife were watching. And when the flame went up toward heaven from the altar, the angel of the LORD went up in the flame of the altar. Now Manoah and his wife were watching, and they fell on their faces to the ground.

The angel of the LORD appeared no more to Manoah and to his wife. Then Manoah knew that he was the angel of the LORD. And Manoah said to his wife, "We shall surely die, for we have seen God." But his wife said to him, "If the LORD had meant to kill us, he would not have accepted a burnt offering and a grain offering at our hands, or shown us all these things, or now announced to us such things as these." (vv. 6–23)

Don't you love this? At one level it's so ordinary—a man and a woman speaking as men and women do—especially couples—when they're excited. But at the same time it's so totally extraordinary, because God has shown up and miracles are happening. And Manoah and his wife are trying to process it all by talking, talking, talking. But they don't quite get it or know *how* to talk about it or exactly what to do.

I especially sympathize with Manoah here. He's the head of the family.

He's supposed to be in charge. But he doesn't have a clue what's going on. Everything is going past him. In verse 8 he prays that the "man of God" will come again and tell them what they need to know to bring the boy up correctly. And the angel *does* come, but only to his wife again, while Manoah is not there (v. 9). So his wife runs to get him and brings him to meet the man (v. 10). He asks, "Are you the man who spoke to this woman?" "I am," he says (v. 11). Well that's a start, I guess. So Manoah presses on, saying in essence, "How are we to bring up the boy? What kind of life will he live? What is his mission?" (v. 12). The man replies in summary, "I've already told your wife" (vv. 13, 14). Now Manoah doesn't know *what* to do. So he says, "Would you like to stay for dinner?" (v. 15). "No," says the man, "but sacrifice a burnt offering to the LORD" (v. 16). By now Manoah is nearly out of his mind. "*Who are you?*" he blurts out. "What's your name?" (v. 17). "Why do you ask that?" the man says, "seeing it is wonderful" (v. 18)—which can mean either (a) "I'm not telling," or (b), "Even if I did tell you, you wouldn't understand," [2] or (c), "I am God, the wonder-working God of the exodus, 'awesome in glorious deeds, doing wonders.'"[3] Then, at the climax of this whole exchange, the One whose name is "wonderful" does a wonderful thing: as Manoah and his wife watch, he ascends in the flame of the altar fire (v. 20). And then, at last, when the man has gone, Manoah finally knows who he is (v. 21). And when he knows that, he also knows something else—he is going to die (v. 22)! Hadn't God said in the Law of Moses, "Man shall not see me and live"? (Exodus 33:20). Manoah's logic is sound as far as it goes, and his fear appears to be well founded. But he's wrong. His wife's logic is better:

> If the LORD had meant to kill us, he would not have accepted a burnt offering and a grain offering at our hands, or shown us all these things, or now announced to us such things as these. (v. 23)

In other words, "If the Lord meant to kill us, he wouldn't have said I was going to have a baby, would he?" Men, when you have an argument with your wife, just give in straightaway. It saves a lot of time and nervous energy, and she's probably right anyway! I joke, of course. But there's also something serious here that we men need to hear, especially Christian men. So much pain and so many mistakes could be avoided if only we learned, early in our marriages, to value the commonsense and spiritual insight of our godly wives. Manoah's wife was certainly right here. Whatever might normally be true, this was an exception. This appearing of God to a man and a woman meant life, not death. It was a gift of sheer, life-giving goodness.

Poor Manoah. He's been running backward and forward trying to look as though he's doing something. Always following his wife and never catching up to her. Trying to act like the head of the family, but always being sidelined. And what's the coded message in all of this? Just this: Manoah *can't* be in control, and neither can his wife. They've been caught up into something too big for them to control. The baby will never really be theirs to control. He will belong to God and will be moved by God to do what God wants him to do. And they will have to let him go. This is going to be very hard for this couple. Remember what Simeon later said to Mary when she brought her baby to him:

> Behold, this child is appointed for the fall and rising of many in Israel, and for a sign that is opposed (and a sword will pierce through your own soul also). (Luke 2:34, 35)

It would be hard for Mary to be the mother of Jesus. And it would be hard for Manoah's wife to be the mother of Samson, and Manoah would share her pain. But bearing that pain would be their contribution to something quite wonderful that God was going to do for his people.

The Dawn of Deliverance (v. 25)

Before we leave this part of the Samson story I want you to notice carefully one particular thing the woman has said. We were moving so quickly you may not have noticed it, but it's very, very important. In verse 7 she repeats what the angel has said to her, but with one difference. In verse 5 the angel said, "Behold, you shall conceive and bear a son. No razor shall come upon his head, for the child shall be a Nazirite to God from the womb, and he shall begin to save Israel from the hand of the Philistines." But when she reports this to her husband she says, "the child shall be a Nazirite to God from the womb *to the day of his death*." Isn't that remarkable? She seems to know, from the very beginning, that Samson's Naziriteship, his separation to God—the very purpose for which he was born—will be consummated in his death.

So the background of Judges 13 is dark. Israel's situation is desperate, and Samson's own death casts a long shadow before it. But the foreground is bright and full of promise. Look how the chapter ends:

And the woman bore a son and called his name Samson. And the young man grew, and the LORD blessed him. And the Spirit of the LORD began to stir him in Mahaneh-dan, between Zorah and Eshtaol (vv. 24, 25).

Into the dark world in which Manoah and his wife lived, light has come. God has broken through their barrenness and given them hope. A savior has been born. The Spirit of the Lord rests on him and begins to claim him for his life's work of delivering Israel. It's like the sun rising over the horizon and flooding the world with light and promise. A new day has begun to dawn.

The Significance of Samson

Everything about this chapter tells us that Samson is a very, very special person. He is holy, separated to God from the womb. His birth is announced beforehand by an angel. He is declared to be a savior—*God's* savior. Early in life he is claimed by the Spirit for his divine destiny. And if we read on we'll see that he is rejected by his own people, arrested and handed over to their enemies, tortured and made a spectacle by them, until at last his calling is consummated in his death. But in dying he destroys Dagon, the god of Israel's enemies. It's a theological victory, not just a material one. It was only a beginning, of course.[4] The Philistines didn't go away immediately. There were more battles to be fought and more dark days to live through. But those who knew about Samson could never believe, anymore, that the Philistines were all-powerful or that Dagon ruled the world. And eventually the work of delivering Israel from the Philistines that Samson began was completed by David (2 Samuel 5:17–21; 8:1).

But the story didn't end there either. Other enemies arose. Other gods claimed to be all-powerful. More dark days came, until eventually the angel of the LORD appeared to another childless woman and said:

And behold, you will conceive in your womb and bear a son, and you shall call his name Jesus. He will be great and will be called the Son of the Most High. And the Lord God will give to him the throne of his father David, and he will reign over the house of Jacob forever, and of his kingdom there will be no end. (Luke 1:31–33)

And to her bewildered husband the angel said, "You shall call his name Jesus, for he will save his people from their sins" (Matthew 1:21).

And the word spoken that day outlived the Roman Empire and still holds true today. So, brothers and sisters, when you feel that all is lost, when you want to be in control and can't be, when everything is going past you, remember this: a Child has been born, a Son has been given (Isaiah 9:6), and by his death he has overcome the god of this world. He has begun our salvation and will complete it on the last day (Philippians 1:6). And if you believe that—however dark your present situation may be, and however powerless and hopeless you may feel—you need never despair (2 Corinthians 4:16–18)!

19

Samson: Saint and Sinner

JUDGES 14:1—16:31

GIVEN HIS BEHAVIOR IN JUDGES 14—16, the fact that Samson is a sinner is incontrovertible. But to call him, in the same breath, a saint seems to violate the English language, destroy morality, and make nonsense of the book's theology. How can God's anger at Israel's evildoing in chapters 3—12 be squared with the view that the blatant sinner of chapters 14—16 is a saint? It seems to imply that the book is morally and theologically incoherent. Nor does there seem to be any support in Christian tradition for regarding Samson as a saint. There is Samson of Dol, a Welsh missionary monk and bishop who died in 565 AD and has long been venerated as a saint in Wales and Brittany.[1] There is also Saint Sampson[2] the Hospitable of Constantinople, who died in 530 BC and is renowned for his charitable works. He was revered as "the Father of the Poor," especially in Byzantine Christianity.[3] The Cathedral Church of Saint Sampson in St Petersburg is named after him.[4] And there may have been others, but none with any connection, except in name, with the Samson of the book of Judges.

However, a number of things should make us hesitate before dismissing the idea of Samson being a saint as unthinkable. The most obvious is the presentation of him as such a significant savior figure in chapter 13. This has led such giants as Augustine and Luther to take Samson as a type of Christ,[5] and who would question *his* sainthood? The second reason is the reference to Samson as an exemplar of faith in Hebrews 11:32, 33. The third is the designation of Samson as "a Nazirite to God" in 13:4, 5. We will have more to say about this shortly. But first let us assume that there may, after all, be some warrant for seeing Samson as both saint and sinner and see where that takes us in terms of our understanding of Judges 14—16.

Where it will lead us essentially is into the inner life of Samson. In the previous chapter, "Samson: The Savior No One Asked for," was viewed Samson from the outside, in terms of his function—what God accomplished through him. Now we will consider him from the inside, in terms of his own understanding of who he *was* and who he *wanted* to be. This will expose the struggle at the heart of Samson's life and enable us to see how directly and powerfully the story of Samson addresses our own inner struggles as fallible, sinful human beings caught up in God's great purpose.

We will begin with something that is said about Samson at a fateful moment toward the end of his life, because this, and what immediately follows it, will provide us with an ideal vantage point from which to understand all that has gone before.

Samson's Loving (16:4)

"After this he [Samson] loved a woman." That's not an unusual thing for a man to do, especially, we may think, this man. If we've read up to this point in Judges we'll be aware that this is the third woman in Samson's life, or at least the third woman we've been told about.

First there was the girl we read about in chapter 14. She was from Timnah, and she was a Philistine. That's all we know about her. We're not told her name; she's just "one of the daughters of the Philistines" (v. 2). They are all much the same to the author. But Samson saw her, wanted her, and demanded to have her. "Get her for me," he told his parents, "for she is right in my eyes" (v. 3). This is the language of lust and possession. It's the language of a man who thinks women exist for his pleasure and that he has a right to any of them he wants. And predictably this relationship does not bring happiness to either Samson or the young woman. The way it starts tells it all.

Next there's the prostitute in Gaza that we read about at the beginning of chapter 16. She doesn't have a name either. There were plenty of them in Gaza. She was just one of them. And again it's Samson's eyes that lead him: he "saw" a prostitute in Gaza and "went in to her" (v. 1). At least he doesn't demand what he wants this time; he digs into his pocket and pays for it. But that again sets the limit to what can be expected. It's a business relationship. She sells, he buys, and he leaves. It's over in a night.

But with the third woman it's different. For the first time the word "love" is used, and this time the woman has a name: "He *loved* a woman in the Valley of Sorek, *whose name was Delilah*" (v. 4). This time Samson demands nothing and buys nothing. He doesn't come with money in hand; all he brings is himself. He loves her, and that's all he wants—to love her and be loved in return. Here at last is the prospect of a lasting relationship— marriage, home, and family. Samson has sown his wild oats and is ready to settle down. He's come of age and is starting to be sensible.

Of course, Delilah is almost certainly a Philistine.[6] But so were the other two. Samson seems to have no stomach for fighting the Philistines. In fact he rather likes them, especially their women. He never wanted to fight them in the first place. His idea was to get along with them. They, not Samson, were the ones who started the trouble, and he fought back only when he was provoked. But now Samson is weary of it all. All he wants now is a quiet life with this woman he loves.

But what of Delilah? Does she love Samson? Well, no. Not much anyway. Certainly not as much as she loves eleven hundred pieces of silver from each Philistine lord who approaches her (v. 5). She's only in it for the adrenaline rush it gives her and the takings. Samson is an impressive man, and Delilah is flattered that he finds her so attractive. What woman wouldn't be? But it's no more than a thrill trip for her. Basically she's a flirt, and if she can make it pay, so much the better. Delilah is a harlot too. But unlike the harlot of Gaza, Delilah is devious. She's not what she appears to be, and Samson is completely taken in by her.

His Secret Desire (16:17)

Try to see it again from Samson's point of view. "Please tell me where your great strength lies," Delilah says (v. 6). The woman he loves wants no secrets between them. She wants him to make himself vulnerable to her, to tell her all his heart (v. 15). That's natural enough, isn't it? It's a reasonable price to pay for closeness, intimacy, a lasting relationship. But Samson hesitates, because he knows there's a lot at stake. So he stalls by trying to turn it into a game. He teases her by giving her false answers about the secret of his strength. But every time he says something he edges closer to revealing the truth. "Do this to me, do that," he says, "and I'll become just like anyone else. Go on, try it and see." And then at last he tells her the truth.

> And when she pressed him hard with her words day after day, and urged him, his soul was vexed to death. And he told her all his heart, and said to her, "A razor has never come upon my head, for I have been a Nazirite to God from my mother's womb. If my head is shaved, then my strength will leave me, and I shall become weak and be like any other man." (vv. 16, 17)

Delilah doesn't need to test the truth of this. With unerring intuition she knows that this time she has him and immediately summons the Philistines (v. 18).

Why does Samson tell her his secret? He must have known that she would shave him. He is virtually challenging her to do so. Why? The text gives us two reasons and suggests a third that I think is the key to the whole story. He told her because he loved her and because she wore him down with nagging, but also, and more profoundly, because he *wanted* to be "like any other man" (v. 17). His Naziriteship had become a burden to him, and he wanted to be released from it. He wanted the ordinary pleasures of an ordinary man—a woman to love, a family, a place to call home—an end to the battles he'd been fighting. Was he wrong to want such things? Yes, he was. Not that these things are wrong in themselves. They're every one of them good and desirable things that God gives to most people. But for Samson to want them as much as he did was to want release from the call of God upon his life. And he knew it: "I have been a Nazirite to God from my mother's womb" (v. 17).

This recalls the words spoken to Samson's mother before his birth: "the child shall be a Nazirite to God from the womb, and he shall begin to save Israel from the hand of the Philistines" (13:5). There is some doubt about precisely what Nazirites did. What is perfectly clear, though, is that they were not as other men. They had taken a vow that meant that they had laid aside, for a time, the ordinary affairs of life to devote themselves to the service of God. For the period of their vow they had to abstain from wine and other strong drink, they were not to touch a dead body or even go near one, and they were to let their hair grow long. No razor was to be used on their head. Their very appearance showed that they were not ordinary. And they were not allowed to cut their hair until the time of their separation to God was over, and then it was burnt as an offering to God. You can read all about it in Numbers 6.

Samson was a Nazirite, but with a difference. He hadn't taken the vow. The matter was settled before he was born. He was a Nazirite by *divine* decision. He had no choice about it. And the purpose of his separation to God was clear: to begin to deliver Israel from the Philistines. Only when that was accomplished would his Naziriteship be over. Not before. Furthermore, Samson was equipped to do what God had chosen him to do. The Spirit began to stir him in his youth (13:25). And that same Spirit continued to propel him toward his destiny. It was by that Spirit that he killed the lion (14:6) and slew the Philistines at Ashkelon (14:19) and again at Lehi (15:14, 15). Significant battles have already been fought and won. Samson is God's man. God's hand is upon him. He is not as other men.

But Samson has never really wanted what God wants for him. One by one he has discarded all the outward signs of his Naziriteship. He has drunk wine (14:10),[7] he has scraped honey from the carcass of a lion (14:8, 9), and he has handled the "fresh" (raw) jawbone of an ass (15:15). He has wined and dined with the Philistines and tried to intermarry with them instead of ridding Israel of their rule. What has been accomplished has been accomplished because he was driven to it by God, not because he went to it willingly. The only thing he has really enjoyed about his separation to God has been his extraordinary strength, and now even that has become a burden he wants to be rid of. He's tired of being a "holy" man. Now, alone with a woman he loves, he wants to be as other men, and deep down he always has. That's why he tells Delilah "all his heart" (16:17).

His Humiliation and Glory (16:18–30)

What happens when Samson opens his heart to Delilah? Well, he gets his wish—and the exact opposite. He becomes weak, like other men (v. 19). But this time the Philistines really *are* in the next room (vv. 18, 20). They seize Samson, gouge out his eyes, bind him, and take him down to Gaza, where he finally does what he was set apart to do in the first place. He pulls down the temple of Dagon and begins the deliverance of Israel (vv. 21, 23–30). And the key to all this is that marvelous line in verse 22: "But the hair of his head began to grow again after it had been shaved." Samson may want to be as other men, but God won't let him be so. There in that dank, miserable, degrading prison God reclaims his wayward child. Samson is God's servant at the end, as he was at the beginning. His death is glorious, in a fashion. But we are left wondering how much more glorious a servant of God he might have been if only he had embraced his calling instead of resisting it.

Samson and Us

The great English poet John Milton wrote a wonderful poem about Samson.[8] Toward the end he has Samson sitting, exhausted and dejected, outside the prison in Gaza, "his hair hung ridiculous about him," a great ruin of a man. A group of Israelites come to console him. When they first see him they are shocked and, like Job's friends, are silent for a time. When they do find words, they speak to themselves rather than to Samson, but what they say shows they have had a moment of profound insight. "O mirror of our fickle state" (line 164), they say. In other words, "That's us. When we look at Samson, we see ourselves." They are right, of course. And so is Milton. Samson's story is also the story of Israel. Israel was to be a holy nation, separated to

God for the purpose of revealing him to the world. But Israel could never be what it was called to be. It was always looking over its shoulder at the other nations and wishing it could be like them, worshiping their gods and adopting their ways. Of course, God *was* finally revealed to the world through Israel, but he had to take it down into the shame and horror of the exile first. Listen to God's lament over them in Isaiah 48:18:

> Oh that you had paid attention to my commandments!
>   Then your peace would have been like a river,
> and your righteousness like the waves of the sea.

Samson was a holy man; Israel was a holy nation. Samson went after other women; Israel went after other gods. In his extremity Samson called out to God to save him (16:28). In its extremity Israel too cried out to Yahweh, as we have seen again and again in Judges. Samson was finally handed over to his enemies and taken down to exile in Gaza. Israel was handed over to the Babylonians and taken away in exile to Babylon. Both outcomes were tragic, and both could have been avoided if other choices had been made.

Samson's story is Israel's story. But it is also our story, and his tragedy may be ours too if we resist God's call as he did. We too are holy people, or "saints" in the proper Biblical sense of that term (1 Corinthians 1:2; 6:1, 2; 14:33; Philippians 1:1; Colossians 1:2). In the words of the Apostle Peter we are "a chosen race, a royal priesthood, a *holy* nation, a people for his own possession, that [we] may proclaim the excellencies of him who called [us] out of darkness into his marvelous light" (1 Peter 2:9). Incredible though it may sound, it's God's intention to take the fight to the enemy through us, reveal his glory to the world through us, and expose its gods for the hollow shams they are. The question for us is, will we embrace that? Will we run with it and find our whole joy and reason for living in being what God has called us to be? Or will we be reluctant saints, as Samson was, always looking over our shoulder and wishing we could be as other people? Will we, too, be led by our eyes and the covetousness of our hearts? Will we serve God because we must or because we love him? And how will it be ten years from now, or twenty, when we've fought many battles and know there are still harder ones ahead? Will we want out, as Samson did? Or will the call of God to be his saints and servants still captivate our hearts, still fill us with a sense of wonder and privilege, and nerve us to continue as his faithful servants to the end?

The fact is, we are called to be saints. That is the word that has been spoken over us. It was settled by God's own decree, not just before we were born, but in eternity: "he chose us in [Christ] before the foundation of the world, that we should be *holy*" (Ephesians 1:4). It's not fundamentally our choice, but God's. And we're in this for life. There's no early discharge. It won't be over until we cross the finishing line and stand on the victory dais. And we are not in this alone. Many have gone before us, including Abraham, Moses, Joshua, Ruth, Deborah, Mary, Peter, John, Paul, and James, and since then a host of others—Augustine, Luther, Wesley, and the many pioneers and martyrs, both men and women, of the modern missionary movement. And above all, Jesus himself has gone before us, "the Holy One of God" (Mark 1:24; Luke 4:34), "the founder and perfecter of our faith, who for the joy that was set before him endured the cross, despising the shame, and is seated at the right hand of the throne of God" (Hebrews 12:2). It was not easy for Jesus to be a saint; nor will it be easy for us. And we cannot match the perfection of his unblemished obedience to God. But we can look to him, follow him, and find our joy, as he did, in what God has called us to be and do. God has chosen us to be saints. We are not as other people, and we will not in the end find true joy in wishing to be.

20

Religious Chaos:
Micah and His Idols

JUDGES 17:1—18:31

RELIGION IS NATURAL. It is an expression of something deep and intrinsic to our humanity. God has put an awareness of his existence in each human being. We all know instinctively that God is there and have a desire to connect with him, and religion is the cultural expression of this desire. That is why religion is universal and why the worldwide religious scene is so chaotic. There are as many sets of gods as there are cultures and almost as many individual gods as there are human beings, because religion is human beings reaching out to the God they are aware of but do not know.

The existence of religion as a human, cultural phenomenon is understandable and inevitable. But not all religion is as good as it should be, and some religion is not good at all. Indeed, according to the Apostle Paul, God has revealed enough of himself in creation to make idolatry, in particular, inexcusable.

> For what can be known about God is plain to [human beings], because God has shown it to them. For his invisible attributes, namely, his eternal power and divine nature, have been clearly perceived, ever since the creation of the world, in the things that have been made. So they are without excuse. For although they knew God, they did not honor him as God or give thanks to him, but they became futile in their thinking, and their foolish hearts were darkened. Claiming to be wise, they became fools, and exchanged the glory of the immortal God for images resembling mortal man and birds and animals and creeping things. (Romans 1:19–23)

Idolatry is wrong because it misrepresents God. God, the maker of all things, is not like anything that human beings create. And even if people think that these things of their own making are only *aids* to the worship of God, they nearly always end up turning into gods themselves and being venerated as such. It's also wrong (and this is harder for us to understand and, perhaps, accept) because it is a form of rebellion against God. "Although they knew God, they did not honor him as God or give thanks to him" (Romans 1:21). Instead of being an expression of thanks to God and humble submission to him, idolatry nearly always becomes a means of trying to manipulate him to either ward off evil or get what we want from him. It dishonors God by making him less than he is and distorting our true relationship with him. The story of Micah in Judges 17—18 is about idolatry and what it does to those who get involved in it.

Something Completely Different

In chapter 17 we enter a quite different part of the book of Judges. The central section of the book has been about a series of external threats to Israel's security and the leaders God raised up to deal with them. In chapter 17 the focus shifts to the internal state of the nation and the religious and moral decay that was weakening it from within. We have already had glimpses of this in the preceding chapters in the refrain that "Israel did [or again did] what was evil in the sight of the LORD" (2:11) and in the religious and moral failings of some of the judges themselves. But here in chapter 17 the focus shifts entirely to what was happening at the local level and in the lives of ordinary people. And the picture is not a pretty one; in fact it is one of chaos—religious chaos in chapters 17 and 18 and moral chaos in chapters 19—21. This closing part of the book shows us a society that has lost its way and is on the verge of complete collapse.

We begin with a man and his mother who seem to have no idea of what being Israelites is supposed to look like.

Making Up Your Own Religion (17:1–6)

The opening scene unfolds in "the hill country of Ephraim" (v. 1). We have been there several times before in Judges. The mighty Joshua was buried there in 2:9; Ehud sounded his trumpet there in 3:27; Deborah held court there in 4:5; and Gideon sent messengers there to call the men of Ephraim to arms against the Midianites (7:24). Now, though, all that's happening there is a squalid little pact between Micah and his mother to set up an idol-shrine

(vv. 2–5). The details are not entirely clear,[1] but the basic sequence of events is as follows: eleven hundred pieces of silver are stolen from Micah's mother. She pronounces a curse on the thief, not knowing it is her son. Micah hears his mother's curse and tells her that he took the money but will return it to her. On hearing this, his mother (greatly relieved) blesses him in the name of the Lord. Micah returns the money as he said he would, whereupon his mother dedicates it to the Lord to be made into an idol[2] for him. She then takes two hundred of the eleven hundred silver pieces and gives them to the silversmith, who uses them to make the idol, and gives the finished product to Micah, who has a shrine in or near his house.[3] He makes some household gods and an ephod[4] and puts them in the shrine as well. Job done!

On one level this is a good news story. A thief owns up to his wrongdoing. Stolen money is returned. A mother and son are reconciled. A curse is turned into a blessing. A gift is given and received. The plans of both mother and son succeed. But at the same time everything is absurdly irregular. A woman consecrates money to *the Lord* and has an *idol* made with it! A man whose name is Micah ("who is like Yahweh?") manufactures household gods (v. 5)! Someone who (as we will soon see) knows that only Levites should be priests makes his own son a priest (v. 5). And of the eleven hundred silver pieces that Micah gave back to his mother, what happened to the nine hundred that were *not* used for making the idol (v. 4)? The whole scene is farcical, and the tragedy of it all is that neither Micah nor his mother give any indication of knowing that what they are doing is wrong. It is a scene of complete religious confusion. Why? Verse 6 gives us the answer: unbridled individualism. "In those days there was no king in Israel. *Everyone did what was right in his own eyes.*" This will become a refrain that will run right through the closing five chapters of Judges.[5] Already in this opening scene of chapter 17 we are beginning to see the kind of situation that develops when there is no center to hold a society together and no generally accepted standard to which its members adhere. In that situation the only possible kind of religion is idolatry—religion that is self-made and self-serving and therefore essentially the worship of oneself.

Applying a Veneer of Orthodoxy (17:7–13)

This scene opens with a young Levite leaving his home at Bethlehem in Judah, seeking a better situation for himself. In due course he comes to Micah's house (vv. 7, 8). This is apparently not a prearranged visit, since it is "as he journeyed" (v. 8) that he comes there, most likely seeking accommodation for the night. But when Micah finds out that his visitor is a Levite

(v. 9), his interest is aroused, and he loses no time in making the young man an offer he can't refuse: "Stay with me, and be to me a father and a priest, and I will give you ten pieces of silver a year and a suit of clothes and your living" (v. 10). The Levite can't believe his good luck and accepts the offer at once (v. 11). Micah ordains him forthwith, and he moves in and takes up his duties (v. 12). It is all very businesslike. Everything seems straightforward and above board. The interests of the parties happily coincide, and they have arrived at an arrangement that suits them both—a win-win-situation. It's a commonsense arrangement. Things appear to have taken a turn for the better at Micah's shrine. A closer look, though, shows that everything is just as irregular here as in the preceding scene: it just has an *appearance* of normality.

First, the Levite's situation and behavior are both abnormal. According to Joshua 21 the Levites had been allocated cities to live in, with adjacent pastureland for their livestock (Joshua 21:2). The family of Aaron were to serve as priests, and the rest of the Levites were to assist them (Numbers 8:5–22 [esp. vv. 19, 22]). In addition to the income from their pasturelands, they were supported by the tithes of their fellow Israelites (Numbers 18:21). So why was this Levite seeking employment? And why has he (and presumably his parents) been living in Bethlehem? It was not a Levitical city; nor is there any indication that the young Levite was heading for one. The Levite cannot necessarily be blamed for his situation; it was probably an accident of birth rather than his own fault. However, this willingness to accept Micah's offer shows that he either had no idea what *was* normal or had no regard for it. In other words, his situation and behavior are at the very least symptomatic of the general disorder of the times.

So are Micah's actions here, just as they were in the previous scene. But they are less excusable than those of the Levite. In spite of the impression of total confusion created by Micah's previous actions, he shows here that he is at least aware of a traditional connection between the Levites and priesthood. But by what authority does he personally "ordain" one to that role (v. 12)? And what has happened to his son, whom he had already installed in that position back in verse 5? Has that son been replaced or demoted or simply gone missing, like the nine hundred pieces of silver that went missing in verses 1–4? No one seems to care, least of all Micah and his new employee, who settle into a new father-son relationship of their own making (v. 11). The reality is that nothing has changed in Micah's shrine except the officiating priest. The homemade ephod is still there, and the household gods, and the image his mother has given him. The appointment of a Levite may, on the surface, be a move toward orthodoxy, but in reality it is nothing of the kind. In fact it has only increased the scandalous nature of Micah's shrine by bringing someone who should have been devoted to the service of Yahweh alone into connection with the worship of idols. And to cap it all off, verse 13 closes the scene by taking us below the surface and showing us *why* Micah has acted as he has: "*Now I know that the* LORD *will prosper me,*" he says, "because I have a Levite as priest."

Judges 17 is full of religious words, objects, activities, and persons, but none of it has been governed by respect for God's Law or a desire to honor him as an end in itself. Rather this has all been about people using religion to serve their own interests—a mother to indulge her son, a Levite to secure a better life for himself, and Micah to achieve prosperity by adding a veneer of orthodoxy to his idolatrous shrine. He may be confident of success, but in fact he is standing on the brink of a precipice. His personal fortunes, which have risen steadily though the opening two scenes, are about to suffer a sudden reversal. From now on nothing will go right for him. Idolatry is still idolatry, even if God's name is invoked and a Levite is employed to give it an appearance of respectability. And it is not the way to real prosperity. On the contrary, it is the way to tragic loss.

Losing Everything (18:1–26)

Micah's downfall is triggered by a situation that at first sight has nothing to do with him. Chapter 1 of Judges has already alerted us to the fact that the tribe of Dan had trouble securing the territory that had been allotted to it. Its land bordered on the coastal plain in the south, where the local Canaanite population was firmly entrenched and had proved impossible to dislodge. Eventually they drove the Danites back from the coast into a much more limited holding in the hills (Judges 1:34), and the subsequent arrival of the Philistines made their tenure even there more and more precarious.[6] Eventually, as the opening verses of chapter 18 tells us, they decided to send out spies to try to find somewhere else for them to live. Like the wandering Levite of the previous scene, the spies headed north and came, as he had done, to the house of Micah and stayed there for the night (vv. 1, 2). Finding the Levite in residence as the priest in charge of Micah's shrine, they decide to ask him to inquire of God on their behalf whether or not their journey will be successful. The Levite is only too glad to oblige; this is now his bread and butter, and although we are not told so, the Danites probably paid him for his services.[7] The response he gives them must have been music to their ears: "Go in peace. The journey on which you go is under the eye of the LORD" (v. 6). The last part of this sentence may mean nothing more than that the Lord sees all that the Danites are doing, but preceded here by "Go in peace" it must mean more than this—namely, that the Lord views their journey favorably and will give them success. It echoes Micah's confident assertion at the end of the previous chapter: "Now I know that the LORD will prosper me, because I have a Levite as priest" (17:13). This Levite is a good person to know! And this time events seem to confirm rather than undermine the confidence that is expressed. The spies continue their journey and discover just what they are looking for—Laish, a city in the far north of Palestine that is isolated, defenseless, beautifully situated, and ripe for conquest (v. 7). God has blessed their journey just as the Levite said he would! The excited spies hurry back home and share the good news with their fellow Danites and urge them to go and seize Laish at once: "God has given it into your hands" (v. 10). However, chapter 17 has given us ample reason not to share too readily the enthusiasm of the characters in this story. There will be losers[8] here as well as winners. Micah himself has already fallen into the background, and unbeknown to him the exchange that has recently taken place between his Levite and the Danites will soon bring about his own complete undoing.

For the Danites, though, everything looks promising, and they can hardly wait to cash in on their good fortune. They immediately dispatch a force of six hundred armed men to retrace the spies' steps back to Laish and claim what they believe God has given them (vv. 11–13). On the second day, as they approach the area where Micah's house is situated, the wily spies hint that it might pay the Danites well to drop in there as it contains something that would nicely complement the prize that awaits them further north (v. 14). The armed men are quick on the uptake and do as the spies suggest. They approach Micah's house. Somewhat surprisingly, it is the Levite rather than Micah himself who apparently hears them coming and goes out to meet them. They allay any concerns he may have had by greeting him warmly (v. 15), but then wait outside with him—ready to use force if necessary—while the spies go in and raid Micah's shrine, bringing out its entire contents (vv. 16, 17). Seeing, too late, what has happened, the Levite challenges them to explain their actions (v. 18). Their immediate response is to tell him to be quiet (v. 19a). This is probably to avoid attracting the attention of his master (Micah has still not appeared and is apparently unaware of what is taking place). But finally the full intent of what the spies had in mind is revealed: they don't just want Micah's idols, they want his priest as well! They urge the Levite to break with his current employer entirely: "Come with *us* and be to *us* a father and a priest. Is it better for you to be priest to the house of one man, or to be priest to a tribe and clan in Israel?" (v. 19b).

Employment as "a father and a priest" is what Micah had offered the Levite back in 17:10. Now the spies use the same phrase to outbid him by offering the Levite far more—not just father and priest to one man's household but to an entire tribe! The Danites have played their cards well. They present the Levite with a fait accompli; there is simply no more shrine for him to serve at in Micah's house, and the deal they offer him is one that a man of this Levite's character cannot refuse. He shows his acceptance by taking the idols from the five men who have just stolen them and goes along with the Danites (literally, "moves into the midst" of them), committing himself totally to their service and trusting them to protect him from whatever consequences may follow for his act of betrayal. In reality, though, he has nothing to fear, for there is nothing that Micah can do.

When Micah finally discovers what has happened, he hastily gathers a small force and goes in pursuit of the Danites (v. 22). When they catch up Micah succeeds in getting their attention by "shout[ing]" to them (v. 23). But from then on he has no success at all. The Danites have been expecting him, and from the moment they turn to respond it's clear that Micah is powerless. Micah and his men are outnumbered, and the Danites are in no mood to make any concessions. Their opening question, "What is the matter with you?" (v. 23) is effectively a taunt rather than a genuine query, calculated to enrage Micah rather than draw him into any meaningful engagement with them. They doubtless listen to his response with amused satisfaction, for there is nothing dignified about it. Literally Micah protests, "My gods that I made for myself—you have taken! And the priest! And you have gone away! What do I have left? How can you say to me, 'What is the matter with you?'" (v. 24).[9]

The broken syntax and the contents are both expressive of Micah's agitated state. It is the speech of a man who is so beside himself with anger that all he can do is blurt out accusations. But to no avail. He had made his own religion and prided himself on having a Levite for his priest. But his gods and priest have both failed him, and the confidence he had placed in them has been exposed for the folly it is. His life has revolved around these things, and without them he is nothing. His question, "What have I left?" is an admission of this painful reality. He has been completely undone. All he can do is turn and go back to his empty house and his empty life (v. 26). God will not bless idolatry.

Micah's Legacy (18:27–31)

Micah has been sidelined and pushed into the background. But sadly, the story of his idols goes on. Worse things follow from Micah's idolatry than his personal loss. The Danites continue on to Laish, conquer it, rename it Dan, and "set up the carved image for themselves" (v. 30). In other words, Micah's idolatrous shrine has an afterlife, as the Danites had said it would— it expands into a shrine for a whole tribe. The Levite expands, too, from a nameless priest at a local shrine at the end of chapter 17 to "Jonathan the son of Gershom, son of Moses," whose descendants served at the shrine in Dan for more than 450 years (18:30).[10] Micah may have lost out, but for the Levite, idolatry *does* seem to have paid off. At what cost, however? The shrine the Danites created in Laish/Dan in the time of the judges turned out to be the precursor to the infamous sanctuary that Jeroboam later established there when the northern tribes broke away and formed a separate kingdom after the time of David and Solomon (1 Kings 12, esp. vv. 25–30). Micah's idol was replaced by a golden calf that Jeroboam made, and "this thing became a sin" because the Israelites went there to prostrate themselves to it (1 Kings 12:30) and continued to do so despite the warnings of the prophets until the northern kingdom was destroyed by the Assyrians and its population taken into captivity.[11] So Micah's legacy was an idolatry that infected the whole nation and eventually led to its destruction. It produced, in the end, no winners at all, only losers.

Two particular comments near the end of chapter 18 underline what a travesty Micah's legacy was of all that Israel was supposed to be. The first we have already noted in passing. It is the identification of Micah's Levite in verse 30 as "Jonathan the son of Gershom, son of Moses." Gershom was the literal son of Moses by Zipporah according to Exodus 2:22, and the Levite may have been his literal grandson. More probably his genealogy has been compressed, and he was born one or two generations later.[12] What is clear, though—and shocking—is that this Levite was a direct descendant of *Moses*, the great lawgiver of Israel!

This revelation of the ancestry of Micah's Levite comes as a complete surprise, and has almost certainly been withheld until now precisely to achieve this effect. The Levite's bad character has been too clearly established by this point for the revelation that he is a descendant of Moses to redeem him. Indeed, it does exactly the opposite. Here is the crowning scandal of the Danites' idolatrous shrine: it brought dishonor even on the revered name of Moses![13]

The second and final damning reflection on Micah's legacy is in the last verse of the chapter: "So [the Danites] set up Micah's carved image that he made, as long as the house of God was at Shiloh" (v. 31). Shiloh, like Micah's house, lay in the central hill country of Ephraim. It was there that the tabernacle was first erected after Israel's arrival in Canaan and there that the land was divided up among the various tribes (Joshua 18:1, 8–10; 19:51). The ark of the covenant was there, reminding Israel of their obligation to keep God's Law (Exodus 25:16; Deuteronomy 10:1–5). But at the same time Micah created for himself an idol-shrine in his own house, and later the Danites used the contents of that shrine to establish their own idolatrous shrine in Laish/Dan and continued to worship there "as long as the house of God was at Shiloh." In other words, Micah's house of "gods" (17:5) was the complete antithesis of Shiloh's house of "God." It epitomized Israel's flagrant disregard of its covenant obligations and was the perfect symbol of the religious chaos that characterized the judges' period and continued to plague northern Israel throughout its history.

The Way of the World

Idolatry is the way of the world—a state of affairs in which people pursue their own interests. "The God who made the world and everything in it" (Acts 17:24) is either explicitly rejected or paid only lip service, and people's lives revolve around other things. These other things may be literal idols or things that have effectively become idols because they have taken the place in their lives that only God should have.

Idolatry is typical of the pagan world. But the story of Micah and his idols is not about pagans—it's about Israelites. It's about idolatry in the life of the people of God, those for whom it was least excusable. They not only had the revelation of God in creation, as the heathen did, but also his revelation in their own history and in the Law he had given them. His Law was close at hand. The name Yahweh was on their lips (Judges 17:2, 3, 13; 18:6), and an annual festival to Yahweh was held at Shiloh (Judges 21:19). But the combined pull of the surrounding culture and their own sinful desire to make everything, including religion, a means of gain made the drift toward idolatry irresistible. And in the end they became so self-deluded that doing "what was right in [their] own eyes" (17:6) seemed not only excusable, but natural and good.

What remedy is there for such perversion? The hint that our text gives us is a king—"in those days there was no king in Israel" (17:6)—and that was the problem, or at least part of it. A king was needed to sort out the chaos and impose some sort of order again on Israel's religious life. And in due course such a king appeared—David, who established Jerusalem as the place God had chosen for Israel to worship and centralized worship there where his royal authority could guarantee its proper observance (2 Samuel

6). And Solomon completed the process by building the magnificent temple to Yahweh that David had planned (1 Kings 5—8). No such solution should have been needed, of course. God was already Israel's king, and the way out of idolatry was always open to his people if only they would recognize *his* authority and return to a proper observance of *his* law. And the provision of a merely human king could not guarantee this would happen—at least not permanently, as the sad end of Solomon's life showed only too clearly (1 Kings 11). Something more was needed—something that would go to the root of the problem and provide a genuinely new start.

That solution came with the incarnation of God, the divine King, in Christ, the great Son of David. Here at last was the one *true* image of God (Hebrews 1:3), the complete answer to our fallenness, and a meeting place between God and man that could never be corrupted. Here, surely, is the end of all idolatry and the way out of the chaos that we have created by our addiction to it. Yes, indeed, but also no—or at least not yet. There is nothing deficient in Christ himself or in what he has accomplished for us. Forgiveness is ours, the Spirit has come, we are new creatures in Christ. Things are not as they were. But neither are they yet as they *will* be. This side of Heaven we are still sinners and still susceptible to the tug of the fallen world around us. As Wordsworth famously put it, "the world is too much with us,"[14] dulling our sensibilities and luring us away from an undivided loyalty to Christ. That world, though, with its chaos of worldviews and bewildering array of false gods, is passing away (1 Corinthians 7:31; 1 John 2:8, 17), and the coming day of judgment will expose idolatry, in all its forms, for the folly that it is (Isaiah 2:20–22). No wonder then, that the Apostle John ended his first letter—so full of loving concern for those in his care—by saying, "Little children, keep yourselves from idols."[15]

21

Moral Chaos: The Levite and His Concubine

JUDGES 19:1—21:25

IT'S SURELY NO ACCIDENT but part of the wise design of the author that a story about idolatry is followed so closely by a story about immorality. Only the God who made the world and everything in it, including ourselves, has the absolute right to tell us how to live our lives. He who brought order out of *physical* chaos by separating light from darkness (Genesis 1:3–5) also gave order to the *moral* universe by separating right from wrong (Genesis 2:15–17). The creator of the world is also its lawgiver and judge. Once we displace him from his rightful place in our lives and allow other things to take his place, we cut ourselves adrift from the only thing that can give moral stability to our lives. There is then no truth, just "*my* truth" and "*your* truth." Nor is there any right or wrong (only what *seems* right or wrong to me), and no common authority we can appeal to when our personal judgments or preferences differ. Without God we are afloat on the shifting currents of relativism. Everyone "[does] what [is] right in his own eyes"—the effective refrain of Judges 17 to 21—and the result is moral chaos (Judges 17:6; 21:25; cf. 18:1; 19:1). Idolatry and immorality are bedfellows; where you have one, you also, sooner or later, have the other.

The last five chapters of Judges are about a decaying society in which all the institutions that should give stability to life are failing because of the character of those who operate them. It is the story of a nation collapsing in on itself because it has lost its anchorage in God and no longer knows how to deal with the chaos it has unleashed by its own folly. And tragically that nation is Israel. It is like post-Christian Europe or Australia or the United

States or any number of other nations that once, at least nominally, acknowledged their Christian heritage and sought to be true to it, but no longer do so. Or like a Christian denomination that was birthed in the fires of revival, but is now enfeebled by false teaching and false living. The only doctrine still preached is tolerance, but the church is torn with dissent and cannot heal itself because it has no means of accurately diagnosing its sickness. The last part of Judges is not pleasant reading, especially chapters 19—21, but if we read carefully we will find that even here God is present and therefore there is hope.

Marriage Breakdown (19:1, 2)

In those days, when there was no king in Israel, a certain Levite was sojourning in the remote parts of the hill country of Ephraim, who took to himself a concubine from Bethlehem in Judah. And his concubine was unfaithful to him, and she went away from him to her father's house at Bethlehem in Judah, and was there some four months.

This story opens in a way that links it with the previous one. The absence of a king in chapters 17, 18 was associated with chaos—everyone doing "what was right in his own eyes" (17:6). So the echo of that here ("no king in Israel," v. 1) leads us to expect that the chaos will continue. The only question is, what form will it take this time? At first it seems that it will be more of the same, because again we have an apparently unemployed Levite living temporarily somewhere (cf. 17:7). In other words, the generally disordered state of Israel's religious life continues. The Levite is even staying in "the hill country of Ephraim" (v. 1) and therefore not far from Micah's house. Will he perhaps replace the Levite who used to work there? But this Levite is less ambitious than the previous one. All he aspires to, as far as we know, is a quiet life with a woman of his choice. Unfortunately, he seems to have no more idea about how to go about this than Micah's Levite did about religion: he "took to himself a concubine" (v. 1).

The expression "took to himself" is unexceptional. It may not sit well with modern sensibilities about male-female relationships, but it was normal language for betrothal in Old Testament times (Genesis 24:3; cf. Genesis 28:1; Leviticus 21:13; Jeremiah 16:2). Whether or not the Levite regarded this woman more as his property than his partner remains to be seen. But why is there no talk of love here,[1] and why take her as his concubine rather than as his wife? In the last (and only) other passage in which the word "concubine" occurs in Judges it spelled trouble,[2] and as we are about to see, the same will turn out to be the case here.

The relationship did not last; in fact the way verse 2 follows verse 1 without interruption or explanation suggests it was very short-lived indeed: "And his concubine was unfaithful to him, and she went away from him." Literally, she "played the harlot against him," but the ESV is probably right to use the more moderate term "was unfaithful" because as far as we know the concubine did not leave her husband for other men but went straight home to her father and stayed there. Her only motive, it seems, was to escape a situation she found intolerable. In other words, her harlotry was metaphorical rather than literal, and her behavior reflects more badly on her husband than on herself. She "played the harlot" because, rightly or wrongly, she felt she had no alternative. Sadly, it is not uncommon for women to find themselves in that situation, especially in a society that has lost its way morally and where marriage no longer functions as it should. Marriage breakdown, especially when it becomes endemic, is a symptom of a decaying society. The present passage is about only one such relationship breakdown. But it, too, is indicative of a more general problem.

Pseudo-Reconciliation (19:3–9)

> Then her husband arose and went after her, to speak kindly to her and bring her back. (v. 3a)

The previous scene has raised some questions about the Levite's character. The way this one opens, however, seems to indicate that he has some redeeming features. After "four months" (v. 2)—long enough to reflect on what has happened and perhaps accept his own at least partial responsibility for it—the Levite sets out for Bethlehem to get his estranged concubine back. Samson, we recall, had done the same thing in similar circumstances (15:1). There is no reference to a gift here as there was with Samson, who brought his wife a young goat, but the reference to a "servant and couple of donkeys" (v. 3b) is an indication of serious intent. This is no casual affair, but a mission planned and undertaken with care. And the fact that he goes to "speak kindly" to his concubine (literally, "speak to her heart") shows that the Levite intends to win her back with gentle persuasion rather than simply demanding that she return and that her father hand her over to him. The way he is greeted on arrival, too, suggests that both the concubine and her father are eager for reconciliation rather than confrontation. She brings him "into her father's house," and her father comes forward "with joy to meet him" (v. 3). All this is very promising. Alas, though, as so often in this part of Judges, things deteriorate as the scene progresses.

The girl's father seems almost too eager to cultivate a positive relationship with the Levite. He entertains him lavishly for four nights and most of five days, plying him constantly with wine and food and urging him repeatedly to stay longer (vv. 4–9). There is no offer of employment here as there was with the Levite in the previous story, but given the confused environment of the times a family connection with a Levite may have had some superstitious value and may have been regarded as socially advantageous. What seems to be strangely lacking, though, is any interest in the host's daughter or any attempt to mediate between her and this man who has come to seek reconciliation with her. In fact, even the Levite himself seems to have forgotten the purpose of his visit. The socializing is all between the two men. The Levite's concubine has receded into the background and is not even mentioned. At no point does the Levite request time alone with her as Samson did when he visited his estranged wife in 15:1, and he never "speak[s] kindly" to her as we were told he would do back in verse 3. She is completely ignored! Only after the Levite has at last insisted on leaving and has begun his journey home are we told, in verse 10, that "his concubine was with him." But how has this come about? Has some kind of deal been done between the two men? Has there been a reconciliation of sorts and she has agreed to go with him willingly? Or has he simply "taken" her, as by right? We don't know. What is clear, though, is that this scene has left us with a strong sense of the concubine's vulnerability and a lot of unanswered questions about the moral character of her husband. Sadly, the next episode in this story is going to confirm our worst fears.

Rape (19:10–30)

The return journey gets off to a bad start. Because they don't set off until the afternoon, the travelers arrive opposite Jebus, just six miles (ten kilometers) north of Bethlehem, as the day is drawing to a close, and they already need to think about finding lodgings for the night. Jebus was later conquered by David and renamed Jerusalem, but at this time it was still a Canaanite city. So rather than stay with foreigners, they press on to Gibeah, a Benjaminite town, and arrive just as the sun is setting (vv. 10–14). Unfortunately, they do not receive the kind of welcome they expect: they go in and sit down in the open square of the city, "for no one took them into his house" (v. 15). It's not a good beginning to their stay there. After some embarrassed waiting, though, things look up. An old man from Ephraim, a temporary resident in Gibeah, does take pity on them and invites them in (vv. 16–21). He is welcoming and generous, and they seem set for a pleasant evening with him. But it is not to be.

As they are beginning to enjoy their supper there is a beating on the door, with loud shouting, and a nightmare scenario begins to unfold, similar in many ways to the terrible night in Sodom described in Genesis 19. A crazed mob of low-life males—"worthless fellows"—have seen the visitors arrive and demand that "the man" (the Levite) be brought out so that they can "know" him (have sex with him, v. 22).[3] It's uncertain whether the motive is to humiliate the old man who has done what the rest of the townspeople refused to do, or xenophobia (the Levite and his host are both non-Benjaminites), or straightforward, out-of-control lust. But the fact that they ask specifically for "the man" makes it clear that what they intend is homosexual rape.

The old man of the house is shocked. But his response is even *more* shocking and shows that he is just as perverted as those outside his door. In order to protect his male guest he offers his own virgin daughter and the Levite's concubine as substitutes.

> And the man, the master of the house, went out to them and said to them, "No, my brothers, do not act so wickedly; since this man has come into my house, do not do this vile thing. Behold, here are my virgin daughter and his concubine. Let me bring them out now. Violate them and do with them what seems good to you, but against this man do not do this outrageous thing." (vv. 23, 24)

Everything is twisted here—the man's misunderstanding of his responsibilities as a host, his use the of the terms "wickedly," "vile," "violate," "outrageous," and "good" in a way that subverts their real moral value, his sexism (women are disposable, men are not), and his appalling blindness to his responsibility as a father. Furthermore, a special edge is given to the awfulness of it all by his reference to his daughter as a "virgin," recalling the terrible plight of Jephthah's virgin daughter back in chapter 11, "weeping for [her] virginity" (11:37).

Paradoxically, however, the old man's daughter appears to have been saved at the last moment by an even more reprehensible act by the Levite, who seizes his concubine and makes her "go out to them" (v. 25), and from then on all attention is focused on her. The men outside seem to forget both their original demand for "the man" (v. 22) and the host's offer of two women and satisfy their lust by abusing the poor concubine "all night until the morning" (v. 25). When they finally let her go, she staggers back to the door of the house and falls there (v. 26). She has no strength to open the door or even cry out.

Then when we think that things can't get any worse, they do. Inside the Levite gets up (he has apparently had a good night's sleep) and prepares to go on his way (v. 27). When he opens the door, there is his concubine, lying "with her hands on the threshold" (v. 27) as if in silent entreaty. But the Levite is utterly unmoved. "Get up," he tells her, "let us be going" (v. 28). No answer. So he puts her on his donkey and goes home. Is she unconscious or perhaps even dead? And if so, why doesn't he just leave her there, since he obviously cares nothing for her? By this point she has been emptied of everything—her virginity, her dignity, her personhood (she is just an object), and probably life itself. The Levite's relationship with her is now defined purely in terms of ownership. She is still his property, and he takes her home because he apparently still has some use for her. Unfortunately, we are about to see what "use" that is.

Horror (19:29, 30)

> He took a knife, and taking hold of his concubine he divided her, limb by limb, into twelve pieces. (v. 29a)

When he gets home the Levite calmly takes a knife, grabs his concubine, cuts her up into "twelve pieces"—one for each tribe—and sends them to all parts of Israel. This is the final, ultimate violation of the concubine's personhood. She is denied even the dignity of burial. And a special horror is added by the lingering doubt about whether she was already dead or merely unconscious when the dismemberment took place. In any case the Levite would not care; he had no further use for her as a person—only as an object to inspire horror and bend others to his will. It is the most appalling abuse of a woman in Biblical literature and perhaps in any literature. But it has exactly the effect the Levite intended.

> And all who saw it said, "Such a thing has never happened or been seen from the day that the people of Israel came up out of the land of Egypt until this day; consider it, take counsel, and speak." (v. 30)

Wherever the grizzly remains of the concubine go, they evoke the same horrified response: an unspeakably terrible crime has been committed, and something must be done. This at least indicates that some residual sense of right and wrong remains in Israel's consciousness, and therefore the possibility of something good happening. But even this is going to be perverted, because the Levite (who now stands unmasked as totally reprobate) has not yet finished his dastardly work. He will corrupt the process of justice by misrepresenting the situation and release a tsunami of horror that will all but destroy Israel itself.

Manipulation (20:1–7)

Representatives of all the tribes except Benjamin gather at Mizpah, near Gibeah,[4] to decide what action to take. It's an impressive gathering, including four hundred thousand armed men.[5] This Levite is no deliverer raised up by Yahweh, but the tribes have clearly taken his action as a call to war[6] and ironically, have responded in far greater numbers than for any of the judges in the previous chapters. It gives the Levite a large platform to stand on and a huge audience to play to, which is probably just what he wanted. Having said that, it's hard to get inside the head of a man like this and know for sure what his motives are. His actions are one indication, but his words are the most revealing.

> And the people of Israel said, "Tell us, how did this evil happen?" And the Levite, the husband of the woman who was murdered, answered and said, "I came to Gibeah that belongs to Benjamin, I and my concubine, to spend the night. And the leaders of Gibeah rose against me and surrounded the house against me by night. They meant to kill me, and they violated my concubine, and she is dead. So I took hold of my concubine and cut her in pieces and sent her throughout all the country of the inheritance of Israel, for they have committed abomination and outrage in Israel. Behold, you people of Israel, all of you, give your advice and counsel here." (vv. 3–7)

In his warped mind the Levite has convinced himself that he himself is the principal victim. He wants revenge on the people of Gibeah and intends to use his fellow-Israelites to get it. So he gives a carefully tailored version of events. The facts are not grossly distorted, but he gives a quite different impression of what happened than the author did in chapter 19. In the author's account it was a bunch of hooligans ("worthless fellows," v. 22) who committed the crime; in the Levite's version it was "the *leaders* of Gibeah" (v. 5). The author said they wanted to "know" (have sex with) the Levite; he says "they meant to *kill* me" (v. 5). The author said that the Levite "seized" his concubine and "made her go out" to them (v. 25); he says only that "they violated my concubine" (v. 5). The author left it unclear whether it was the mob who killed the concubine by raping her or the Levite himself who did it by dismembering her. He says, by implication, that it was the rapists who killed her (v. 5). In short, he portrays himself entirely as the aggrieved party and lays the blame for the "abomination and outrage" that has taken place entirely at the feet of the leading men of Gibeah (v. 6). He has taken the high moral ground, but it is all pretense, and entirely for his own ends. The Levite is no truth-teller, but a truth-manipulator, and here it is Israel as a whole that is being manipulated by his deception. His appeal to the assembly to "give your advice and counsel" (v. 7) is effectively a call for them to take sides with him against the men of Gibeah and to take vengeance on them on his behalf. However, given the manipulation that has taken place, the action that follows will be compromised from the start. It will fall short of complete justice because it will be based only on half-truths. The corruption of justice is a terrible thing, and that is what the Levite—for all his assumed moral outrage—is guilty of here. The result is going to be horrendous.

Bloodbath (20:8–48)

What erupts from the assembly the Levite convened is civil war on a scale never before seen in Israel. The Israelites who have heard the Levite's account of what happened demand that the people of Gibeah hand over the culprits to be punished (vv. 8–13a). When the men of Gibeah refuse to do so and instead come out to do battle with them, the Israelites respond by mustering a massive fighting force of their own (vv. 13b–17). But before the battle is joined, something is done that seems to offer hope.

> The people of Israel arose and went up to Bethel and inquired of God, "Who shall go up first for us to fight against the people of Benjamin?" And the Lord said, "Judah shall go up first." (v. 18)

This is the first of three inquiries the Israelites will make of God (vv. 18, 23, 28). These inquiries and God's responses to them are very significant because they show us what is happening in the minds of the Israelites and between them and the Lord as the war unfolds.

The first inquiry shows that the Israelites are confident about the rightness and eventual outcome of their cause. They are already committed to the war, and God's approval is assumed. So they ask a purely procedural matter: *How* is the campaign to be conducted? Who will lead the others into battle? And the answer is that Judah will do so (v. 18), as seems fitting since the ravished concubine was from Judah (19:1). But there are some unsettling things about this first inquiry and the reply that is given. It is the same question Israel asked at the very beginning of the book and receives a similar response (1:1, 2). But there Israel was united; here they are divided. There they were fighting Canaanites; here they are fighting one another. There they were acting on orders they had been given by Joshua; here they are acting under the influence of the devious Levite. And most significantly, there they were promised victory; here they are not. In 1:2 the reply was, "Judah shall go up; *behold, I have given the land into his hand.*" Here it is simply, "Judah shall go up first" (v. 18), and what follows is a terrible *rout* in which twenty-two thousand die, and the defeated Israelites are left weeping before the Lord (vv. 19–23a).

The Israelites are shattered. So they go to God again before taking the matter further. "Shall we again draw near to fight against our brothers, the people of Benjamin?" (v. 23b). The phrase "our brothers" is new and suggests the Israelites are beginning to doubt the rightness of their cause. Perhaps they are even hoping that God will tell them to desist. But it is not to be. This time the reply is even shorter, and again there is no promise of victory; just "Go up against them" (v. 23b). The Israelites must have been very confused and troubled at this point. "What is God doing? What will happen if we just repeat what we did yesterday?" But God has left them no option, and to their credit they obey him. The Levite's baleful influence is beginning to wane, so much so that he features no more in the story, which gives hope that some good may yet come of all the pain. But not yet. The Israelites are defeated again, and another eighteen thousand of their men lie dead on the battlefield (v. 25).

Now they are desperate.

> Then all the people of Israel, the whole army, went up and came to Bethel and wept. They sat there before the Lord and fasted that day until evening, and offered burnt offerings and peace offerings before the Lord. And the people of Israel inquired of the Lord . . . "Shall we go out once more to battle against our brothers, the people of Benjamin, or shall we cease?" (vv. 26–28a)

These are broken people. They are at an end of themselves. They want release—an end to their torment and healing of their wounds that only God can give them. It's like 2:1–5 all over again—Israel at Bethel, offering sacrifices and weeping before the Lord. But there it was clear what had gone wrong: they had broken God's covenant and disobeyed what he had told them to do, and the angel of the Lord appeared to explain it all to them. Here the reason is still hidden from them. Haven't they done their best to right a terrible wrong? How were they to know that the Levite had misled them? Perhaps if they had consulted the Lord at the beginning rather than at the end things might have been different, but it is too late for that now. Their only option is to go forward, hoping that God will eventually have mercy on them and that all may finally become clear. And at last they are assured that the nightmare will soon be over: "And the Lord said, 'Go up, *for tomorrow I will give them into your hand*'" (v. 28b). Here at last is the word they have been longing for. Just one more battle, one more painful struggle, and victory will be theirs.

Energized by what they have just heard, the Israelites attack Gibeah for a third time. But this time they don't just do what they did before; they go about it in a much more creative, strategic way. They first set an ambush (v. 29a), then feign a full-frontal assault, only to retreat when the Benjaminites come out to engage them, drawing them away from the city, leaving it defenseless. When those who had been set in ambush come out and cut off any possibility of the Benjaminites fleeing back into the city, the Israelites turn on them and begin attacking them. The Benjaminites are weakened by having to fight on two fronts now, and when the tide begins to turn against them they have nowhere to go. They stand and fight, but when they see that Gibeah is going up in flames behind them they know their situation is hopeless. They break ranks and begin to flee, with the Israelites in hot and merciless pursuit (vv. 29b–42). The slaughter continues all day, until only six hundred Benjaminites are left hiding in "the Rock of Rimmon," a site with hundreds of small caves about six miles (nine kilometers) northeast of Gibeah itself (v. 47).[7] With light fading, the Israelites decide they have better things to do than try to flush them out. They leave them there for now, turn back, and go on a rampage, killing every remaining Benjaminite they can find and setting all their towns on fire. Even their animals are not spared. By the time they are done, twenty-five thousand Benjaminites are dead (vv. 43–48).

So justice has finally been done—or has it? There are huge, perplexing moral issues here. The concubine's death has been avenged. Retribution has been visited on the rapists and on those who protected them. But at what cost? More than fifty thousand fighting men have died, plus all the civilians—men, women, and children—who have been caught up in the conflict. Can this be justice? And in particular, what of the wholesale destruction of the rest of Benjamin's towns that was carried out after the battle proper? Is this justifiable action or unjustifiable overreaction? Can a bloodbath like this ever be right? Is this the restoration of moral order or a travesty of all that Israel was called to be and do? More importantly, what are we to make of *God's* involvement in all of this? Why did he prolong the carnage by sending the Israelites into battle twice without success? And does the fact that he did finally give them victory mean that he approves of their actions? Finally, what has become of the Levite whose misrepresentation of what happened set the whole chain of events in motion? There's no indication that his deception was ever unmasked. So where is he? Alive? Dead? Hiding in

Rimmon Rock? Will he ever be made to pay for what *he* has done? One thing is certain: Israel has turned on itself, and a huge rift has been made in the fabric of its national life. And there is still unfinished business. What is to be done with the six hundred men still in hiding? They are all that's left of the tribe of Benjamin. Can Israel ever recover from this and become the united twelve-tribe nation it once was? The moral outrage committed in Gibeah has had terrible consequences. We have entered a very dark place, where Israel seems to have been given over[8] to the full consequences of "everyone [doing] what was right in his own eyes" (17:6).

Blaming God (21:1–7)

With the frenzy of battle over and their blood beginning to cool, the Israelites become conscious at last of the full import of what they have done. The tribe of Benjamin has been brought to the brink of extinction. And to make matters worse, now (too late) they remember an oath they had sworn at Mizpah: "No one of us shall give his daughter in marriage to Benjamin" (v. 1). So the six hundred remaining men still in hiding are either doomed to die childless (all their women and children have been slaughtered) or to marry foreigners. In either case the tribe of Benjamin will cease to exist. It is perhaps strange that the rest of Israel should care about this, given the orgy of destruction in which they have just engaged. But the fact is that things often look very different after a battle than they do in the midst of it, and kinship was fundamental to the whole way ancient societies like Israel were structured and who they understood themselves to be. The Israelites have almost destroyed themselves, and they know it. They want to fix the damage, to heal themselves if possible. But how?

Their first attempt to deal with the situation is to go to God again.

> And the people came to Bethel and sat there till evening before God, and they lifted up their voices and wept bitterly. And they said, "O Lord, the God of Israel, why has this happened in Israel, that today there should be one tribe lacking in Israel?" (vv. 2, 3)

On the face of it, this is good. It seems to show genuine sorrow and a desire to hear whatever God may have to say about the situation. But in reality it falls well short of this. There is no admission of responsibility on Israel's part or appeal for God's help. In this case the question "Why?" is more like an accusation: "God, why have you allowed, or even caused, this terrible situation to come about? Didn't you order us to keep going when we wanted to stop?

Didn't you send us into battle against Benjamin again and again? Isn't *that* the reason why we are in this terrible mess? Why, God, have *you* done this to us?" It's an understandable question, and not without some justification. God *has* punished the Benjaminites severely and has made all Israel suffer in the process,[9] because what happened in Gibeah is symptomatic of a moral malaise that is not confined to that tribe alone. The problem, though, is the failure or refusal of the questioners to recognize their own responsibility for the particular situation they are in now. The real reasons why there are no wives for the remaining Benjaminites are, first, because the Israelites themselves have slaughtered them all—not in the battle itself, but in the orgy of destruction that followed it, in which all the towns of Benjamin and all the people in them were destroyed (20:48); and second, because of their oath (also without warrant) not to give any of *their* daughters in marriage to Benjamin (21:1). It is they, not God, who are to blame, and the attempt to deny it will only make matters worse. Blaming God for trouble we have brought on ourselves is an age-old strategy. But it never works because God cannot be fooled. If healing is to happen at all it must begin with us taking responsibility for our own actions. God can see right through the implied blame-shifting of the Israelites here and is unmoved by their tears. They get no answer from him.

Making Others Pay (21:5–23)

Concluding that they have been left to their own devices the Israelites cast about desperately for a solution and at this point conveniently remember *another* "oath" they had sworn at Mizpah—to put to death any who had not come to the assembly (v. 5). The Benjaminites had not come, of course, and had already been dealt with. But what of others? Were there other parts of the federation that had not sent any representatives?

The People of Jabesh-gilead (vv. 8–15)

A review is conducted, and it is discovered that "no one had come to the camp from Jabesh-gilead" (v. 8),[10] and immediately a force of twelve thousand men is sent to serve justice on them (v. 10). But of course, this has actually nothing to do with justice. It's just a ruse to solve the problem at hand in a way that has a *show* of legitimacy. And again the violence is extreme. All the people of the city are slaughtered, including women and children, except "young virgins who had not known a man by lying with him," who were seized by the raiders and carried back to their base in Shiloh (vv. 11, 12). The one slightly mitigating element of this whole horrible episode is the word "compassion" in verse 6: "the people of Israel had *compassion* for Benjamin their brother," which is why they did what they did. But as we have seen, they themselves were the real cause of the problem they were trying to solve. They were making others pay for their own wrongdoing. The decision to victimize the people of Jabesh-gilead smacks much more of expediency than justice, and of compassion horribly distorted by the lack of any sound moral basis. And in spite of all the additional carnage involved, it did not achieve what it was supposed to do. Only four hundred virgins were found, two hundred short of the six hundred they needed (vv. 12–15). So the chaos continued.

The Daughters of Shiloh (vv. 16–23)

After some more fruitless wrestling with the issue (vv. 16–18), the leaders hit on a plan[11] that might hold the key to finally solving their problem. They remember that there is an annual "feast of the LORD" (v. 19) (religious festival) nearby at Shiloh[12] and that as part of the celebrations the "daughters of Shiloh" (the local girls) come out to dance in the vineyards (v. 21a). So they tell the two hundred Benjaminite men still needing a wife to go and hide until the right moment, then seize a girl each and carry them off (v. 21b)!

Now we really have hit rock bottom. *Everything* is wrong here. The festival itself is not easily identifiable as any of the three great annual festivals (the Passover, the Feast of Weeks, and the Feast of Tabernacles; Deuteronomy 16:1–17; cf. Exodus 23:14–17; 34:18–23; Numbers 28:26) prescribed in the Law of Moses, none of which involved girls dancing in the vineyards! The association with the grape harvest suggests it may, at best, have been a semi-pagan, corrupt version of the Feast of Tabernacles.[13] The festival itself is a manifestation of what is at the heart of the moral malaise that has overtaken the whole nation: the Lord is paid lip service, but people do as they please. In that situation the foundations of morality have been destroyed. Worse, an assumed obligation to *obey* God (and thereby honor him) has been used here as a pretext for doing evil—first by slaughtering the people of Jabesh-gilead and then by abducting (effectively stealing) the young women of Shiloh. The justification for both has been oaths sworn to the Lord in Mizpah (vv. 1, 5). Here is a dishonoring of God's name that is almost beyond belief. And at a purely human level, the most shocking aspect of what happens here in this final ploy to solve a problem caused by all the moral chaos is the total objectification and abuse of women. What started with the rape of the concubine in Gibeah has led to the abduction (and effective rape) of four hundred virgins in Jabesh-gilead, and ended with the seizure of two hundred more in Shiloh. To make matters even worse (is it possible?), the perpetrators of the crime, even before they commit it, have worked out a justification that will absolve everyone involved from guilt.

> And when their fathers or their brothers come to complain to us, we will say to them, "Grant them graciously to us, because we did not take for each man of them his wife in battle, neither did you give them to them, else you would now be guilty." (v. 22)

So there you have it. Women have been abducted, protest has been stifled, and no one has done anything wrong because all has been done out of compassion for Benjamin and in fulfillment of solemn oaths taken before the Lord! But the truth is that Israel's leaders have forced others to do what they themselves had sworn not to do (give their daughters as wives to Benjaminites) and papered it all over with sophistry. They have solved their problem, but in such a way as to overturn all canons of truth and morality. They have created a world in which right is wrong and wrong is right and landed the nation in complete moral bankruptcy. And the book of Judges is almost finished. Is this the way it is to end, though, in complete moral and spiritual darkness? Not quite. There are a few sentences left, and they contain some glimmers of hope.

Unexpected Hope (21:23b–25)

> Then they went and *returned* to their *inheritance* and *rebuilt* the towns and *lived* in them. And the people of Israel departed from there at that time, every man to his *tribe* and *family*, and they went out from there every man to his *inheritance*. (vv. 23b, 24)

Amazingly, after all the chaos and the apparent death-dive that Israel has been on in these closing chapters, there is not oblivion here but return, rebuilding, living in towns, and community (tribes and families)— the recovery of something approaching normality. How can this be? It is not what Israel deserves, and certainly not something they have achieved. Their actions have been flawed from the start, and even when they have tried to make things better they have made them worse. The key lies in the word "inheritance": "Then they went and returned to their *inheritance* . . . they went out from there every man to his *inheritance*" (vv. 23, 24). "Inheritance" speaks of connection with the past and the possibility of a future. More specifically it speaks here of God—of his promises and his faithfulness to them. God's promise to give Israel the land of Canaan as their inheritance arcs right across the Pentateuch from Genesis to Deuteronomy and on into the book of Joshua (Numbers 26:53, 54, 56; 33:54; 34:2; 36:2; Deuteronomy 4:21, 38; 15:4; Joshua 11:23; 24:2). After his successful military campaigns, Joshua "gave [the land] *for an inheritance to Israel according to their tribal allotments*" (Joshua 11:23), and his way of describing what had happened was this: "Not one word of all the good *promises* that the LORD had made to the house of Israel had failed; all came to pass" (Joshua 21:45). The book of Joshua ended, after Joshua had dismissed the people, with "every man [going] to his inheritance" (Joshua 24:28). The fact that after all that has happened the book of Judges ends in the same way is nothing short of miraculous. What it tells us is that God has not abandoned his wayward people, and therefore there is hope. The promise of an inheritance still stands.

Even the last verse, with its reminder of the problem that was nearly Israel's undoing, contains a thread of hope: "*In those days* there was no king in Israel. Everyone did what was right in his own eyes" (v. 25). These are the words of someone who looks *back* to dark days that have now passed. Under God Israel *did* have a future. After the Levite and his concubine and the civil war of chapters 20 and 21 came Boaz and Ruth, Hannah and Samuel, Saul, David, and Solomon—and eventually One greater than Solomon who established a new covenant, a greater inheritance, and a hope of which Israel could only dream. Later writers could even look back to the period of the judges as a time when some had exemplary faith (Hebrews 11:32–33)! It's hard to find anyone like that in the closing chapters of Judges, but they did exist; the book of Ruth will show us some. But before we leave the book of Judges itself, there are some final reflections to be made on the terrible story we have just read.

Reflections

First, the story of the Levite and his concubine shows us the kind of society we finally get when "everyone [does] what [is] right in his own eyes" (21:25). It is not a community of glorious freedom, and certainly not one of love. It is a chaotic and cruel society in which everything that is worst in human nature comes to the fore, where the institutions that should give order and deliver justice fail, where everyone suffers, and women in particular are abused.

Second, it shows us that even a nation like Israel, with all the experience of God that it has had and all its privileges of revelation, can become this kind of society if it abandons faithfulness to God's word. Benjaminite

Gibeah can become no better than a Canaanite city, and those who come to it seeking hospitality and nourishment can find themselves in a virtual Sodom. What a solemn warning this is to the church of our own day, which is departing more and more from obedience to God's Word and is accommodating itself more and more to the values of the world around it!

Third—and this is the good news—it shows that the presence of chaos does not mean the absence of God. God is referred to frequently in chapters 20, 21. People assemble to him (20:1), inquire of him (20:18, 27), weep before him (20:23, 26; 21:2), offer sacrifices to him (20:26; 21:4), take oaths in his name (21:1, 5), and attend an annual feast to him in Shiloh (21:19). He is certainly present in their speech at times and in some of their actions. And sometimes they obey him, even when it is costly to do so. When he commands them to continue their action against Benjamin, even though they want to stop, they obey—twice (20:23, 24 and 20:28, 29). The problem is not that they are not religious or not willing to take God seriously at certain moments and in certain situations, and certainly not that he is absent. The problem is that he has ceased to have any *moral* authority over them. Most of the time in their approach to everyday matters such as sex, marriage, hospitality, justice, and the treatment of women (among other things), "everyone did what was right in his own eyes" (21:25). This is why there is moral chaos and why all their institutions are breaking down. It is why their common life has ceased to be the wholesome, good thing God intended it to be and why their society has become so chaotic and cruel. But God has been *in* the chaos! And twice we have been shown what he has been doing. By withholding victory twice he has made all Israel suffer, because *all* of them have been guilty of doing what is right in their own eyes—not just the rapists in Gibeah. In other words, *he has disciplined his people without abandoning them.* And as we have seen, the end result has been better than anything they could have imagined when things were at their worst, something that only God could have brought about.

So brothers and sisters, when you are dismayed at the state of the church in our own day, especially its departure from the Word of God and its moral confusion, take heart. God is still present. The church has existed for more than two thousand years and will continue to do so, because it is *God's* church, and he has not abandoned it and never will. And the end that he will bring about in his time will be glorious beyond all our imaginings.

> Then I saw a new heaven and a new earth, for the first heaven and the first earth had passed away, and the sea was no more. And I saw the holy city,

new Jerusalem, coming down out of heaven from God, prepared as a bride adorned for her husband. And I heard a loud voice from the throne saying, "Behold, the dwelling place of God is with man. He will dwell with them, and they will be his people, and God himself will be with them as their God. He will wipe away every tear from their eyes, and death shall be no more, neither shall there be mourning, nor crying, nor pain anymore, for the former things have passed away" (Revelation 21:1–4).

RUTH

22

Emptiness:
Going Away and
Coming Back

RUTH 1:1–22

GOING AWAY AND COMING BACK is part of the normal rhythm of life. We've all done it countless thousands of times. It starts when we're children; we go to school and come home; we go to the playground and come back; we go to a friend's house and return. And it continues throughout our adult life. We go to work and come home; we go on vacation and come back; we go shopping and return; we go on an overseas business trip and come home. Where I live there's a TV soap opera called *Home and Away*. It has run continuously since 1988 and is one of the most popular TV programs in Australia. It's about a family that lives in a trailer park near Sydney, where people are always coming and going. The regulars come for summer vacations, go home, and come again next year. Their lives literally consist of being "home" and "away." Going away and coming home is *life*: it's what we *do*. But sometimes it's different, because going away is forced on us by circumstances, and coming back is not always possible. Old people typically dread the transition from home to a care facility. Refugees flee intolerable situations and may never be able to return. And even if return becomes possible, it may not be easy. Going away changes people, and returning may mean finding others have changed too; and returnees may have to face hardships they had not expected and for which they are unprepared. The first chapter of Ruth is like that. It's a going away and coming back story in which both the leaving and returning are painful.

Losing Everything (vv. 1–5)

As the book of Ruth opens we are still "in the days when the judges ruled" (v. 1a), and we are back in Bethlehem, where the Levite went to reclaim his concubine at the beginning of Judges 19. But this time a very different kind of story is about to unfold. Bethlehem seems to have been untouched—directly at least—by the wars of the judges period. Life proceeded according to custom. The seasons came and went, crops were sown and harvested, people met and fell in love, children were born; and when disputes arose they were settled by the elders of the community at the town gate. But like everywhere else Bethlehem was still vulnerable to the vagaries of the weather, and sometimes life there turned hostile with devastating consequences—consequences just as life-threatening, in their own way, as invasion and warfare: "there was a *famine* in the land" (v. 1a). And as it dragged on, people became desperate. Everyone was affected, of course, but the opening verses of Ruth zero in on one particular man and what he eventually decided to do.

> A man of Bethlehem in Judah went to sojourn in the country of Moab, he and his wife and his two sons. The name of the man was Elimelech and the name of his wife Naomi, and the names of his two sons were Mahlon and Chilion. They were Ephrathites from Bethlehem in Judah. They went into the country of Moab and remained there. (vv. 1b, 2)

Moab (modern-day Jordan) was a small kingdom, east and south of Bethlehem, across the Jordan River, on the other side of the Dead Sea. It had ties with Israel reaching right back to the time of Abraham (Genesis 19:30–37, esp. v. 37). But it was now another country, a completely independent state with its own leadership, laws, religion, and customs. Once there Elimelech and his family will be foreigners, completely at the mercy of Moab's own people. This is a story about displaced people crossing borders, seeking help; of refugees taking risks to survive. It's a situation that, sadly, is all too familiar in the world we all still live in, though I suspect most of us find ourselves on the receiving end of such people movements rather than the departure points.

Given the pace at which the story is told, it's hard to judge the passing of time, but the impression we are left with in verses 3, 4 is that any benefit the family gets from their move quickly evaporates. First Elimelech himself, the head of the family, dies, and Naomi is left with her two sons, Mahlon and Chilion. They take Moabite wives, Orpah and Ruth. But after ten years of relative normality the two sons also die, and Naomi is left with no men at all—just her two Moabite daughters-in-law. And given the realities of life in a patriarchal society, to be left without men, as Naomi is, is to be utterly bereft. Naomi becomes, in the end, simply "the woman" (v. 5b). It's as though she has lost not just her family but her name. That is the symbolic end of her descent into emptiness. The focus of the story has quickly narrowed to this one woman, and the implicit question hanging in the air at the end of verse 5 is: what future does Naomi have? Can she ever recover from this? Can her emptiness ever be filled?

Hearing of Home (v. 6)

Famines can be long and terrible, but they are normally cyclical and do not last forever. So it was in Bethlehem. At length bad times gave way to good, and Naomi heard about it: "She . . . heard in the fields of Moab that the LORD had visited his people and given them food" (v. 6b).

Such news can lift the heart and bring hope flooding back. But it can also intensify feelings of loss and even guilt. God has visited "his people" (v. 6)? Is she not one of them? Why is she no longer among them? Why are they *there*, where there is now abundance, and she *here*, where there is only pain and loss? Has her going away perhaps been a terrible mistake? It's not just Bethlehem she's gone away from, it seems to her now, but God and home and people, and the sense of distance and alienation is terrible. Naomi at this moment is like the prodigal of Jesus' parable, sitting hungry in a far country and remembering the abundance in his father's house. And like him she concludes that there's only one realistic thing for her to do. "She arose with her daughters-in-law to return from the country of Moab" (v. 6a).

Going Back (vv. 7–18)

We now follow Naomi as she heads back to Bethlehem, and most of the chapter is taken up with what happens on the way. There are two main things to be noted about *how* Naomi returns.

First, she does not go alone. Her two daughters-in-law go with her (v. 7). Naomi is now a broken woman, but there must have been something about her during her first several years in Moab to account for the fact that Orpah and Ruth do not let her go alone. Their initial connection was with her two sons, whom these girls found attractive enough to marry. But there must also have been something about Naomi that attached the girls to her as well, not just to her sons. Perhaps it was her courage in coming to Moab in the first place to provide for her family; perhaps it was the way she picked herself up after the death of Elimelech and cared for her family alone. It may even have been her faith in one God—the God of Israel and the Creator of the whole earth—that drew the two young women to her, a faith so different and somehow nobler and stronger than the polytheistic, idolatrous religion in which they had been raised. We cannot know for sure, but attached to her they were, and that cannot have been without reason. Even when one of them turned back halfway, it was not without tears and a sad kiss good-bye (v. 14). And the other, Ruth, stayed loyal to Naomi to the end and proved to be a link to a future that Naomi could scarcely have imagined at this point. She did not go alone.

Second, she went back with low expectations. This comes out particularly in her words to the two girls when she urges them to leave her.

> Turn back, my daughters; go your way, for I am too old to have a husband. If I should say I have hope, even if I should have a husband this night and should bear sons, would you therefore wait till they were grown? Would you therefore refrain from marrying? No, my daughters, for it is exceedingly bitter to me for your sake that the hand of the LORD has gone out against me. (vv. 12, 13)

Her low expectations are driven, first of all, by her appreciation of commonsense realities. She cannot replace the husbands the girls have lost. She is too old to bear any more sons, and even if she could, the girls could not wait for them to grow to marriageable age. By then the girls themselves would be too old to bear children. And even though they *might* hope to find other men to marry in Bethlehem, their foreignness and the fact that they are widows, not virgins, would count against them; so their marriage prospects would surely be much better back in Moab. They have too much to lose by sticking with Naomi. There is a generosity in her concern for the girls' future rather than her own needs. But there is also evidence of a depressed state of mind that is driven by guilt and has led her to have low expectations, even of God. She expects very little from God herself and even less for her daughters-in-law, should they continue to accompany her. Note what she says to Ruth in verse 15: "See, your sister-in-law has gone back to her people *and to her gods*; return after your sister-in-law."

In her present state of mind Naomi thinks Ruth can expect more from the gods of Moab than from the God of Israel! But this daughter-in-law will have none of it.

> But Ruth said, "Do not urge me to leave you or to return from following you. For where you go I will go, and where you lodge I will lodge. Your people shall be my people, *and your God my God*. Where you die I will die,

and there will I be buried. May the LORD [Yahweh] do so to me and more also if anything but death parts me from you." (vv. 16, 17)

The irony is that although Naomi is returning to Israel, Ruth the Moabitess has more faith in the *God* of Israel than Naomi herself does. She is willing to commit herself to him unreservedly and be accountable to him for her loyalty to Naomi. But Naomi's own faith in God hangs by a thread at this point. She is more inclined to turn those she loves away from him than bring them to him. Her expectations on every level are at a very low ebb.

Arriving (vv. 19–22a)

Naomi's arrival in Bethlehem causes quite a stir and starts tongues wagging, as they do all too readily in small communities. She is recognized, but her appearance causes consternation. "The whole town was stirred because of them. And the women said, 'Is this Naomi?'" (v. 19). Naomi and Ruth are like storm-battered ships limping into the harbor. Neither of them are in good shape after their long journey. Ruth is a complete stranger in Bethlehem, and Naomi, while still herself, is also not herself. She is not like the Naomi that went away, and she knows it.

> She said to them, "Do not call me Naomi; call me Mara, for the Almighty has dealt very bitterly with me. I went away full, and the LORD has brought me back empty. Why call me Naomi, when the LORD has testified against me and the Almighty has brought calamity upon me?" (vv. 20, 21)

Now what we suspected earlier becomes quite clear. Naomi believes she did wrong to go away and has been punished for it. Is she right, though, or is this just a further manifestation of her depressed state of mind? After all, the famine was real, and she was a mother with a family to feed. What else could she have done? Would staying in those circumstances have been any better than going away? And in any case the decision to leave had not been hers: "there was a famine in the land, and *a man of Bethlehem in Judah went to sojourn in the country of Moab, he and his wife and his two sons*" (v. 1). Naomi lived in a patriarchal society, and when her husband went away, she went with him, as she was bound to do. Others may have stayed—rightly or wrongly, wisely or unwisely—but Naomi had no choice in the matter. For Naomi, though, all this is irrelevant. She offers no justification and no excuses. "I went away"—that's how she sees the situation—"and God has punished me for it," she says in essence. So bad does Naomi feel at the moment, and so ashamed, that she doesn't even want to be called Naomi ("pleasant") anymore. That's who she *was*; Mara ("bitter") is who she has become. And she is doubly bitter. Back in verse 13 she said, "it is exceedingly bitter *to me* for your sake that the hand of the LORD has gone out against me." There "bitter" referred to how she *felt* about what had happened. But in verse 20 it has more to do with the severity of the events themselves, especially the loss of her husband and her two sons: "the Almighty has *dealt* very bitterly with me." She comes home full of bitter memories.

All this is very understandable. Less understandable, though, and certainly less justifiable, is the word "empty" in verse 21: "the LORD has brought me back *empty*." That is simply not true. She may *feel* empty, but the truth is that she comes back with two significant assets. The last chapter of the book will reveal that she still has a "parcel of land" she has inherited from Elimelech (4:3). And more significantly she has at her side a daughter-in-law who has pledged undying loyalty to her (vv. 16, 17). How sad Ruth must have been to hear that word "empty" fall from Naomi's lips, because it rated her own value at zero, and perhaps even *below* zero. If Naomi was even *aware* of Ruth at this moment she seems to have seen her as an embarrassment—a liability rather than an asset. Naomi's perception at this point is so distorted by pain that she can see nothing good in her situation. Worst of all, her perception of *God* is twisted. She can see him only as her judge, so that even bringing her back is a further humiliation that he has inflicted on her. So she arrives back in Bethlehem a bitter woman, with a very poor view of God and very low expectations. But she's in for a surprise.

An Ending and a Beginning (v. 22b)

Ruth and Naomi's arrival in Bethlehem was the end of a journey, not just from one place to another, but from one chapter of their lives to another. At this point the focus is still on Naomi. It is she who went away and has come back. The chapter of her life that closes at this point has been full of pain. And the question that hangs in the air as she arrives is: Can there be closure? Can the pain be left behind or at least assuaged? Can there be a new beginning in which the memory of the pain will fade? Naomi seems incapable of imagining such a thing, let alone expecting it. Yet this first chapter of the book ends with a statement that is full of promise: "And they came to Bethlehem *at the beginning of barley harvest*" (v. 2). The famine is over. There is a harvest, and Ruth and Naomi have arrived at a time of reaping. The rest of the book will be about Naomi discovering, or rediscovering, God as her Redeemer and being overwhelmed by his rich generosity to her. And in the process Ruth, too, will be rescued and revalued.

Seeing the Bigger Picture

In spite of her warped perspective and downcast frame of mind, there are some good things about Naomi in this chapter. As we noted earlier, she must have been a woman of character to have influenced her daughters-in-law so profoundly. In particular Ruth's willingness to abandon everything for Naomi and pledge herself for life to Naomi's God and people is testament not only to Ruth's sterling character but to Naomi's as well. Naomi had not always been as she is at the end of this first chapter of the book.

The second thing to her credit is that she came back. She came back bitter, she came back empty, *but she came back*, and that is good news. And whether she was right or wrong to think that she had done wrong by going away, there is something deeply impressive about the fact that she takes full responsibility for it. She does not blame Elimelech or make excuses. "I went away" (v. 21)—that is all; and this willingness to come home without apportioning blame or making excuses again shows us a side of Naomi that is reassuring and makes her an excellent candidate for rehabilitation.

Furthermore, even in Naomi's bitter talk about God punishing her there is an acknowledgment of his sovereignty. She doesn't attribute even her coming back to herself but to God: "the LORD has *brought* me back" (v. 21). And she's right. It wasn't just destitution that brought her back, but news—*good* news about something that God had done: "the LORD had visited his people and given them food" (v. 6). It was this good news—this gospel—that had called her home, and those who respond to such news are not just coming home to Bethlehem or elsewhere, but are coming home to God. And as Naomi is about to discover, those who come to God will never be rejected (John 6:37; Matthew 11:28–30).

We began this chapter by noting that this part of the book of Ruth is a going away and coming back story and that going away and coming back is part of the rhythm of life. It's also part of the rhythm of Scripture. There are many such stories in the Bible. Abraham goes away to Egypt and comes back (Genesis 12:10—13:1). Jacob flees to Aram (Syria) and returns (Genesis 27:41—33:20). The people of Jerusalem go into exile in Babylon and come back (Ezra 1:1–3). In the New Testament the prodigal son goes away from his father's house and comes home again (Luke 15:11–32). In fact the whole Bible is such a story. It's about the entire human race going away from God, and his great plan of salvation to bring them back again. At the center of that plan is our Lord Jesus Christ, and the good news that calls us back is about something else that God has done in Bethlehem—not just for those who live there, but for all of us, whoever we are, and however far we are from God. It's a new and infinitely greater gospel than the one that Naomi heard and that turned her thoughts to home, and it's an open invitation to all of us: Come home. Come home to the God who made you and loves you and is the only One who can fill your emptiness and meet your deepest need. Come back empty, come back with only small expectations if that's all you have, come back bitter if you must, but come back. You may have been away ten years, as Naomi was. It's too long. So is one year, or one month, or even one day, for we were made for God, and our true home—our only place of true wholeness—is with him.

One Wednesday night, three weeks before I wrote this, I had a telephone call from a man I didn't know. He told me his name was James[1] and that he'd lost his faith because of something that had happened many years ago, but wanted to get it back again. He said that someone had told him I had a men's Bible study in my home every Thursday night, and would it be alright if he came? He said, "I don't even have a Bible." I replied, "No problem. I print out the Bible passage and give it to everyone." "Do I need to bring anything else?" James asked. "No," I said. "Just come." And he did. He came the following night and the following week and has kept coming. James told us how one of his children suffered brain damage at nine years of age and became mentally handicapped and how he has had a running argument with God about it ever since. James was bitter and empty for thirty years, but he's heard God calling him and is on his way home. Ruth 1 is a story about someone who went away *but came home*, and it's an invitation to all of us to do the same.

23

Seeking:
The Kindness of God

RUTH 2:1–23

SEEKING IS BASIC TO LIFE and an activity we share with all living things. Animals seek food and water, acceptance in a social group of some kind, mates, a place to live and breed, and protection from predators. Human beings seek these things too, although we would describe them differently. We seek the means to earn a living and provide for ourselves, acceptance, companionship, a life partner, a home to live in, career opportunities, and the joy of having children and raising a family. We also seek more than this, because we have greater capacities and aspirations than animals. We seek moral purity, spiritual experience, and fulfillment. We are aware of God and desire a relationship with him (Ecclesiastes 3:11; Psalm 42:1, 2). The search for food, though, is the most basic search of all, and for some—the very poor or those in situations of famine or war—it can become a never-ending, daily obsession that takes precedence over everything else. For them seeking food is the most basic form of the struggle to stay alive or keep their children alive. Begging may be the only option they have left.

Venturing Out (vv. 1, 2)

When Ruth and Naomi arrived in Bethlehem they were in great need. They desired—and needed—all the things that you and I do. They needed acceptance, love, family life, and emotional and spiritual wholeness. But the first issue was sustenance. How could they survive long enough to get everything else they needed? Begging would be an unbearable humiliation. Fortunately, however, they had come into an environment where law and custom were

255

shaped by the Law of Moses, and that law obligated landowners to make provision for people in precisely Ruth and Naomi's situation, especially at harvesttime.

> When you reap the harvest of your land, you shall not reap your field right up to its edge, neither shall you gather the gleanings after your harvest. . . . You shall leave them for the poor and for the sojourner: I am the LORD your God. (Leviticus 19:9, 10)

> When you reap your harvest in your field and forget a sheaf in the field, you shall not go back to get it. It shall be for the sojourner, the fatherless, and the widow, that the LORD your God may bless you in all the work of your hands. (Deuteronomy 24:19)

Gleaning may not have been much better than begging, but at least it was a form of work and therefore enabled the poor to retain a modicum of dignity. It also gave the rich an opportunity to show generosity in a way that God had commanded and promised to bless. With her Israelite background Naomi should have known about this. She probably still did somewhere in the back of her mind. She was still too depressed, though, to seize the opportunity that it gave her. It is Ruth, who may have had little, if any, acquaintance with Israelite law, who sees what must be done and takes the initiative. "And Ruth the Moabite said to Naomi, 'Let me go to the field and glean among the ears of grain after him in whose sight I shall find favor'" (v. 2).

Naomi simply acquiesces. "Go, my daughter" (v. 2). If Naomi were in a different state of mind it might be reasonable to attribute either shrewdness or blame to her for letting Ruth go like this. As a younger woman, Ruth would be more likely to catch the eye of the men working in the fields and perhaps get a favorable response from them. On the other hand, as a female and a foreigner she may have been vulnerable to abuse—especially given the moral and spiritual chaos of the judges period, in which case Naomi could be seen as careless of Ruth's welfare. More likely Naomi was incapable of anything *but* acquiescence. She was too immobilized by depression to act herself, and if Ruth was willing to go, so be it. What this does show very clearly, though, is Ruth's strength of character and determination to support Naomi, whatever risk that may expose her to.

Being Noticed (vv. 3–7)

Ruth was a woman of resolve, but it must nevertheless have been with some trepidation that she ventured out among the reapers, being careful to keep to the margins of the field and not impede their work in any way. In particular she must have been acutely aware of her foreignness and (to her eyes) the foreignness of her surroundings. John Keats sought to capture this moment in his "Ode to a Nightingale," imagining how the delightful song that he heard one summer's day in England might have been heard by others in times and places very different from his own.

> Perhaps the self-same song . . . found a path
>   Through the sad heart of Ruth, when, sick for home,
> She stood in tears amid the alien corn.[1]

However, "sad" and "tears" are not quite the right words to describe Ruth. She was more resilient than that. But she would not have been human if she was not apprehensive and perhaps a little wistful for home, where she would not have evoked the kind of curiosity and gossip that she might here in Bethlehem. She need not have worried, though, because things were going to go well for her today, and even better in the days to come.

Her fortunes begin to rise with an apparent stroke of good luck: "she *happened* to come to the part of the field belonging to Boaz, who was of the clan of Elimelech" (v. 3). As the book progresses we will have more and more reason to reflect on whether what we are seeing in such events is just good fortune or the hidden hand of God. But this "happenstance" is certainly a most promising one. As the owner of the field—at least the part of it that Ruth finds herself in—Boaz is in a position to offer her protection and, if he is generous, material help. And as a relative of Naomi's former husband, he is likely to feel himself *obligated* to help her, something Ruth stands to benefit from, at least indirectly. More of this later. But much depends on the kind of person Boaz is and whether or not he will show any interest in Ruth or even notice her.

The first indication we are given of Boaz's character is the way he greets his employees and how they respond: "And behold, Boaz came from Bethlehem. And he said to the reapers, 'The Lord be with you!' And they answered, 'The Lord bless you'" (v. 4). Boaz is apparently a godly Israelite who has the respect of his workers; and the double reference to "the Lord" suggests that there may indeed be more than luck involved in Ruth being in this particular field at this moment. There is a further hint of this, too, in the word "Behold," which carries the idea of suddenness or surprise (v. 4). No sooner did Ruth "happen" (v. 3) to arrive in this particular field than behold, so does Boaz—the landowner, a relative, and a God-fearing Israelite! Can this just be chance? And things just keep getting better for Ruth, because Boaz *does* notice her, and his curiosity is aroused.

> Then Boaz said to his young man who was in charge of the reapers, "Whose young woman is this?" And the servant who was in charge of the reapers answered, "She is the young Moabite woman, who came back with Naomi from the country of Moab. She said, 'Please let me glean and gather among the sheaves after the reapers.' So she came, and she has continued from early morning until now, except for a short rest." (vv. 5–7)

Boaz is given a lot to think about here. Ruth is young, she's Moabite, she arrived with Naomi (and therefore is possibly related to her), she's poor (which is why she's gleaning), she's humble and courteous (she's politely asked permission to do it), and she's hardworking (she's toiled all day). Our first impressions of Boaz were positive, and so are *his* general impressions of Ruth. Is it chance or providence that is bringing them together? That is the question this intriguing scene poses for us.

There is a serious impediment, however: Ruth's ethnicity. Israel's relationship with the Moabites was a complicated one that went right back to the time of Abraham (Genesis 19:30–37, especially verse 37) and had taken a particularly nasty turn in the time of Moses. As a consequence of the latter a permanent ban had been placed on the Moabites. They were never to be admitted into Israel; the Law of Moses forbade it.

> No Ammonite or Moabite may enter the assembly of the LORD. Even to the tenth generation, none of them may enter the assembly of the LORD forever, because they did not meet you with bread and with water on the way, when you came out of Egypt, and because they hired against you Balaam the son of Beor from Pethor of Mesopotamia, to curse you. But the LORD your God would not listen to Balaam; instead the LORD your God turned the curse into a blessing for you, because the LORD your God loved you. You shall not seek their peace or their prosperity all your days forever. (Deuteronomy 23:3–6)

Given this background, if Boaz the pious Israelite finds himself attracted to Ruth the Moabitess, this has the potential to become a very complicated story indeed!

Experiencing Human Kindness (vv. 8–16)

The sense that Ruth and Boaz are being drawn together grows stronger here in a scene full of need on the one hand and gentle solicitude on the other. Boaz speaks of reward: "The LORD *repay* you for what you have done, and a full *reward* be given you by the LORD" (v. 12). But Ruth, acutely aware of her vulnerability, speaks only of finding favor, comfort, and kindness.

> Then she fell on her face, bowing to the ground, and said to him, "Why have I found *favor* in your eyes, that you should take notice of me, since I am a foreigner? . . . I have found *favor* in your eyes, my lord, for you have *comforted* me and spoken *kindly* to your servant, though I am not one of your servants." (vv. 10, 13)

Binding these two complementary perspectives on the situation together is the hint of obligation inherent in family ties and the duty of care, particularly to the poor, that comes with the possession of wealth. And a special quality is given to all this, of course, by the fact that Boaz is a man and Ruth is a young woman.

Boaz's concern for Ruth is driven partly by an awareness that not all men are as he is. He orders his men not to "touch" Ruth (v. 9) and warns her not to go elsewhere, "lest in another field you be assaulted" (v. 22). All is not sweetness and light in quiet Bethlehem; dark threats lurk in the wings. Against this background Boaz acts as Ruth's provider and protector. He allows her to glean in his field, gives her food and water, draws her in from the margins to the center of the social group he superintends, and sends her home with plenty to share with Naomi. There is a generosity here that borders on extravagance; he even instructs his men to deliberately pull out some stalks from the sheaves for Ruth to gather (v. 16). It may be nothing more than true piety as Boaz observes the spirit of the law, not just its letter. But it may also be right to see more in his actions than even Boaz himself does, or perhaps more than he *allows* himself to see at this stage. At any rate, this is kindness that is not mere compliance with legal obligation; it is far richer than that. There are other "young women" in this scene (v. 8), but Boaz has eyes only for Ruth.

Interestingly, however, nothing is said about Ruth's appearance. Whether or not she was beautiful appears irrelevant to Boaz. What has impressed him is her character.

> All that you have done for your mother-in-law since the death of your husband has been fully told to me, and how you left your father and mother and your native land and came to a people that you did not know before. (v. 11)

Ruth is a woman who has suffered and has shown resolution, loyalty, and courage. Above all, she has shown kindness to her bereaved mother-in-law and has been willing to sacrifice her own prospects to do so. This is what Boaz finds so impressive about Ruth and what moves him to show kindness to her in return. In this scene kindness answers to kindness, and in the pointed way in which it is expressed shows promise of blossoming into something more.

Moreover, there is something else about Ruth that Boaz has noted, and this seems to have taken precedence in his mind over her foreignness. In fact, for him it has effectively removed her from the category of "foreign" altogether. Ruth has not just left her native land and her father's house, she has also left her foreign gods: "The LORD repay you . . . *the Lord, the God of Israel, under whose wings you have come to take refuge!*" (v. 12). We can almost see the wheels turning inside Boaz's head at this point. Moabites had been placed under a ban of eternal exclusion for cursing and seducing them into worshiping their gods (Numbers 22:1–6; 25:1–3). But what of a Moabite who abandons those gods and embraces the Lord God of Israel? And what if she is also poor, an alien, and a widow—one of the very people the Law commanded Israelites to protect? What does it mean to truly keep the Law in these circumstances? Would Boaz be wrong to embrace such a one? The answer that seems to be forming in his mind and showing itself in his actions is that he would not. And the rest of the book confirms that he is right.

Discovering God's Kindness (vv. 17–23)[2]

All this is pulled together and set in a larger theological framework as Ruth returns to Naomi and the chapter draws to a close. Naomi is suddenly aroused from her emotional torpor by the news that Ruth has met Boaz, for Naomi knows something about him that Ruth does not. Boaz is not just a relative, but a "redeemer" (v. 20). It is one of those crystallizing moments in a story when the plot changes gear and latent possibilities suddenly rise to the surface. Naomi is aware of the special obligations that belong to a redeemer in Israelite law and custom.[3] More about this will emerge as the story progresses. But Naomi is already energized by hope and suddenly able to see not only her circumstances but God himself in a new light, which she voices in a double blessing:

> Blessed be the man who took notice of you. . . . May he be blessed by the LORD, whose kindness has not forsaken the living or the dead! (vv. 19, 20)

In the kindness of Boaz Naomi perceives the kindness of God and knows herself to be the object of it. All Naomi had done was let Ruth go; she was incapable of anything else. But one apparently chance event had followed another, and yet another, until the evidence of God's hand in it all had become unmistakable. And the grain that Ruth brings home to Naomi (there is a lot of it)[4] is a handsome foretaste of even better things to come, for which Naomi can now dare to hope. There is the hint of a complication in the phrase, "*one of* our redeemers" (v. 20), but for the moment it scarcely registers on anyone's consciousness. Nothing can cloud Ruth's satisfaction and Naomi's joy at what has just taken place. Boaz is the only redeemer who matters. Ruth continues to glean in his field and stay with Naomi (v. 23), while they, and we, await further developments.

Seekers

Our observations on this chapter have focused mainly on Ruth. There are also other seekers here, however. Naomi's seeking has been feeble and lacking energy. In fact, it has been almost entirely passive. All she has contributed to Ruth's seeking is to allow it to take place. But she has found God to be kind not just to Ruth but to her as well. When she refers to God being kind to "the living [and] the dead" (v. 20), she describes the change that his kindness has already begun to bring about in her own life. Once she was dead (or virtually so); now she lives, because God has had mercy on her, even though her seeking has been so feeble. Boaz, too, is a seeker of sorts, trying to work out the right course of action for him as a pious Israelite faced with a very complex situation. Should he exclude Ruth the Moabitess or welcome her, given her situation and his own perplexing, apparently conflicting obligations under the Law of God? And we sense by the end of the chapter that this seeker has found godly discernment and has begun to see clearly what is right and pleasing to God in his particular situation. And finally, God himself is a seeker in this chapter. Behind all the chance events that work for Ruth and Naomi's good is his hidden providence as his kindness eventually seeks them out in their need and provides for them. Ruth and Naomi make the wonderful, heart-stopping, surprising discovery by the end of the chapter that *God* has been seeking *them*!

Two great lessons emerge for us from this second chapter of Ruth. First, applying the Word of God to the messy business of life requires great wisdom. All of it is inspired by God and carries the stamp of his authority. So all of it is to be honored and obeyed. However, treating it as a set of absolute rules that must all be applied in the same direct way in every situation, regardless of the intention behind them or the complexities of particular cases, simply will not do. Jesus rebuked the Pharisees of his day for failing to distinguish between the lesser and greater matters of the Law, magnifying the former and neglecting the latter (Matthew 23:23). The result was a harsh legalism that failed to express the divine concern for justice and compassion that was the real heart of the Law and lay behind all the commandments. The truth is that the ban on Moabites was given to prevent Israel from ever again being harmed by Moab, or seduced into worshiping its gods. It was never intended to exclude someone like Ruth who had abandoned those gods and taken refuge in the Lord, any more than the ban on Canaanites was intended to exclude the harlot Rahab, who was in awe of Israel's God and decided to cast in her lot with him and his people. If proof is needed, it is found in the way Ruth and Rahab are both included in the genealogy of Jesus that opens the New Testament![5] The way the book of Ruth ends, with blessing upon blessing, leaves us in no doubt that Boaz was a lawkeeper, not a lawbreaker. In Ruth's case he was absolutely right in letting his concern for the poor, the alien, and the widow take precedence over the ban on Moabites. This is something that evangelicals in particular need to note very carefully. We are right to honor the Bible as the inspired Word of God and make it the final judge of our beliefs and practices. But we, too, need discernment in knowing how to apply it to the complexities of life, lest we make the same mistake the Pharisees did and end up out of step with the very God whose word it is. May God grant us such discernment.

The second great lesson of this passage has to do with the kindness of God. He rewards seekers,[6] whether they seek resolutely as Ruth did or in perplexity like Boaz or whether, like Naomi, they barely have the energy or desire to seek at all. In particular, those like Ruth who seek refuge in the God of Israel will find, to their great surprise, that *he* has already been seeking *them*. And the treasure he has hidden in a field,[7] so to speak, for them to find is nothing other than a redeemer—someone who is able and willing to meet their deepest need. More riches are yet to unfold from the book of Ruth, but we have already discovered its greatest treasure—the astonishing kindness of God.[8]

24

Finding:
The Promise of Rest

RUTH 3:1–18

REST IS ESSENTIAL FOR OUR WELFARE. We are not creatures of infinite capacity. We cannot live by striving alone. Sooner or later our strength is depleted. Without rest we cannot carry on. And since it's clear from both the Old and New Testaments that rest is part of God's good intention for us, there is a very proper place for planning for it. Wise people plan vacations if they can afford to do so. Sensible people go to bed at a reasonable hour, if possible, to give themselves the best chance of a good night's sleep. In some cases rest is a reward. This is the thought behind the reference to the "sweet[ness]" of a laborer's sleep in Ecclesiastes 5:12. He has earned his rest by honest, hard work, and because his gains are not ill-gotten he sleeps with a good conscience.

However, the full Biblical understanding of rest is much richer than this. Rest is a journey's end, the fulfillment of promise, and the celebration of completion. The promise of "rest . . . in the land" was what sustained the Israelites during their long journey though the wilderness (Deuteronomy 12:9, 10; 25:19), and their entry into that rest was celebrated annually in the great Feast of Booths.[1] This rest was not their own achievement, and certainly not a reward for faithfulness (they had been anything *but* faithful in the wilderness); it was pure gift (Deuteronomy 8, 9). In a similar way the rest of the Sabbath day was not simply relief from labor or a reward for it, but an opportunity to remember and celebrate God's finished work of creation (Exodus 20:8–11) and redemption (Deuteronomy 5:12–15). And the New Testament tells us that an even greater rest awaits us in Heaven (Hebrews 4:1–10)—

a rest we already begin to taste when we accept Jesus' gracious invitation to come to him and lay our burdens down (Matthew 11:28–30). Such rest is a covenant blessing of God, a gracious gift to his children.

Rest is also a central theme of Ruth 3, which begins with Naomi seeking "rest" for Ruth (v. 1) and ends with the confidence that Boaz will not "rest" until he has provided it (v. 18). As we will see, however, the promise of rest in this chapter is actually a gift of God, who is sovereignly overruling all things for the good of those involved.[2]

A Shrewd Plan (vv. 1–5)

Naomi has been energized by the news that Ruth has met Boaz and quickly devises a plan to capitalize on the possibilities this presents. The "rest" she seeks for Ruth is marriage, home, and the prospect of children, which will mean her full integration into Israelite society—and indirectly the rehabilitation of Naomi herself. Furthermore, although all that we see directly here is human initiative, the fact that she has already perceived the *Lord's* kindness in the direction things have begun to take[3] suggests confidence that God will bless her efforts. There's an important principle we could note here. Properly understood, a belief in God's sovereignty does not lead to fatalism or passivity. Quite the contrary; it provides hope and the confidence to move forward. That is certainly the effect it has on Naomi here.

The particular opportunity Naomi sees is presented by the new stage that has been reached in the harvesting process. As we move from chapter 2 of Ruth to chapter 3, reaping gives way to winnowing, which brings the threshing floor into focus as the center of activity. To expedite matters, the winnowing will continue into the night, and those involved will sleep there rather than return to their homes, so that the work can be resumed early the next morning. And Naomi knows Boaz well enough to expect that he will camp there with his men (v. 2). It is a perfect opportunity for Ruth to approach Boaz under cover of darkness, hopefully without anyone knowing. However, there are obvious dangers involved. Given that Boaz has previously had to command his men not to "touch" Ruth (2:9), there are dangers to her person in a nighttime situation like this. At least some of those present will be these same men. And second, there is the risk of scandal, for harlots too saw nights like this as opportunities and were known to ply their trade at threshing floors (Hosea 9:1). In view of this, Naomi puts Ruth at considerable risk by telling her to approach Boaz in such a place. But the fact that Ruth is young and has already attracted Boaz's attention, plus the signs of God's providential involvement, have evidently convinced Naomi that it is a risk worth taking.

Her plan is a clever one. Ruth is to bathe, anoint herself—presumably with perfume—and put on a cloak for warmth (she will be sleeping out, v. 3a).[4] In others words, she is to enhance her feminine attractiveness, but in a way that is consistent with the impression she has already made on Boaz as a practically-minded woman of good character. Then she is to go to the threshing floor, find the place where Boaz is lying, uncover his feet, lie down herself, and wait until he stirs and tells her what to do (vv. 3b, 4). It is a bold move and can hardly be seen as anything other than an invitation to love. But given what we have already been shown of Boaz's and Ruth's character it would be going too far to see it as a crude seduction scene. It is far too delicate for that. It is not instant sexual gratification that Ruth is after, but a commitment to marriage and the secure future this would provide for her. Her uncovering of Boaz's feet is best seen as a way of ensuring that he will stir in the coolest, early morning hours and notice her. This nicely balances audacity and restraint and is designed to leave Boaz in no doubt about what is being asked of him without forcing his hand by entrapment. Naomi and Ruth must have discussed the plan, but it was Naomi's first and shows how keenly her mind is now working and how determined she is to make the most of the opportunity God has given her to secure the "rest" for Ruth that she feels bound to provide (v. 1). Ruth, resolute as ever, promises to do everything Naomi has told her (v. 5).

A Whispered Conversation (vv. 6–14)

Ruth's movement to the threshing floor in verse 6 marks the transition to the next, central scene of the chapter. Ruth follows Naomi's instructions exactly, and all goes according to plan—including Boaz's waking at midnight, when all his weary men are fast asleep (v. 8). But the fact that he wakes "startled" threatens to spoil everything, especially when his alarm is heightened by discovering that a woman is lying at his feet (v. 8)! If he cries out, all will be lost. Somehow though (is it God again?) he has the presence of mind not to do so. Instead all that comes from his lips is the whispered question, "Who are you?" (v. 9a). It's one of those pregnant questions that tease us with possibilities beyond its surface meaning. It's like the "Where are you?" of Genesis 3:9—not simply a request for information, but a probing for something more. Given the encounter that had taken place the day before and the impression Ruth had made on Boaz, what woman could have been more on his thoughts as he fell asleep than Ruth was? Who was more likely to be his first thought when he awoke? And what more hoped for answer could there be than the one Ruth gave him—"I am Ruth, your servant!" (v. 9b)? He could hardly have *expected* her to be there; but he may well have *longed* for it. If so, nothing could have given him more joy at that moment than to hear her whispered response.

This is the moment for which Naomi and Ruth had planned. True to her instructions, Ruth had remained silent until she was addressed. Now, though, is the time to speak, and speak she does, with exactly the right blend of respect and boldness: "Spread your wings over your servant, for you are a redeemer" (v. 9c).[5] Ruth is pointedly alluding to what Boaz said to her in their previous meeting: "The LORD repay you for what you have done, and a full reward be given you by the LORD, the God of Israel, under whose *wings* you have come to take refuge!" (2:12). She is challenging him to translate his pious words into action by being the means by which the blessing he pronounced on her will be fulfilled. But the contrast between this scene and the one in chapter 2 is striking. Ruth no longer refers to her foreignness or to the fact that she is not one of Boaz's workers. On the contrary, she identifies herself simply as "Ruth, your servant" (v. 9). Her tone is deferential, but she presses her claim pointedly by referring to Boaz as her "redeemer," someone obligated to help a relative in need (v. 9).

Boaz is clearly smitten. Instead of brushing off her appeal as an embarrassment he responds by reaffirming his previous blessing (v. 10a), addressing her for a second time as his "daughter" (v. 10a, cf. 2:8), and reiterating his high opinion of her by referring particularly to her *kindness*: "You have made this last *kindness* greater than the first in that you have not gone after young men, whether poor or rich" (v. 10b). He too alludes to their earlier conversation in which he has commended Ruth for her remarkable loyalty to her mother-in-law (2:11). This "first" (v. 10) kindness has made a powerful impression on Boaz. Why he should regard Ruth's appeal to him as a second, even greater kindness is at one level obvious: he feels it more personally because it answers the unspoken desire of his own heart for a closer relationship with her. That can now be taken for granted. But the particular way he refers to her kindness contains the first hint of a complication that is about to cast a cloud over all this happy prospect. It is a kindness because there were, and are, alternatives—other men, younger than Boaz, who also know of Ruth's fine qualities and whom she might have approached with hope of success.[6] In mentioning these other men, though, Boaz is doing more than underlining the extraordinary privilege he feels that Ruth has chosen to approach *him*. He is also edging toward a disclosure that he dreads but knows must be made—the existence of one particular man whose potential interest in Ruth must be reckoned with. There is a kinsman-redeemer who is nearer to Ruth than Boaz himself (v. 12).

In reality, of course, it is Naomi rather than Ruth who has chosen Boaz, because it was her plan rather than Ruth's to approach him. Ruth is just following instructions. And it is Naomi who has been aware of other possibilities, as we can now recognize in her earlier words, " [Boaz] is *one of our redeemers*" (2:20). But in calling Ruth's act a "kindness," (v. 10) Boaz indirectly declares his love for her and encourages her to make her choice of him her own and to hold to it in the face of the disclosure he now feels bound to make. This is another element in his wooing of her. But it also shows us an aspect of his character that will be displayed more fully in the final chapter of this story. Boaz is noble, but he is also shrewd.

The night scene at the threshing floor is handled delicately and with an apparent concern to avoid any suggestion of sexual misconduct. The possibility of scandal certainly exists and is implicitly acknowledged by Boaz's warning to Ruth that no one should know of her visit (v. 14b). It was hardly necessary, however, because Ruth herself was well aware of the danger: she "arose before one could recognize another" (v. 14a). Everything has been done discreetly and within proper bounds. The only misconduct of which they could justly be accused is pursuing their relationship so far without first consulting the nearer redeemer. The whispered conversation at the threshing floor has made this matter urgent and created the momentum for the opening scene of the next chapter. The present chapter, though, does not end in foreboding about what the next day may bring. On the contrary, it finishes on a note of bold confidence.

A Promise (vv. 13, 15–18)

This chapter, like the previous one, ends with Ruth's return to Naomi. This time, though, she returns with even stronger grounds for hope than she did before. The most significant outcome of her meeting with Boaz has been a promise, and what a promise it is: "As the LORD lives, I will redeem you" (v. 13). These are no idle words, but a solemnly sworn commitment by Boaz to come to the aid of Ruth and rescue her (and therefore Naomi) from their plight. Promises, of course, can be cheap things. They are only as good as the character and capacities of those who make them. On both counts, however, Ruth has firm grounds for confidence here. Boaz is "a worthy man" (2:1) with considerable resources at his disposal, and everything we have seen of him in chapters 2 and 3 has confirmed his good character. Here is a man whose word can be relied on and who has both the determination and means to do what he has promised. Nor does the promise stand alone. Boaz adds to it a sign to confirm the pledge he has made, like an engagement ring that is given in anticipation of a marriage. He tells Ruth to bring "the garment" she is wearing, and when she holds it out he pours "six measures of barley" into it, enough to fill it to overflowing (v. 15).[7] Given the way it is handled, "the garment" in question could hardly be Ruth's main item of dress. It was probably a shawl of some kind, the sort of garment commonly used by working women to carry their babies. So the filling of this garment by Boaz is more than simply a convenient way of giving Ruth grain; it is also an acted sign of the promise he has made to her. It foreshadows the child Ruth can now look forward to having when Boaz's promise to her is fulfilled.

So Ruth returns home bursting with good news, and Naomi's breathless question, "How did you fare, my daughter?" (v. 16a) is all the encouragement she needs to pour it out. "Then she told her *all* that the man had done for her" (v. 16b), but she particularly emphasizes the six measures of barley and the words that Boaz had spoken as he gave them to her: "You must not go back *empty-handed* to your mother-in-law" (v. 17). It's the clearest possible evidence that Ruth has grasped the larger significance of what Boaz has done. The expression "empty-handed" is literally just "empty"[8]—the same word Naomi had used to describe her own condition (and by implication Ruth's as well) when they arrived back in Bethlehem (1:21). So not only is Ruth no longer "empty" as she returns to Naomi this time, but neither is Naomi. Boaz's promise to redeem Ruth effectively banishes the emptiness of both of them. They don't yet have the fullness of what is promised, but they have good reason to believe that they soon *will* have it. Naomi's exhortation to Ruth in the last verse of the chapter expresses her absolute confidence in a way that recalls how the chapter began: "Wait, my daughter, until you learn how the matter turns out, for *the man will not rest* but will settle the matter today" (v. 23). Paradoxically Boaz's restlessness ("the man *will not rest*") is the guarantee that the "rest" Naomi has sought for Ruth (v. 1) will soon be hers. All she has to do is wait.

Two Ways to Find Rest

This third chapter of Ruth is about a quest for rest: "My daughter, should I not seek *rest* for you, that it may be *well* with you?" (v. 1). The quest for rest is a search for "wellness," the opposite of emptiness and alienation. It is a search for acceptance, inclusion, provision, a future, and a life worth living. It is the essential search of every man and woman. It can become obsessive and neurotic, but it is basically a normal, healthy thing, and this third chapter of Ruth has shown us two things that are fundamental to the success of this search.

The first is initiative—the ability to spot an opportunity when it presents itself and the will to seize it. There is a proper place for planning and risk-taking in this, provided no moral boundaries are crossed. This is what we see Naomi and Ruth doing in the first half of the chapter. Naomi sees the opportunity she has been given in Ruth's meeting with Boaz in chapter 2 and the chance she has of capitalizing on it that very night now that winnowing has begun at the threshing floor and Boaz is likely to be there. It's an opportunity not to be missed. But spotting an opportunity is only half of the initiative that is needed; there must also be a plan, and action to match it. Naomi's mind works quickly. Her plan is a bold one, as we have seen. Even this, though, would not have been enough if Ruth was not willing to take the risk of putting the plan into effect.

There is a synergy here between the two women that was absent at the beginning of chapter 2. There Naomi was passive, and Ruth had to act alone. Naomi had no plan; all she was capable of was acquiescing in what *Ruth* wanted to do. The contrast here in chapter 3 is a very positive sign that Naomi is on the road to recovery. She is has broken out of her depression and is now well enough herself to actively seek wellness for Ruth. She has become a woman with the initiative and energy necessary to make the most of the opportunity she has been given. She can see and think clearly. She is well enough to strategize and take calculated risks. And combined now with Ruth's own resolve and willingness to act, Naomi's initiative is a powerful catalyst for change. Such initiative is healthy and liberating, and a very positive factor in the search for rest in this chapter.

It is not the whole story, however. Indeed, it is only a beginning. If persons are ever to arrive at the rest they are seeking, they must also know when to stop striving and begin waiting. Or to put it another way, they must learn to leave the outcome of their seeking in the hands of another. The truth is that Naomi's quest in this chapter would not have been successful if Boaz had not made a promise. And the peace of mind that Ruth and Naomi have at the end of the chapter would not have been reached if they had not trusted his promise. This is the second principle this chapter teaches us: rest, in the way the Bible speaks of it, is fundamentally a gift and cannot be achieved by striving alone. One must also learn to trust.

Furthermore, there is also a more profound aspect of this second principle that emerges when the present chapter is read with the previous two in mind. On the road between Moab and Bethlehem, when she had been given the opportunity to turn back, Ruth decided to embrace Naomi's God and people (1:16). In Boaz's words in 2:12, she had taken refuge in the Lord God of Israel. And although she may not have realized it at the time, that Lord had made provision in his law for just such persons as she and Naomi were—the widow, the poor, and (in Ruth's case) the alien.[9] More than this, there have been repeated hints in chapters 1 and 2 of God sovereignly moving to bring Ruth into contact with Boaz, the person he intends to use to meet their need. Near the end of chapter 2 Naomi has clearly shown her awareness of this by saying to Ruth, "May he [Boaz] be blessed by the LORD, whose kindness has not forsaken the living or the dead!" (2:20). In other words, behind Boaz's promise lies the commitment of God himself to meet Ruth and Naomi's need. To believe the promise of Boaz is in effect to believe the promise of God and to recognize that even the opportunity to seek this rest is his gift. Without his prior initiative there would be no rest to be found, and no redeemer to provide it.

So in its own subtle but powerful way this chapter too bears witness to a truth that lies at the very heart of the Christian gospel. The Lord blesses those who seek him (Isaiah 55:6, 7), and his promise to them is rest, not just from poverty and social isolation, but from spiritual emptiness and alienation from God. And his means of delivering that rest to them is a Redeemer whom he has provided. Only two things are necessary for our quest for this rest to be successful: to seek it and to believe God's promise to give it to us. Jesus summed this up perfectly in his challenge to "ask," "seek," and "knock" (Matthew 7:7) and in his promise, "Come to me, all who labor and are heavy laden, and *I will give you rest*" (Matthew 11:28). We can seek and find many other things without believing the promise of God, but we will never find *this* rest, *this* wellness, *this* wholeness by searching elsewhere or by human initiative alone. It is found in Christ alone, and the only strategy we need in order to have it is to come to him.

25

Fullness: Four Redeemers

RUTH 4:1–22

IT'S ASTONISHING how our brain stores childhood memories and, seemingly at random, suddenly brings them to mind again after, in my case, nearly sixty years. Some of them are completely trivial, and one wonders why they are remembered at all. I recall traveling with my mother on a bus one day on the way into the city to do some shopping (hardly a memorable outing for a child) and seeing a sign on the back of another bus that read, "Stay alive in 55." It was the year 1955, and the sign was part of a government-sponsored road safety campaign. I was born in 1945, so I must have been ten years old at the time, but why seeing that sign should have interested me, let alone lodge in my mind for fifty-eight years, I have no idea. Nor do I know why I suddenly remembered it recently. It's just not that interesting.

The retention of other things, though, is much more understandable. On another occasion I remember my mother taking me to a magic show in a large department store. It was school break, and I was probably getting on her nerves at home, and she needed to find a way of diverting me. And it worked! I was spellbound. The most memorable moment came for me when the magician produced a large sword and held it out to his left at arm's length. There was a black cloth draped over it, which was clearly concealing something about the size of a cabbage. We knew it was there because we could see its shape under the cloth. And we could see that it was making small movements this way and that. Imagine my utter amazement when the magician whisked the cloth away to reveal an apparently disembodied human head with a frilly collar, balanced delicately on the edge of the sword and very much alive, a fact he demonstrated by engaging it in conversation for several minutes! Then with a theatrical flourish he placed the cloth over the sword again, raised it to show that the head had disappeared, and then produced the entire person, head plus body, from stage right! I have no trouble at all understanding how I've remembered that!

I've always been fascinated by magicians—not only by their seeming ability to do the impossible, but by the sheer extravagance of some of their feats. The same magician who produced the disembodied head also produced a live dove out of thin air, or was it from his sleeve? That's a pretty standard trick—in fact one of the oldest in the trade—but still amazing to a child seeing it for the first time. What really set the place buzzing, though, was the fact that he then produced another, then another, two more, and so on until the whole auditorium seemed to be filled with flying doves! That really *did* take our breath away!

My experience of writing this chapter on the final part of Ruth and Naomi's story has been something like watching the magic of the dove extravaganza. I knew chapter 4 would be a movement from expectation to fulfillment, from emptiness to fullness. The whole development of the story in chapters 1—3 had led me to expect that. So "Fullness" came easily to mind as a suitable caption for the whole. I also picked up quickly that "redeemer" and "redeem" were key words here; they occur too often not to be noticed. This is a chapter about redemption. So I began by looking for redeemers. I was sure Boaz would be one, but then found another, and another, and thought I had finished. Perfect. I now had the subtitle I needed for the chapter: "Three Redeemers." But then to my surprise I discovered one more and had to revise the subtitle to reflect the reality of what I had found: "Fullness: *Four* Redeemers." There is an extravagance of redemption here that is amazing. The Bible is like that, especially the book of Ruth. Better than any magic trick. Truly astonishing. And the rewards you get from studying it stay with you. They are not easily forgotten.

The DNA of Redemption

First, some background. Israel had redemption in her DNA. In the Old Testament the idea of a redeemer goes right back to the time of Moses when God rescued the Israelites from slavery in Egypt. They were his people, and they were in deep trouble; so God came to their aid. He sent plagues on the Egyptians until they gave in and let the Israelites go. And when Pharaoh changed his mind and went after them and tried to recapture them, God parted the Red Sea so they could escape. That was a mighty act of rescue, and from then on Israel referred to God as their Redeemer—the One who had rescued them from slavery in Egypt (Exodus 15:11–13; Psalm 78:35;

Proverbs 23:11; Isaiah 47:4; 63:16; etc.). So their history as a nation really began with redemption, and this principle became enshrined in the Law that God gave them through Moses. God told them in his law that he wanted *them* to be redeemers too. This is how it worked:

- When an Israelite family became very poor and had to sell their land to survive, the nearest male relative (the kinsman-redeemer)[1] had the responsibility of rescuing them from poverty by buying their land back and restoring it to the family. This was called redemption of property (Leviticus 25:23–34).
- If they'd become so poor that they'd had to sell themselves into slavery, a rich relative had to rescue them by buying their freedom. This, too, was redemption (Leviticus 25:47–55).
- Finally, if a man died leaving his widow without children (the situation Ruth and Naomi have found themselves in), their nearest male relative had to step in and marry his widow and enable her to have children, so they could inherit their father's property and keep it in the family—a third kind of redemption.[2]

In this kind of situation marriage was not fundamentally about love, at least not in the romantic sense. It was much more about ensuring that families survived and about keeping property in the family. For Boaz, though, it was different, because he loved Ruth and wanted to marry her. But first there was Naomi to consider and what remained of the family property. Naomi was not entirely destitute; she did own a piece of land (v. 3), but was going to have to sell it to survive. Which brings us to the opening scene of chapter 4 and the first of our four redeemers.

The First Redeemer (vv. 1–13)

Chapter 4 begins with Boaz going to the town gate and sitting down there (v. 1). The town gate was a very important place. It was there that the village elders would gather to hear complaints and settle disputes between members of the community. It was also the place where business was done, especially business that required formalities to be observed, such as the witnessing of agreements. Boaz was probably expecting *his* business, about Ruth and Naomi, to be settled there that day. And he seems to be in luck, because no sooner has he got there than someone comes along who holds the key to what Boaz wants to do. He's the person referred to simply as "the redeemer" (v. 1)—the first mention of a redeemer in the passage. And immediately tension builds, because as Boaz has already told Ruth back in 3:12, this man is "nearer" (more closely related) to her and Naomi than Boaz himself is; so he is the relative with the most entitlement to act on their behalf if he chooses to do so. Therefore everything depends on what this other man decides to do, and this has to be resolved before there can be any future for Ruth and Boaz. Of course, Boaz could have ambushed him somewhere down a dark lane and forced him to withdraw by threats or worse! But that's not Boaz's way. He's an honorable man, determined to resolve the matter in an honorable manner. That's why he has come to the town gate at the beginning of this chapter.

Boaz explains the situation in verses 3 and 4:

> Then he said to the redeemer, "Naomi, who has come back from the country of Moab, is selling the parcel of land that belonged to our relative Elimelech. So I thought I would tell you of it and say, 'Buy it in the presence of those sitting here and in the presence of the elders of my people.' If you will redeem it, redeem it. But if you will not, tell me, that I may know, for there is no one besides you to redeem it, and I come after you." And he said, "I will redeem it."

So the matter of Naomi's property is taken care of: the first redeemer will buy it to keep it in the family. For Boaz, though, this is potentially bad news because there's more to this than property, and the next item on the agenda is the critical one. What's this man going to do about Ruth? Boaz has a lot to lose here, but the issue must be faced. So he goes on:

> Then Boaz said, "The day you buy the field from the hand of Naomi, you also acquire Ruth the Moabite, the widow of the dead, in order to perpetuate the name of the dead in his inheritance." (v. 5)

Ah! A woman—and young! Fortunately for Boaz, however, this first redeemer is not the romantic type. He's a money-wise, number-crunching, cool head and looks at the whole situation in strictly business terms. If he goes ahead he'll have to buy the field *and* marry Ruth, and in the end that means he's going to lose out. He'll have another person to support—two in fact, because Ruth will bring her mother-in-law with her. Any gain he may make from using the field will be used up in supporting them. And if Ruth has children (which is what is meant to happen), those children will inherit the field when she dies. So he will eventually lose it, and the money he paid for it will have reduced rather than increased his assets, meaning he'll have less to leave to his *own* children. So he declines and effectively deals himself out of the whole situation. "Then the redeemer said, 'I cannot redeem it for myself, lest I impair my own inheritance. Take my right of redemption yourself, for I cannot redeem it'" (v. 6).

I don't know whether Boaz was able to keep a straight face at that moment, but his heart must have been bursting with joy. This is what he was hoping for, and he almost certainly introduced the property matter first and then Ruth in that order, hoping this would work in his favor. Boaz may have been shrewd, but he hasn't done anything underhanded or dishonorable. He hasn't tried to get Ruth by crooked means. And now the way is open for him to marry her with a clear conscience, which he does in verse 13a. And God puts his seal on their marriage by blessing them with a son (v. 13b). So their marriage is doubly blessed: it is blessed by the Lord who opened up the way for it to happen and blessed them with a son. And it is also blessed by "all the people who were at the gate and the elders," who wish them well and pray for them (v. 11). The first redeemer's withdrawal has made way for the second[3]—and, in fact, for the third and fourth. But more of that in a moment.

The Second Redeemer

The second redeemer is Boaz, and he is a complete contrast to the first. The first redeemer was not willing to accept his responsibilities; Boaz is. The first redeemer was motivated by self-interest; Boaz is motivated by love. The first redeemer was dishonorable,[4] the second honorable. The first is a failed redeemer, the second a true one. But wait, there's more . . .

The Third Redeemer (vv. 14–16)

Ruth has a baby, which means that Naomi now has a grandson! And as she takes him in her arms, the women of Bethlehem pronounce a blessing on her too. Listen carefully to what they say in verses 14 and 15:

> Then the women said to Naomi, "Blessed be the LORD, who has not left you this day without *a redeemer*, and may his name be renowned in Israel! He shall be to you a restorer of life and a nourisher of your old age, for your daughter-in-law who loves you, who is more to you than seven sons, *has given birth to him.*"

This can only mean one thing: the baby boy that Naomi holds in her lap is a redeemer too! He's a gift from Ruth, who has stuck with her mother-in-law and loved her all the way through the grief and loss she has suffered. He's also a gift from Boaz, who has acted honorably by taking Ruth as his wife. But most of all he is a gift from God, and his final answer to Naomi's bitterness and emptiness. Naomi is not an old woman yet; there's time for this baby to grow into a young man who will renew her life and support her in her old age. Moreover, this third redeemer is *a baby born in Bethlehem,* which opens this story toward the future—not just the near future, but the distant future as well, as shown by the way the book ends.

The Fourth Redeemer (vv. 17–22)

This chapter, and the whole book, concludes with the naming of the newborn son and an account of what followed from his birth.

> And the women of the neighborhood gave him a name, saying, "A son has been born to Naomi." They named him Obed. He was the father of Jesse, the father of David.
>
> Now these are the generations of Perez: Perez fathered Hezron, Hezron fathered Ram, Ram fathered Amminadab, Amminadab fathered Nahshon, Nahshon fathered Salmon, Salmon fathered Boaz, Boaz fathered Obed, Obed fathered Jesse, and Jesse fathered David. (vv. 17–22)

The fact that the baby lies in Naomi's lap rather than Ruth's and is named by the women of Bethlehem rather than by Boaz suggests that something is going on here that the parents could not have predicted and cannot control. The child has a larger significance than being simply theirs. The baby born in Bethlehem turned out to be the grandfather of King David! And that was only the beginning. The royal line of David continued right through the Old Testament and into the New until it reached its climax in *another baby born in Bethlehem* in Matthew 1. And just in case we are too dull to grasp the magnitude of this, Matthew reproduces the last few verses of Ruth there in the genealogy of Christ (Matthew 1:4–6). What happened in Bethlehem in "the days when the judges ruled" (1:1) was small, but it was also big—very big! Was this second baby born in Bethlehem also a redeemer? He certainly was. "You shall call his name Jesus [Savior]," the angel said to Joseph, "for he will save his people from their sins" (Matthew 1:21), and "save" is just another word for "redeem." Jesus came to redeem people (Mark 10:45), and as what follows shows us very clearly, his mission was to extend far beyond Israel to include people of all nations.[5] With Jesus, "his people" was to take on a whole new meaning—not just Jews but Gentiles as well, people like us, of whatever background we are. So the acceptance of Ruth into Israel in the time of the judges was a sign of this greater reality to come. And from what did Jesus come to redeem us? From our sins that had broken our relationship with God, from the emptiness of a life without God, and from the judgment we deserved for rejecting God. And how did he do it? By his death for us on the cross. The Apostle Peter says, speaking to us as followers of Jesus, "you were ransomed [redeemed] . . . not with perishable things such as silver or gold, but with the precious blood of Christ" (1 Peter 1:18, 19). Jesus is the fourth redeemer, and the greatest redeemer of all.

"There Is a Redeemer"

The second half of the twentieth century saw a fresh outburst of singing in the church. It was sparked partly by the amazing sight of thousands of people at a time responding to Christ in Billy Graham's great evangelistic crusades. I was one of them. I still remember the wonderful, inspiring singing of the large choirs at those meetings and the way that singing continued to be echoed in the churches I was part of for the next several years. In the 1970s and 1980s the Scripture in Song movement emerged in New Zealand and spread worldwide, and then, in the 1980s and 1990s came the great outpouring of worship songs that was ignited by the charismatic movement and continues to the present day. Not all these songs are of equal quality, of course, and only time will tell which of them will endure, but enough time has already passed for some to have begun to emerge as classics. Among these, and arguably the one that best captures the passionate love for Christ that the Spirit has reawakened in the church, is Keith Green's "There Is a Redeemer." And no song of recent times could be a more apt theme song for the book of Ruth, especially its last chapter.

This theme is prepared for with the description of Naomi's desperate condition in chapter 1 and then subtly hinted at with the introduction of Boaz as "a relative" of her husband and "a worthy man" at the beginning of chapter 2. It is introduced directly with the revelation that he is "one of our redeemers" in 2:20 and taken further by his *promise* to "redeem" Ruth (and therefore Naomi) in chapter 3. It is not until chapter 4, though, that the theme bursts into full bloom and opens out toward its fulfillment in Christ. The book of Ruth is a story of redeeming love. First there is the redeemer who didn't go ahead because he didn't love, then the redeemer who did go ahead because he did love. Then comes Obed, who was God's love gift to Ruth and Naomi. And finally, already beginning to lighten the sky like the rising sun in the closing verses of Ruth, comes Jesus, the great Son of David, God's love gift to you and me. Watching these four redeemers emerge has been like watching a magician produce rabbits from his hat. But this is no magic; it's the work of a sovereign God quietly but powerfully working all things together for good for the sake of those who love him and are called according to his purpose (Romans 8:28). It is also part of a much larger story in which the full outworking of that same loving purpose can be seen.

God in Chaos

Our reflections on Judges and Ruth in this book have taken us on a journey with many harrowing moments and surprising outcomes. We have gone from the chaos of the judges period to the calm of Bethlehem, from the apparently insoluble problem of Israel's cyclic sin to the birth of a redeemer. Judges ended with the muted hope of a king; Ruth ends with King David. Who can help but see here the work of a sovereign God who never gives up on his people in spite of their sin? And who cannot see here the great, reassuring, shining truth that chaos is not all-powerful, but God is? That truth is laid down at the very beginning of the Bible as a foundation stone for all that follows: "The earth was without form and void, and darkness was over the face of the deep," but "the Spirit of God was hovering over the face of the waters" (Genesis 1:2). Genesis 1, 2 are about God bringing order and life and beauty out of the chaos of unformed matter. The rest of the Bible is about him bringing order out of the moral and spiritual chaos caused by human sin, and the end result is the new heavens and new earth of Revelation 21 and 22, where there is no more chaos. And the key to it all is a Redeemer born in Bethlehem. The Old Testament looks forward to his coming; the New Testament announces his arrival and recounts all that followed from it. The books of Judges and Ruth are just one part of that great story of creation and redemption.

There is a Redeemer! That's the message with which Judges and Ruth leave us. It's a wonder to marvel at, something to sing about, and a truth never to be forgotten, especially when we find ourselves betrayed again by our own sinfulness. And when the moral and spiritual chaos all around and within seems overwhelming, we need never despair, because a baby has been born in Bethlehem. Light has come into this world, and the darkness never has, and never will, be able to put it out (John 1:5).

Soli Deo gloria!

Notes

JUDGES

Chapter One: After Joshua

1. For an example of Joshua's efforts and success in keeping Israel united, see his handling of the incident involving the boundary altar erected by the Transjordan tribes in Joshua 22. In this he was following the precedent set by Moses (Numbers 32:20–22; Deuteronomy 3:18–20).

2. The Law of Moses indicates that the Urim and Thummim were normally involved in seeking direction from God. The high priest carried these two stones in the breastpiece that he wore over his heart and somehow used them to determine what God wanted his people to do (Exodus 28:29, 30; Leviticus 8:8). However, it would be hazardous to assume that anything was completely normal in the period of the judges, including the manner of asking God about things.

3. E.g., 2:3; 4:4–7; 6:7–12; 10:11–14.

4. E.g., Joshua 3:12; 8:10; 14:1; 19:51; 21:1; 22:30.

5. Cf. Joshua 1:9; Matthew 28:18–20.

6. See Numbers 14:24; Deuteronomy 1:36; Joshua 14:9, 13; 15:13, 14.

7. See also 1 Chronicles 4:13.

8. E.g., 2 Corinthians 9:6–14.

Chapter Two: Judgment Day

1. Manasseh and Ephraim, the first two sons of Joseph, became the ancestors of the two leading tribes of northern Israel (Genesis 41:51, 52).

2. In pre-Israelite times the Hittites, based in what is now Turkey, ruled a large part of the Middle East, including Syria and parts of Canaan. In Joshua 1:4 "the land of the Hittites" refers to Canaan as a whole, but that cannot be the case here, where it almost certainly refers to the locality of the seven city states in Syria that perpetuated the name "Hittite" for several centuries after the fall of the Hittite empire. See 2 Samuel 24:6; 1 Kings 10:28, 29; 11:1, 2; 2 Kings 7:6.

3. Claytons is the brand name of a non-alcoholic drink resembling whiskey that was the subject of a major marketing campaign in Australia and New Zealand in the 1970s and 1980s in an attempt to counteract the rising toll of alcohol-related driving fatalities. The term *Claytons* subsequently become a common way of referring to "a poor substitute," "not the real thing." See "Claytons," http://en.wikipedia.org/wiki/Claytons.

4. In the underlying Hebrew the verb *'alah* ("to go up") occurs in verses 1, 2, 3, 4, 16, and 22.

5. My own view is that this particular polarisation is a false one and particularly unfortunate. Since the Scriptures themselves are inspired by the Spirit, faithfulness to Scripture and sensitivity to the leading of the Spirit should not be set over and against each other in this way. Sensitivity to the Spirit necessarily involves a commitment to being faithful to the clear teaching of Scripture that the acting out of

same-sex attraction is wrong. See Barry G. Webb, "Homosexuality in Scripture," in *Theological and Pastoral Responses to Homosexuality*, ed. B. G. Webb, Explorations, vol. 8 (Adelaide: Openbook, 1994), 65–104.

Chapter Three: Losing Our Children

1. E.g., Daniel I. Block, *Judges, Ruth*, The New American Commentary, vol. 6 (Nashville: Broadman & Holman, 1999), pp. 122, 123.

Chapter Four: The Program

1. I owe the substance of the previous two sentences to Roger J. Ryan, *Judges*, Readings: A New Biblical Commentary (Sheffield, UK: Sheffield Phoenix Press, 2007), p. 12.

2. For the approximate length of the judges period, see Barry G. Webb, *The Book of Judges*, New International Commentary on the Old Testament (Grand Rapids: Eerdmans, 2012), pp. 10–12.

3. Collins Dictionary, www.collinsdictionary.com/dictionary/english/willfulness.

4. *Merriam-Webster's Collegiate Dictionary Eleventh Edition*, 2011, p. 1433.

5. This tells us, incidentally, that the judges had a prophetic role as well as a saving and a judicial one in the normal sense. The clearest example of this in Judges itself is Deborah (5:4–14). We see the same thing more fully, beyond Judges, in Samuel (1 Samuel 3:19–21; 7:3–17).

6. Cf. Holman Christian Standard Bible (HCSB) and New Revised Standard Version (NRSV). "Would" is preferable to the ESV's "will" here because the test being referred to is past (and already failed) from the point of view of the present passage. See my comments on this passage in my *Judges*, pp. 146–148.

7. See Romans 1:18–32; cf. Genesis 1:26, 27; 2:15–17; 3:1–24.

8. See Galatians 3:15–18, esp. verse 17: "the law, which came 430 years afterward, does not annul a covenant previously ratified by God, so as to make the promise void."

9. Cf. Isaiah 1:2, 3.

Chapter Five: Othniel

1. In Joshua 11:21 Joshua is said to have cut off the Anakim from Hebron, and later, in 15:14, Caleb is credited with doing so. The difference is probably best understood as being between initial conquest and subsequent settlement. Although the latter is recounted in both Joshua and Judges, it probably belongs chronologically in the period of the judges and is included in the book of Joshua for thematic reasons. But the slightly different way it is described in Judges 1 (as a feat of the tribe of Judah rather than of Caleb personally) is important for the theme of generational change in that chapter.

2. See Jude 17–23.

3. As reflected in the ESV.

4. Similarly see 1 Kings 18:24–29.

5. Or "younger brother." The Hebrew, like the English, is ambiguous. But "nephew" is far more likely, given the fact that Caleb is an old man by this stage, and Othniel's vigor and suitability as a husband for Achsah suggest he is much younger.

6. According to Isaiah 28:21 judgment is God's "strange" or "alien" work.

7. See especially 6:1–6.

Chapter Six: Ehud

1. See Roy L. Heller, *Conversations with Scripture: The Book of Judges* (New York: Morehouse, 2011), pp. 103–106.

2. Note, famously, Job's experience of never knowing the reason for the calamities that befell him. Cf. John 9:1–3.

3. Cf. Luke 15:23.

4. The objects themselves may have been Moabite rather than Israelite, though Israelite worship of idols would not be surprising in Judges. See especially the story of Micah and his idols in chapters 17, 18.

5. In the next few paragraphs the wording follows closely my fuller treatment of the same verses in *The Book of Judges*, New International Commentary on the Old Testament (Grand Rapids: Eerdmans, 2012), pp. 175, 176.

6. Both *bari'* and *shamen* can be used as the opposite of *razah*, "lean." Compare Ezekiel 34:20 with Numbers 13:20. Robert G. Boling, *Judges*, The Anchor Bible 6a (New York: Doubleday, 1975), p. 85 translates *shamen* as "plump." Trent C. Butler, *Judges*, Word Biblical Commentary 8 (Nashville: Thomas Nelson, 2009), p. 53 translates it as "fat."

7. E.g., Judges 2:4, 15, 18; 10:9, 16; 20:23.

8. Daniel I. Block, *Judges, Ruth*, The New American Commentary. vol. 6 (Nashville: Broadman & Holman, 1999), p. 156.

9. Hans Christian Andersen, *The Emperor's New Suit*. For the full text see http://hca.gilead.org.il/emperor.html.

Chapter Seven: Shamgar

1. See Amos 9:7, where "Caphtor" is the Hebrew name for Crete; cf. Deuteronomy 2:23; Jeremiah 47:4.

2. For details see Daniel I. Block, *Judges, Ruth*, The New American Commentary, vol. 6 (Nashville: Broadman & Holman, 1999), pp. 173, 174.

3. It has four consonants rather than the typical three-consonant form of a Hebrew name.

4. The relevant evidence is given by Gregory Moberly in his book *The Empty Men: The Heroic Tradition in Ancient Israel* (New York: Doubleday, 2005), pp. 27–30.

5. Cf. Hebrews 7:1–3. In the words of the Nicene Creed, he is "eternally begotten of the Father."

Chapter Eight: Barak

1. K. A. Kitchen, *On the Reliability of the Old Testament* (Grand Rapids/Cambridge, UK: Eerdmans, 2003), pp. 206, 208 calls the Jabin of the book of Judges "Jabin II."

2. See "the kings of Canaan" in 5:19, and compare the expression, "Hazor . . . the head of all those kingdoms" in Joshua 11:10.

3. Cf. the New International Version and most English versions. The ESV and NASB have "who rides through the deserts."

4. So J. Gray, *Joshua, Judges, and Ruth*, The Century Bible, New Edition (London: Nelson, 1967), pp. 269–271.

5. Cf. 9:53, 54.

Chapter Nine: Singing

1. Gilead is the name of a region that lies in the central and northern areas of Transjordan. It seems to stand here for the tribe of Gad plus the rest of the eastern Manassites (those not covered by Machir, v. 14).

2. Notice his appearance to pronounce judgment on Israel for covenant unfaithfulness in 2:1–5.

3. For acknowledgment of God's servants see the psalms of David, Solomon, and Moses, traditional hymns such as "Hushed Was the Evening Hymn" (about the call of Samuel), and such contemporary songs as "These Are the Days of Elijah." For righteous anger, including the cursing of enemies (which is an appeal to God for justice), see, e.g., Psalm 109:17; 137:7–9.

Chapter Ten: Mothers

1. The LXX, perhaps sensitive to this issue, reads instead, "until *she* arose."

2. Othniel is a possible exception, though I think we are meant to understand that in 3:7–11 it is the basic features of judgeship that are on display rather than the man himself. In contrast, Deborah is a fully-presented character.

3. The Hebrew is obscure. The ESV's "*the* neck" is a valid translation, but "*my* neck" probably reflects what Sisera's mother has in mind. Compare other English versions.

4. E.g., Exodus 12:15, 19; 30:33, 38; Numbers 9:13; 15:30.

Chapter Eleven: Mavericks

1. "Samuel Maverick," http://en.wikipedia.org/wiki/Samuel_Maverick.

2. *Merriam-Webster's Collegiate Dictionary Eleventh Edition*, 2011.

3. *Cambridge Advanced Learner's Dictionary* (Cambridge, UK: Cambridge University Press, 2008).

4. Cf. 2 Chronicles 34:22–28.

5. Anath was the name of a Canaanite goddess.

6. Timothy Dudley-Smith, *John Stott: The Making of a Leader* (Leicester, UK: Inter-Varsity Press, 1999), p. 183.

7. Teddy Saunders and Hugh Sansom, *David Watson: A Biography* (London: Hodder & Stoughton, 1992), p. 27, as quoted in Dudley-Smith, *John Stott*, p. 184.

8. Basil F. C. Atkinson, "Basil's Recollections." Unpublished paper, UCCF, 1966, p. 64, as cited in Dudley-Smith, *John Stott*, 1999, p. 184.

Chapter Twelve: Gideon: The Making of a Leader

1. See 2:1; 5:23.

2. The meaning of Jerubbaal, "Let Baal contend against him," actually mocks Baal by challenging him to a rematch with Gideon if he dares!

3. See the promise to Abraham in Genesis 22:17: "I will surely bless you, and I will surely multiply your offspring as the stars of heaven and as the sand that is on the seashore. And your offspring shall possess the gate of his enemies."

4. None of the places mentioned have been identified with certainty, but the sites that have been suggested all lie south of the Sea of Galilee and just east or west of the Jordan.

5. Gideon is from Manasseh (6:15).

Chapter Thirteen: Gideon: Self-Destruction

1. I take this as a flashback, reverting to the crossing he had already made back in 7:25, in order to mark the crossing as particularly significant and begin to trace the development of new aspect of Gideon's life and character from that point.

2. As David later did (1 Samuel 23:9–12).

3. Cf. Exodus 28:6–14.

4. "Let Baal contend against him" (6:32).

Chapter Fourteen: Abimelech

1. Cf. 11:1, 2.

2. According to Leviticus 27:3–7 a male slave cost fifty silver pieces (or shekels) and a female slave thirty. At seventy silver pieces for the lot, the lives of Gideon's seventy sons were paid for cheaply.

3. In verse 6 "all Beth-millo" is more specific than "all the leaders of Shechem." It refers to those leaders who customarily met at the Beth-millo (the Millo-house). This was a building of some kind, and in view of the use of the word *millo* elsewhere, it may have been fortress-like and quite substantial (2 Samuel 5:9; 1 Kings 9:15; 11:27; 2 Kings 12:20; 1 Chronicles 11:8; 2 Chronicles 32:5). Furthermore, given the association of trees with rule elsewhere in Judges (4:5; 6:11), "the oak of the pillar," a ceremonial oak of some kind, probably marked the Beth-millo as the seat of government.

4. Cf. Isaiah 2:12, 13.

5. "Beer" means "a well." It's exact location is unknown, but it is mentioned in Numbers 21:16 as a place where the Israelites stopped as they were skirting around Moab on their way to Canaan. Its main attraction for Jotham was presumably its remoteness from Shechem and Abimelech.

6. E.g., 3:11 (Othniel), 3:30 (Ehud), 5:31 (Deborah and Barak), etc.

7. Cf. 1 Samuel 16:14, 15; 1 Kings 22:22, 23.

8. "The house of their god" is presumably "the house [temple] of Baal-berith" of verse 4.

9. See 7:16.

10. "The center of the land" is probably the Shechem pass, just west of the city (Barry G. Webb, *The Book of Judges.* New International Commentary on the Old Testament [Grand Rapids: Eerdmans, 2012], p. 285) . "The Diviner's Oak" was another well-known landmark, the location of which is unknown.

11. Arumah is generally identified with Khirbet el-'Ormeh, five miles (eight kilometers) southwest of Shechem.

12. See the discussion of this "salt" ritual in Webb, *Judges*, pp. 289, 290.

13. "El-berith" ("covenant God") is probably an alternative name for the "Baal-berith" ("covenant Baal") of 8:33; 9:4. Cf. "the house of their god" in 9:27.

14. Some identify it with Tübas, nine and a half miles (sixteen kilometers) to the northeast.

15. We might wonder how Abimelech's death at the hands of a nameless woman in Thebez can be seen as the fulfillment of the second part of Jotham's curse. Has fire really come from the Shechemites and consumed Abimelech (v. 20)? Apparently so (v. 56). If the people of Thebez were in league with the Shechemites, as seems likely, then the woman who hurled the stone from the burning tower can be seen as their surrogate.

16. In some cases, of course, the evil that God allows to happen is not related in any way to any particular sin that the person concerned has committed. See for example, the suffering of Job and Jesus' cautionary words in John 9:3.

Chapter Fifteen: First Interlude

1. "Interlude," in *Merriam-Webster's Collegiate Dictionary, Eleventh Edition*; http://www.merriam-webster.com/dictionary/interlude.

2. "Interlude," in *American Heritage Dictionary of the English Language*; http://education.yahoo.com/reference/dictionary/entry/interlude.

3. "Interlude," in ibid.

4. The "cities" in question were in reality only small towns, as indicated by the expression "Havvoth-jair" ("villages of Jair") in verse 4. For his acquisition of them see Numbers 32:41; Deuteronomy 3:14. They were in territory already conquered and settled by Israel in the time of Moses and Joshua. Their later acquisition by Jair is presumably referred to here for thematic reasons. Although the term "captured" is used in Numbers 32 (presumably involving at least some use of force), the present passage in Judges passes over this in silence and focuses instead on the relative peacefulness of Jair's rule and the gifting of these cities to his sons.

Chapter Sixteen: Jephthah

1. The free Merriam Webster's Online Dictionary 11th Edition; www.merriam -webster.com/dictionary/negotiation.

2. Contrast 3:9, 15 and Jonah 3:10, God's response to the repentance of the Ninevites.

3. In 11:1, 2 "Gilead" is probably a substitute for his father's real name, which may have been unknown to the author.

4. Some scholars have identified it as Tel-Aiyibeh in the remote area northeast of Gilead.

5. See 2 Samuel 10:6–8.

6. The reference to "Chemosh" in verse 24 is puzzling, since the god of the Ammonites was not Chemosh but Milcom or Molech (1 Kings 11:5, 7). Chemosh was the god of Moab. But given that the land of Moab does feature in the passage, the likely explanation is that the Ammonites had invaded Moab before they invaded Israel (see Robert G. Boling, *Judges*, The Anchor Bible 6a [New York: Doubleday, 1975], pp. 201–205). Jephthah is willing to concede for the sake of argument that Chemosh may have given Moab to the Ammonites, but not that Yahweh has given Gilead to them.

7. This is the sense of the esv, and is in agreement with other English versions such as the nrsv and the niv.

8. The Hebrew verb *wayehi* normally indicates an event rather than a state. See the translation of this verse in the niv 2011, nrsv, and hcsb.

9. "Manasseh" here probably refers to east Manasseh, north of the Jabbok (Deuteronomy 3:13; 29:8), but may include west Manasseh as well, on the other side of the Jordan (Joshua 13:7).

10. See 10:17.

11. The italics are mine, but reflect the underlying Hebrew, which has the emphatic infinitive: "If you will *indeed* give . . ."

12. See 12:3.

13. The underlying Hebrew specifies neither species (animal or human) nor gender.

14. The same Hebrew verb, "do/done," is used in both clauses. Cf. Barry G. Webb, *The Book of Judges*, New International Commentary on the Old Testament (Grand Rapids: Eerdmans, 2012), p. 332.

15. Contrast Genesis 22:11, 12.

16. Some have proposed that Jephthah dedicated his daughter to God as a perpetual virgin, but this is clearly not what the text implies. For relevant references see Webb, *Judges*, p. 333, n. 77.

17. The other was Manasseh. The tribes of Ephraim and Manasseh were descendants of the two sons of Joseph of the same names. Their importance is confirmed by the way the whole of northern Israel is referred to as "the house of Joseph" in 1:22, 35.

18. Webb, *Judges*, p. 343.

19. See, for example, David F. Wells, *God in the Wasteland: The Reality of Truth in a World of Fading Dreams* (Grand Rapids: Eerdmans, 1994). This book is now dated in some respects, but not in the warning it sounds.

Chapter Seventeen: Second Interlude

1. The six as a group are traditionally known as the minor judges, in contrast to the major judges whose careers are described in much more detail.

2. The Talmud (*Baba Bathra* 19a) identifies Ibzan with Boaz of Bethlehem in Judah, but this appears to be pure midrash, with no historical basis.

3. See *H. G. Oxford Bible Atlas*, Second Edition (Oxford: Oxford University Press, 1984), p. 62.

4. See 4:4, 5.

5. Exodus 17:8–16; Judges 3:13; 6:3; 7:12; 10:12. See also the ESV footnote to Judges 5:14.

6. Judges 6:3 (so Daniel I. Block, *Judges, Ruth*, The New American Commentary, vol. 6 [Nashville: Broadman & Holman, 1999], p. 390).

7. See 5:22.

Chapter Eighteen: Samson: The Savior No One Asked For

1. It is longer than the Jephthah narrative of 10:6—12:7. The Gideon-Abimelech complex as a whole (chaps. 6—9) is longer than the Samson story, but the Gideon narrative itself (6:1—9:28) is shorter.

2. "It is beyond your understanding" (NIV footnote).

3. See verse 19; cf. Exodus 15:11.

4. As the angel had predicted (13:5).

Chapter Nineteen: Samson: Saint and Sinner

1. See "St. Samson Bishop of Dol, Brittany," at www.celticsaints.org/2011/0728a.html.

2. A variant of "Samson."

3. See "Sampson the Hospitable," at en.wikipedia.org/wiki/Sampson_the_Hospitable.

4. See "Russian Orthodox Cathedrals in St. Petersburg, Russia," at http://www .saint-petersburg.com/cathedrals/index.asp.

5. See David M. Gunn, *Judges*, Blackwell Bible Commentaries (Malden, MA: Blackwell, 2005), pp. 175–182.

6. Her name, Delilah, sounds like *hallaylah*, the Hebrew word for "night." So it's possible she was an Israelite. But where she lived and how she behaved make it far more likely that she was a Philistine, and "recent Philistine inscriptions demonstrate a strong tendency among them to adopt Semitic names." K. L. J. Younger, *Judges, Ruth*, The NIV Application Commentary (Grand Rapids: Zondervan, 2002), p. 316, n. 73.

7. The Hebrew word *mishteh*, "feast," in verse 10 is from the verb *shatah*, "to drink," and given the fact that there were vineyards nearby (14:5) Samson's marriage festivities almost certainly involved wine.

8. The tragic epic poem *Samson Agonistes* (about Samson the wrestler).

Chapter Twenty: Religious Chaos

1. See the next two footnotes. The lack of clarity is probably due, in part at least, to damage the text has suffered in transmission.

2. Or two idols, one carved and one molten (esv). But the pronoun "it" in the next sentence implies that it was a single, composite idol.

3. The idol is in Micah's "house" (v. 4), but also in his "shrine" (v. 5), either at the same time or subsequently.

4. An "ephod" was a priestly garment, but given the environment in which we find it here and the fact that Micah "made" it, it's unlikely that it bore much similarity to the splendid high-priestly garment of that name described in Exodus 28:6–13; 39:2–7. More likely it was an idol in the form of an ephod. Cf. Gideon's golden ephod in 8:24–27.

5. Here at 17:6 and then in full or abbreviated form at 18:1; 19:1, and 21:25.

6. As we see in the Samson story of chapters 13—16.

7. For an example of such a fee for service see 1 Samuel 9:5–10. Apparently the "man of God" whose services were sought in this way was normally a prophet, but in the days of the judges it was priests rather than prophets who inquired of God on behalf of the people (e.g., 20:27, 28). This did not necessarily involve payment of a fee, but given the irregularity of affairs at Micah's shrine and the mercenary nature of the Levite, it probably did in this case.

8. Not least the unsuspecting citizens of Laish!

9. Translation from Barry G. Webb, *The Book of Judges*, New International Commentary on the Old Testament (Grand Rapids: Eerdmans, 2012), p. 443.

10. Jabesh-gilead was about 22 miles (36 kilometers) south of the Sea of Galilee, and 1 mile (1.6 kilometers) east of the Jordan River. For its probable pro-Benjamite stance see the discussion in Webb, *Judges*, p. 499.

11. "Until the day of the captivity of the land" in verse 30 probably refers to the devastation of the area in which Dan was located and the deportation of its population to Assyria by Tiglath-pileser III in 734 BC, approximately 475 years after the middle of the judges period. For details see Webb, *Judges*, pp. 1–12, 449. The complete end of the northern kingdom came with the fall of its capital, Samaria, to Sargon II in 722 BC (2 Kings 17:21–23).

12. The omission of one or more generations is common in Biblical genera-tions, "son" in this case being metaphorical for "descendant," as in "the children [literally, sons] of Israel," the Messiah as "son of David," and so on. For details see ibid., p. 448.

13. Ibid. Indeed, so great was the scandal that the scribes who transmitted the passage as Scripture inserted a small superscript *nun* above the name to indicate that it should be read as "Manasseh" rather than "Moses" out of respect for the founder of the nation.

14. This is the opening line of his famous sonnet of that name. Unfortunately, in his romanticism about nature Wordsworth himself was more nostalgic about pa-ganism than drawn to a revived faith in God.

15. 1 John 5:21. Compare the prayer of William Cowper, the great English poet and hymn-writer, in his hymn "O for a Closer Walk with God":

The dearest idol I have known,
Whate'er that idol be
Help me to tear it from Thy throne,
And worship only Thee.

Chapter Twenty-One: Moral Chaos

1. Contrast Samson's "love" for Delilah in 16:4.

2. The evil Abimelech was the son of Gideon's concubine (8:31).

3. Verse 25 makes it clear that this is definitely the intended sense of "know" here.

4. Mizpah is in the central highlands, four miles (six and a half kilometers) north-northwest of Gibeah.

5. The very large numbers in this chapter have presented something of a di-lemma to scholars, as they are out of proportion to the size of comparable armies of the time for which we have extra-Biblical evidence. No workable solution to this problem has so far been found. On balance it is best to take the numbers at face value, as all the proposed adjustments create more problems than they solve. For a discussion see Barry G. Webb, *The Book of Judges*, New International Commentary on the Old Testament (Grand Rapids: Eerdmans, 2012), pp. 71–74.

6. Cf. Saul's use of the pieces of slaughtered oxen to summon Israel to war in 1 Samuel 11:1–7.

7. Webb, *Judges*, p. 494, n. 130.

8. Cf. Romans 1:21–27.

9. See verse 15, where the author himself says that "*the Lord* had made a breach in the tribes of Israel." However, in the words of verse 16 ("the women are de-stroyed out of Benjamin") the Israelites indirectly admit that they themselves had made things worse. It is they, not God, who slaughtered all the potential wives for the Benjaminites.

10. See chapter 20, note 10.

11. The "behold" of verse 19 suggests a sudden burst of inspiration.

12. According to verse 12 their camp was "at Shiloh," but probably in the envi-rons rather than in the town itself.

13. Cf. 9:26, 27, the story of Abimelech.

RUTH

Chapter Twenty-Two: Emptiness

1. Not his real name. I have withheld it to protect his privacy.

Chapter Twenty-Three: Seeking

1. See http://www.poetryfoundation.org/poem/173744.

2. The following section is adapted from pp. 44, 45 of my *Five Festal Garments: Christian Reflections on the Song of Songs, Ruth, Lamentations, Ecclesiastes and Esther*, New Studies in Biblical Theology, 10 (Leicester, UK: IVP, 2000).

3. See Leviticus 25:25–27; Numbers 35:6–28; Deuteronomy 19:4–12.

4. An "ephah" (v. 17) was about three fifths of a bushel or twenty-two liters (ESV footnote).

5. See Matthew 1:1–16, especially verse 5.

6. See Hebrews 11:6; Isaiah 55:6, 7.

7. See Matthew 13:44.

8. Cf. Titus 3:4–7.

Chapter Twenty-Four: Finding

1. Also known as the Feast of Tabernacles; Deuteronomy 16:13–17.

2. Cf. Romans 8:28.

3. See 2:20.

4. According to Exodus 22:25–27 poor people used a "cloak" (*silmah*) for warmth at night. Daniel I. Block, *Judges, Ruth*, The New American Commentary. vol. 6 (Nashville: Broadman & Holman, 1999), p. 683.

5. The following is adapted from pages 46–48 of my *Five Festal Garments*.

6. Cf. Boaz's reference to Ruth as "my daughter" (2:8; 3:10), showing his awareness of the age gap between them.

7. Depending on what "measure" he used (the word is not specific), estimates range from 60 to 100 pounds or even more (Block, *Judges, Ruth*, p. 698).

8. Hebrew *regam*.

9. E.g., Leviticus 25:23–55.

Chapter Twenty-Five: Fullness

1. The *go'el* in Hebrew.

2. This is commonly referred to as levirate marriage, because the person who normally fulfilled this responsibility was the widow's brother-in-law, or *levir* in Latin (Deuteronomy 25:5–10).

3. As formally attested in the customary way in verses 7–10. Cf. Deuteronomy 25:7–10.

4. See Deuteronomy 25:7–10.

5. Matthew's Gospel begins (after Jesus' birth) with magi coming from the east (outside Israel) to worship the newborn king (Matthew 2:1–12) and ends with the great commission to go into all the world and make disciples of all nations (Matthew 28:16–20).

Scripture Index

General Index

Index of Sermon Illustrations

is hostile to the gospel and is becoming more hostile every day, 106–7

There's a warning against confusing godliness with respectability. Deborah may have been respectable even though she broke certain norms. Jael and Shamgar certainly weren't. Respectability has never been a reliable indicator of which side people are on, in either the Bible or in the history of Christianity. The more respectable the church becomes, the less real, the less salty the less authentically Christian it will be. Jesus was not respectable, 131

God was already Israel's king, and the way out of idolatry was always open to his people if only they would recognize *his* authority and return to a proper observance of *his* law. And the provision of a merely human king could not guarantee this would happen—at least not permanently, as the sad end of Solomon's life showed only too clearly. That solution came with the incarnation of God, the divine King, in Christ, the great Son of David. Here at last was the one *true* image of God (Heb. 1:3), the complete answer to our fallenness, and a meeting place between God and man that could never be corrupted, 226

Judgement

Judgment is God's "strange" or "alien" work. We cannot say that God *is* judgment in the way that we can say that he is love, 167

Only the God who made the world and everything in it, including ourselves, has the absolute right to tell us how to live our lives. He who brought order out of *physical* chaos by separating light from darkness also gave order to the *moral* universe by separating right from wrong, 227

Ministry

Example of boundary events that change the course of history including Israel's obedience after the promised inheritance, 19

Story of unprepared students an example of experiencing disappointment in ministry, 109

Story of John Stott and Dr. Basil Atkinson as an example of eccentricity and humility in the Christian life, 129–30

Warning of idolizing leaders and the example of Gideon, 154–55

Leadership of God's people is a terrible responsibility, with great potential for doing both good and harm. Those of us who are called to it need an acute sense of our own sinfulness and the need of God's sanctifying grace in our lives. We also need the humility to be able to acknowl-edge when we have damaged others by our poor judgment or by acting out of insecurity and selfishness rather than out of genuine love for those we lead, 188

Negotiation

In short, the story of Jephthah shows us two things about negotiation. It has a legitimate place in human affairs in a fallen world but has severe limitations; and in the hands of an insecure man like Jephthah it can end up doing more harm than good. More importantly, it shows us that negotiation is the antithesis of faith and has no place at all in our relationship with God, 189

Obedience

Sacrifice is no substitute for obedience, 35

It has been said that God doesn't have problems. Nonsense! You can't have children without having problems, and God has lots of children! Furthermore they are recalcitrant children who refuse correction. The whole world is a problem; the human race as a whole has rebelled against God, 59

Reading the Bible

This can be very hard for us as evangelical Christians because we are committed to being faithful to what the Bible teaches. What we sometimes fail to see is that the Bible itself allows for exceptions to what should ideally be the case and refuses to let us put God into a box. We must always be prepared to acknowledge the blind spots in our Christian cultures and the limits of our theological systems, 131

But reading a Biblical narrative is like playing a violin. As the bow is drawn across one string, others begin to vibrate with it. And the body of the instrument is designed to capture and blend the resonances of the strings to produce the rich sound that we hear. In the same way the canon of Scripture captures and blends the resonances of each of its parts, so that when we read it there is a richness of meaning greater than that of any one part read in isolation, 146

Self-Destruction

The story of aircraft investigations and of Canaanite presence in Israel demonstrate that we bring trouble on ourselves by what we do or fail to do; but instead of accepting responsibility for our misfortune we attribute it to others or to bad luck or the general state of the world or (worst of all) to God, 29–30

Dylan Thomas poem, 31